Harvard
Business
Review
Family
Business
Handbook

The Harvard Business Review Handbooks Series

HBR Handbooks provide ambitious professionals with the frameworks, advice, and tools they need to excel in their careers. With step-by-step guidance, time-honed best practices, real-life stories, and concise explanations of research published in *Harvard Business Review*, each comprehensive volume helps you to stand out from the pack—whatever your role.

Books in this series include:

Harvard Business Review Entrepreneur's Handbook

Harvard Business Review Family Business Handbook

Harvard Business Review Leader's Handbook

Harvard Business Review Manager's Handbook

Harvard Business Review

Family Business Handbook

How to Build and
Sustain a Successful,
Enduring Enterprise

JOSH BARON | ROB LACHENAUER

Harvard Business Review Press

Boston, Massachusetts

Copyright 2021 BanyanGlobal Family Business Advisors
All rights reserved
Printed in the United States of America

10 9 8 7 6 5

No part of this publication may be reproduced, stored in or introduced into
a retrieval system, or transmitted, in any form, or by any means (electronic,
mechanical, photocopying, recording, or otherwise), without the prior permission
of the publisher. Requests for permission should be directed to permissions@
harvardbusiness.org, or mailed to Permissions, Harvard Business School
Publishing, 60 Harvard Way, Boston, Massachusetts 02163.

The web addresses referenced in this book were live and correct at the time of the
book's publication but may be subject to change.

Library of Congress Cataloging-in-Publication Data

Names: Baron, Joshua, 1974– author. | Lachenauer, Robert, author.
Title: The HBR family business handbook / by Josh Baron and Rob Lachenauer.
Other titles: Harvard Business Review family business handbook | Harvard
    Business Review handbooks series.
Description: Boston, MA : Harvard Business Review Press, [2021] | Series:
    [Harvard business review handbook series] |
Identifiers: LCCN 2020036537 (print) | LCCN 2020036538 (ebook) | ISBN
    9781633699052 (hardcover) | ISBN 9781633699045 (paperback) | ISBN
    9781633699069 (ebook)
Subjects: LCSH: Family-owned business enterprises—Handbooks, manuals, etc.
    | Success in business—Handbooks, manuals, etc.
Classification: LCC HD62.25 .B35 2021 (print) | LCC HD62.25 (ebook) | DDC
    658/.045—dc23
LC record available at https://lccn.loc.gov/2020036537
LC ebook record available at https://lccn.loc.gov/2020036538

Paperback ISBN: 978-1-63369-904-5
Hardcover ISBN: 978-1-63369-905-2
eBook ISBN: 978-1-63369-906-9

The paper used in this publication meets the requirements of the American
National Standard for Permanence of Paper for Publications and Documents in
Libraries and Archives Z39.48-1992.

Contents

PART ONE
Cracking the Code of Your Family Business

PART TWO
The Five Rights of Family Owners

PART THREE

Challenges You Will Face

Introduction

Understanding Your Family Business

Are you a leader of a multigenerational family business who wants to keep the business and family growing and thriving?

Are you the founder of a successful business trying to decide whether to hand your business down to your children?

Are you a member of the younger generation in a family business, eager to find a way to contribute but not quite sure how?

Are you trying to navigate your dual roles as owner and employee in your family business?

Are you a family business owner who plays no active role in day-to-day operations but who is committed to the company's long-term success?

Are you the spouse of an owner of a family business who cares about supporting both your spouse and your children, but you don't fully understand the boundaries of your role?[1]

Are you a nonfamily executive, board member, or adviser to a family business you deeply respect, but you're not sure how to help?

Are you a nonfamily employee of a family business, trying to figure out if you have a shot at thriving there?

Are you part of a company that is not technically a family business but operates like one, perhaps because it's employee-owned or a partnership?

If you fall into any of those categories—whether your family business is a global conglomerate or a local pizza parlor—this handbook is for you.

Family and business are two of the most powerful forces in the world. Our families provide our nature in the form of our genes and much of our nurture. Businesses employ our most valuable resources—our people, our time, our capital. When combined, family and business amplify their impact, and their complexity. If you are reading this book, you live and work in this intense nexus and you have insights and experiences that outsiders seldom understand.

The frameworks and practices in this book are based on the decades of experience we have acquired through working with family businesses in a wide range of sizes, industries, and geographic locations. We will share the stories of some of those families throughout this book but will, by necessity, disguise any identifying details. The tactics in this book have worked for hundreds of business families, and we hope you find ways that they can work for you, too. You'll need to assess whether our recommendations will work for your own family under the circumstances and time frame unique to your situation—and what, if any, tweaks you'll need. There are very few best practices that all family businesses should adopt; we'll alert you to the exceptions.

We have enormous respect for family businesses. As family business advisers, we share a passion to help people who need to make important decisions together amid the business's many layers. Both of us started our careers as strategy consultants, Rob at Boston Consulting Group (BCG) and Josh at Bain & Company. Rob has practical leadership experience from being the CEO of three companies, while Josh brings an academic perspective from teaching MBA and executive education at Columbia Business School. Each of us has spent more than a decade advising family businesses all over the world as they have navigated these tricky shoals. We always learn something important from the families we work with, and we deeply admire what they have built and sustained.

Through our work, we have also learned that family businesses can represent both the best and the worst forms of capitalism. At their best, these businesses invest in the long term, in their community, and in working and growing together. At their worst, and as they are often portrayed in the media, family businesses are plagued by terrible conflict, destroying their wealth, scores of jobs, and their family relationships in the process.

So, what separates the best from the worst? The most successful family businesses have three traits in common:

1. **Curiosity:** Successful family businesses are led by lifelong learners. These leaders ask great questions rather than assume they have all the answers. They're always exploring what others are doing and looking for new ideas.

2. **Teamwork:** Effective family businesses know that keeping their business functioning well requires constant effort. They identify emerging problems, they're not afraid of having difficult conversations, they make tough choices—and they recognize the importance of doing these things together.

3. **Adaptability:** They embrace the challenges that come their way and are open to change to meet them. They recognize that just because something has worked brilliantly up until now doesn't guarantee it will work from now on.

What you will learn in the
HBR Family Business Handbook

We have structured this handbook to speak to each of these three traits. In part 1, we share the main insights needed to help you cut through the inherent complexity of a family business and we show how you can use your influence to sustain your business. You will learn two overarching aspects of working in a family enterprise:

- How to decode your family business by understanding the influence of key individuals, multidimensional relationships, and system dynamics

- Why ownership brings with it the power to either destroy your business or position it to thrive across generations

In part 2, we explain the core work that needs to be done in any family business to continue its lasting legacy. You will learn how to take the following steps:

- Identify your type of family business and determine if it needs to change for the business to prosper

- Build the governance structures and processes necessary for good decisions

- Develop an Owner Strategy that defines success for your business

- Create an approach to communication that helps you foster the trusted relationships your family business depends on to thrive

- Establish a transition plan for your business to set up the next generation for success rather than conflict

In part 3, you learn about the core challenges you may face in your family firm. We describe ways to address these challenges, including how to meet the following goals:

- Preparing for the inevitable disruptions to your business family

- Succeeding while working in your family business

- Setting a family employment policy

- Managing your family's wealth responsibly

- Getting the level of conflict just right

- Building a family office

- Minimizing the risk of losing what you have built

You may be tempted to skip to whichever chapter speaks to your present challenge, and you certainly can do just that. But we hope instead that you read this book from end to end. To understand your family business as a whole, you have to consider all its parts and how they are inextricably connected. A "Further Reading" section at the end of the book also provides jumping-off points if you want to delve deeper. This book will be most helpful to you if it triggers new insights and collaborative conversations among the stakeholders in your family business. A healthy family business—and business family—may be well within reach, for future generations, if you are collectively willing to put in the work.

Your role in a family business will ask much of you—your intellect, your emotional intelligence, and even your courage. Done well, your family relationships will be deeper and more rewarding, your business will thrive, and your community will benefit.

This book will help you explore the family business you know and love but perhaps don't always understand. We hope it will engender empathy for others in your business—people who also face complex situations and decisions—and help you identify where you can have a positive influence. If you find this book helpful, you may want to keep it handy, share it with others in your family, and turn to it from time to time as new challenges arise. We wish you a good journey.

PART ONE

Cracking the Code of Your Family Business

1.

Decode Your Family Business

Who cut down Mom's rosebushes? Rosebushes! This fight nearly derailed a successful second-generation family business. We had scheduled a meeting with the company's owners to discuss whether to retain their under-performing nonfamily CEO. Instead they spent almost the entire time arguing over whether one of the brothers had the right to "prune" or "kill" (depending on whose version you believed) their mother's prized rose-bushes at the family cottage. Despite our efforts to change the subject, they couldn't move past the rosebush incident. The meeting ended in a dead-lock, the group unable to make any decisions together.

It's hard to imagine a public company's board coming to a standstill over landscaping. Outsiders often scratch their head at how family busi-nesses seem to defy conventional business rules. That's because family businesses are different. If you're part of such a business or working for one, the business's uniqueness will be no surprise to you. But that doesn't mean you always understand how and why the business operates the way it does. You just know that conventional business wisdom doesn't always apply. But what are the rules?

We have good news. Family businesses can be understood if you stop scrutinizing them like conventional businesses and instead use these three levels of analysis:

- Individuals, especially owners, have a huge impact.

- Relationships are multidimensional and interlocking.

- System dynamics shape everyone's behavior in ways you might not realize.

In this chapter, we will help you identify and understand the influence of critical individuals in your family business, decipher and map key relationships, and recognize the often-unseen system dynamics at play that will shape your future.

The impact of individuals

For all the talk of "imperial CEOs" of public companies, these executives can't touch the influence of a family business leader backed by ownership power. The owners, a relatively small number of people (most family businesses are owned by far fewer than a hundred people), have ultimate authority over every decision in the business. They can fire the CEO, add or remove board members, change the strategy, sell the company, decide who can be an owner, and even cut the rosebushes, to name just a few things in their control. Family ownership keeps power in the hands of a few individuals. Who these individuals are and what they want will have a profound impact on their family business. And that impact will vary, of course, from business to business and family to family.

One US entertainment company has been quietly owned by one family for generations and has managed to grow and thrive with just one global brand, a rarity in the fickle, consumer-driven entertainment business, which is dominated by multibrand conglomerates such as Disney.

While the family CEO has had numerous opportunities over the years to buy competitors and diversify his portfolio, he held firm in his stance. This CEO—we'll call him Frederick—is clear: he just wants to own and run one company. Frederick is a man of routine. His calendar is set a year in advance, lunch is always served at 12:45 p.m., and he leaves the office on time to see his family and read books. "Owning many brands would be a pain in the ass," he told us. "Someone would need to run the businesses. And that someone would be me." Not one for surprises, he structures his life and his business in predictable ways. He likes to perfect his family business incrementally, prudently, and meticulously. And as long as he's in charge, that strategy will never change. Frederick would not have chosen to run his company any differently. His approach is fundamental to who he is.

By contrast, a European family business has a CEO we'll call Ian. During his thirty-year reign as CEO, Ian's family business acquired more than twenty-five companies in industries as diverse as automotive parts, insurance, information technology, and furniture manufacturing. The industry did not matter. Ian would buy low, upgrade management, find where price could be raised, and be off to the next acquisition. He would check in on the previously acquired companies only twice a year in day-long reviews of the firms' balance sheets and profit-and-loss statements—fancy strategy documents were left untouched. "Our strategy is to make money!" Ian would declare. He loved the thrill of the hunt and knew what he needed to be successful. After "retiring" at seventy-five, Ian purchased several businesses in Africa to keep himself busy.

You will find Fredericks and Ians in the story of every successful family business—leaders whose strategies deeply reflect their personalities. Without that person, without their "singular genius," the family business would probably be dramatically different. Put Ian into the entertainment company or Frederick into the conglomerate, and you would probably get radically different outcomes. The average CEO tenure in a family firm is at least thirteen years, compared with five years in publicly traded firms. With both more time in the seat and more decision power as an owner, these family CEOs put their personal stamp on their companies.

Despite the pervasive myth that only founders can have supersized influence on a business (think Sam Walton at Walmart), subsequent generations can also have a profound impact. For example, Rupert Murdoch took the modest foundation of his father's Australian media assets and built a global, multibillion-dollar empire. People such as Frederick (G3, third generation) and Ian (G4) play a role we call *creators*; they sit at the power center of their family companies.[1] As we'll discuss, other owners can play significant roles, too, even if they're not the CEO of the business.

But owners are far from the only people who, as individuals, make and shape important decisions in family businesses. Though they may not show up on the company's organizational chart or the ownership documents, spouses, children, cousins, in-laws, nonfamily executives, and board members can all influence a family business's direction. In a public company, it matters little who the CEO's spouse, parents, siblings, or friends are, but in a family business, these people can matter greatly. A nonfamily CEO who has the full support of the company's owners, even if those owners are relatively uninvolved, can also play a significant role in shaping a family business because of that support. (Think of the power and influence of *Vogue*'s longtime editor in chief, Anna Wintour, who had the enduring support of the legendary S. I. Newhouse, co-owner of Advance Publications, for decades.)

People's personal character plays a key role in directing the fate of a family business. For example, we met a family that is one of the largest landowners in Colombia. The father loved the game of business and passionately pursued creating more family wealth. Because his wife grew up in another, but conflict-ridden, family business, she was determined to give away their family fortune before she died. She urged that the profits from their family business be distributed, instead of reinvested, and then given to charity. Their son was indifferent to both the business and the family's wealth, happily pursuing a career as a ranch-hand on one of the family's cattle ranches. He is probably one of the world's richest cowboys. Their daughter, feeling profoundly guilty about her family's wealth, married a minister, and together they moved to the slums of Bogotá. None of these family members are on the same page about what the family should do with the wealth their business creates—but they all have a say in what happens to it.

To anticipate what will happen to this company in the next generation, we have to understand what the daughter and son want for their family business. Will they divide it so that each of them can make a personal decision about what to do with their wealth? Will they move out of their current professions and take an active role in leading their business? Will one sibling want to sell to the other? The only thing that is certain is that their choices will be driven at least in part by their personal priorities, which have little to do with the business itself.

The seemingly irrational decisions of family businesses often reflect rational choices of thoughtful people who value things beyond higher profits. And since they own the company or influence those who do they can "want what they want"—be it growing through a personality-fitting strategy such as those that Frederick and Ian applied, or focusing on distributing money out of the firm, or directing the firm to combat climate change or poverty. As individuals with unique goals and desires, they get to chart their own course.

Make-or-break relationships

You can also decode your family business by examining the **relationships** inside it. Unlike in a nonfamily business, where clear boundaries usually separate professional and personal relationships, a family business involves multidimensional relationships that influence each other in profound, often unexpected, ways. In fact, three distinct types of relationships are simultaneously at play.

Family relationships are at their best when they are inclusive, forgiving, protective, and supportively challenging. They "trade" in emotions—love and some more negative emotions at times. Families are emotionally connected. And family relationships are the longest relationships of most people's lives.

Business relationships, on the other hand, are hierarchical; there's a boss and a reporting structure. They are usually meritocratic. If you don't make the cut, you are fired or you leave. The average tenure of US employees is now less than five years. Businesses "trade" in competencies. You hire a vice president of manufacturing for the executive's knowledge and experience in the business issues you face. And the person is in the role only as long as the mutual investment makes sense for both parties.

Owner relationships come down to who has the voting control of the firm and who has influence through their voice, even without a vote. Owners "trade" in power and are part of an exclusive club: you are either an owner or not. In family businesses, unlike, say, at Apple, ownership is sticky. Most companies have limits on whom you can sell your shares to, and how. Exit and entry are not simple, quick options.

In your family business, each big decision you make—to curtail a dividend payment to your mom to protect your balance sheet, to buy out your cousin, to skip your family reunion, or to fire your brother—is within a complex expression of family emotion, business hierarchy, and owner power. Your decisions are never just straightforward business or family calls.

This complexity plays out in a staggering number of important relationships, each with a distinct tenor. For example, Ian, the conglomerate creator, is a son, a brother with two siblings, a husband, a father, an uncle, a cousin, a father-in-law, and a grandfather. In the business, he was the CEO, with twelve direct reports, and was chair of the board. As an owner, he has been a trustee, a beneficiary of the trust, an investment partner with his siblings, an investor who bought additional shares from his other family members, and a board member of their foundation. When you add it up, Ian has more than fifty important relationships.

And each family member plays multiple roles with each other. Look at Ian's relationships with his sister, Alison. With Alison, he manages seven relationship roles: (1) her older brother, (2) a fellow board member, (3) the brother-in-law of Alison's husband (who served as CEO of their firm for two years and reported to Ian as board chairman), (4) a fellow trustee, (5) a fellow beneficiary, (6) a fellow foundation board member, and (7) uncle to Alison's son who is a board member. Such multifaceted relationships often lead to role confusion. Famously in the family lore, in a pique of frustration

Family business genograms

To begin to understand the complexity in your family business, identify the individuals in your family system and their relationships with each other. The system is probably more complicated than you think. Start by sketching a genogram (a family tree) with all your family members, including spouses, and going back to the generation that founded your business. A genogram helps you map a business family at a glance—and identify potential issues in the future (see "Further Reading"). In figure 1-1, we map the Dillons, a typical third-generation family business in the pet care industry.[a]

FIGURE 1-1

Sample genogram for the Dillon family

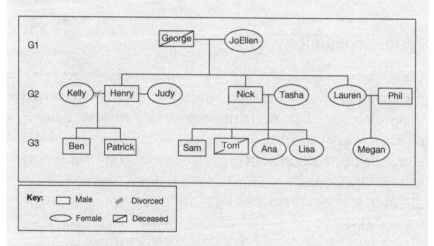

Note: G1, first generation; G2, second generation; G3, third generation.

a. The name and the nature of the business are fictionalized.

at Ian's domineering stance during a discussion, Alison once told him, "Ian, I'm your sister, not your employee. I don't report to you."

Two years after retiring as CEO, Ian, as chairman of the company board, was dissatisfied with the performance of his brother-in-law CEO, who was also Alison's husband. If Ian ousted his brother-in-law, a move that Ian felt was best for the business, how would the change affect his relationship with Alison? Relationships often involve triangles among three people (see "Further Reading" at the back of this book for more on this topic). With his brother-in-law in the hot seat, would Ian, Alison, and her husband still share holiday traditions at their family estate? Would the family fracture into branches? If the demotion were not handled well, would Alison's branch want to sell its shares? Would it trigger conflict among their children?

A single decision can reverberate for years—or even generations. Only family businesses face such relationship challenges.

System dynamics

A family business is a *system*, meaning that the people who are part of it exist within an interconnected environment that affects everything that happens. Yes, individuals and relationships drive much of the behavior in a family business, but each business faces legal, cultural, geographical, and other circumstances that also affect it in fundamental ways. System dynamics shape what happens in a family business, how people act, and even what they want. Four main system dynamics are at play: sameness, mutuality, competing interests, and unintended consequences. Let's examine them.

Sameness

Though your family business is unique, it will behave in predictable ways that are similar to some businesses and different from others, no matter your industry or the size of your business. For example, the stage of development of your family business will shape how it operates. In the seminal family business book *Generation to Generation*, Marion McCollom Hampton and coauthors describe three main configurations of these stages: controlling owners, sibling partners, and cousin consortiums. The distinct patterns of behavior for each configuration are similar the world over. If you meet a family business owned by siblings in Australia or Austria, they will be facing some of the same challenges, no matter the industry or the size of the business.

The laws and taxes of your country and the culture your business operates in will create important similarities with other family businesses in your area. For example, if you live in a country that, like the United States, has high estate taxes, then you are likely to make decisions similar to those made by US businesses to minimize this tax impact. If you live in a country with minimal estate taxes, your choices will be different. Because of differences in these taxes, many large American family businesses are owned through trusts, while most of those in Brazil are not.

Cultural influences also affect the structure of family businesses. In some family businesses, for example, the eldest male in a generation is generally the preferred leader and the other males will usually be owners. The females in these families are seldom the owners but will be cared for by the family. Gender still plays a significant role around ownership in many cultures, with many family businesses bypassing women heirs in favor of men. All of these factors can mean that businesses in a wide variety of industries and sizes have much in common with one another in particular contexts.

Your situation probably has more in common with some other family businesses than you think. You can learn from their experiences.

Mutuality

Family business is a team sport. You win together, and you can lose together. The interconnected nature of a family business means that people can achieve some outcomes, arguably the most important ones, only by working together. Many family businesses want to pass the business on to the next generation. A common interest like this cannot be realized through mandate. Founders may want their children to take over for them, but if the next generation doesn't want to take on the endeavor, there is no family business. You can't simply will it to happen. Even the most powerful people in a family business must learn to compromise if they want to accomplish goals that depend on the actions of others. In the long run, family businesses succeed by mutuality—making decisions that are of mutual benefit to family members. Common interests can only be achieved through collaboration.

For example, spouses can play a significant role in how the next generation sees the family legacy and business. If they are not treated well, they can find ways to keep their children less involved with the family. Unhappy in-laws can discourage their children from attending family gatherings or accepting internships in the family business. They could also advise their children against seeking a career in the business. Your family business will struggle without their support.

Competing interests

System dynamics create competition inside a family business. *Fundamental attribution error* is what social psychologists call the human tendency to attribute people's actions to their personalities rather than any other causes, such as their situation. You might be quick to dismiss the objections of a family member who is the odd one out and you think this person is always just trying to be a contrarian. But in reality, they might be looking at a business decision through a different lens and are just expressing an objection in a clumsy manner. The family member might have a worthwhile point that you will never consider, because you assume they're just being stubborn. Perhaps a better way to understand behavior comes from the expression "Where you stand depends on where you sit." People's wants depend significantly on their position in the family business. Since those positions will differ—consider, for example, the controlling owner versus someone uninvolved in the business but dependent on its dividends for financial security—individuals will have competing interests.

Competing interests typically emerge over time. In the founding generation, one person, or a married couple, often owns all the shares and heads both the business and the family. No competing interests seem to matter, since the founder is viewed as having the power to make all the trade-offs between the business, ownership, and family decisions. The founder's reason behind a rule is often simply "Because I said so!"

But as your business expands to new generations, with many more people involved, multiple competing interests arise. Well-intended people can want plenty of things—dividends, company growth or its sale, status, love, recognition, and jobs for themselves and the next generation, to name a few. Competing demands are put on the business, the owners, and the family.

In the 1980s, two professors at Harvard Business School—Renato Tagiuri and John Davis—created what's known as the *three-circle model*, which shows three overlapping circles—family, business, and ownership—in a Venn diagram. People can occupy multiple sections of the Venn diagram. For example, a family member can also be an owner and an employee of the company, wearing three different hats at any given time.

This simple depiction highlights the likely interests and roles of the people in a complex family business system. The seven roles have distinct, often conflicting, and largely predictable interests (table 1-1).

As families and businesses expand, people inevitably compete for what they want in predictable ways. With this perspective, you won't wrongly attribute behavior to personalities: "Seth is lazy," "Aunt Laureen is a control freak," "Dad never wants us to enjoy our family's wealth; he only cares about the business," and so on. When you consider how each person's role in the family business system influences their interests, you'll better understand the influences on their behavior and decisions—and you can avoid the fundamental attribution error.

Before going any further, fill out your own version of the table (you may not have someone in each role). You'll see that your point of view—and that of others in your family business—may not always be the same.

Think of a recent difficult decision in your family business, such as how to fire a family executive, buy a family member out of the business, create a board, or transfer ownership to the next generation. See if your new knowledge of the connection between people's roles and their primary interests can help you appreciate where people stand, given where they sit. Note their common interests and their conflicting interests. By looking at each person's interests, you will get useful insights on why things are happening at your family firm. The reasons will be varied, of course, but not so perplexing.

TABLE 1-1

The seven possible roles in a family business

Role	Example of the role	Examples of primary interests
1. Family owners who are employees	Creators such as Frederick and Ian	Invest to grow the value of their company, perform meaningful work, steward the company
2. Nonfamily employees	A nonfamily chief financial officer (CFO)	Progress career, protect their job, be fairly compensated
3. Nonfamily owners	An outside investor in the company	Increase the economic value of the company and the financial distributions from the company
4. Family members who are not employed and are not owners	Spouse of an owner	Protect their nuclear family, especially their spouse and children, from harm; have employment and financial opportunities for their spouse and children
5. Family members who are employed by the business but not (yet) owners	A daughter who recently joined the family business at an entry-level job	Build a career, aspire to be an owner of a thriving firm
6. Family owners who are not employed at company	Stay-at-home parent who is an owner	Steward the company well, increase the value of the company and the financial distributions from the company
7. Nonfamily employees who are also owners	A CFO who has been granted equity but is not related to the family	Build their career, protect their job, be fairly compensated, and grow the value of their equity

Unintended consequences

You can never do just one thing.[2] Does this saying sound familiar? You try to fix one problem but, in the process, create a bigger problem elsewhere. We worked with one family business run by three brothers who wanted to avoid a situation where any two of them could gang up on the other. So, they set a rule that any major decision required unanimity. This approach worked out fine when it was just the three of them in the business and their interests were more or less aligned. But it broke down when the next generation entered the company and each brother became more narrowly focused on what was best for his children. Since any of the three brothers could block a decision, they often ended up in a deadlock.

In a complex system, actions have ripple effects. A well-known example is the butterfly effect, where a hypothetical butterfly flaps its wings and sets off a series of events that cause a typhoon on the other side of the world. This hypothetical property of chaotic or complex systems suggests that when actions are interconnected, small things can have major impacts that are nearly impossible to see until much later. You can never really just change one thing in a family business; a single change almost always triggers other consequences as well. When you take a stand or make a major change, you will often create an outcome that is different from, or even the opposite of, what you originally intended.

Family businesses are deceptively complicated. Consider the family arguing over rosebushes at the beginning of this chapter. As we worked with the family, we quickly came to realize that the fight wasn't really about the roses. It was about years of slights, power plays, and lingering wounds, but also about everyone's deep desire to preserve their parents' legacy. The battle over the rosebushes was merely a proxy for their difficulty making decisions together as a group. The family members were eventually able to see this problem for themselves.

Once you grasp how family businesses work, you can see how an apparently irrational decision might make perfect sense in your family business. More importantly, you will come to understand your family and your business better. Focusing on the right problems can help you maintain both a great business and a great business family. And hopefully, you will then avoid wasting precious time arguing over roses.

Summing up

- There are three "levels of analysis" to decode the unique dynamics of a family business: individuals, relationships, and the system. As you read through this book, you'll find many examples of where these three levels are key to understanding what's really going on.

- Relatively few **individuals** shape what happens in a family business. Figure out who those key people are. Then try to understand their personal history and how it influences how they act today, as well as what matters most to them (i.e., their interests) in their various roles.

- Within your family business are complex, multidimensional **relationships** that cut across the different cultures of families, businesses, and ownership. Assess where relationships are strongest in the family (e.g., generations or branches). Look for particular relationships that have significant tension and try to understand why. Consider the potential reverberations across relationships as you make decisions. And look for those with broad relationships that cross boundaries that can help make change happen.

- A family business is a **system** that is shaped by the environment around it. Be on the lookout for the explicit or implicit rules that shape behavior in your family business. As you navigate your system, remember these points:

  - Your situation probably has more in common with some other family businesses than you think. You can learn from their experiences.

  - The most important outcomes require collaboration. No one has absolute power.

  - Competing interests are inevitable. And where each person stands on an issue has as much to do with their position in the system as it has to do with their personality.

  - Actions often have unintended consequences. Try to think through the second- and third-order effects before you make major changes.

- Keep an eye out for changes within your family business that affect dynamics at the individual, relationship, or system levels. When those changes happen, expect that the previous rules may no longer apply.

2.

The Power of Family Ownership

Unlike public companies, in which market forces dictate nearly all decisions, family business owners get to write their own rules, fundamentally shaping not just the business but the family as well. Owners define success for the company. They decide who leads it, whether to stay private or go public, and how much of the profits are kept in the business or distributed.

Whether you are an owner, an in-law, a nonfamily manager, or a competitor, you can't truly know what is going on in a family business until you appreciate the power of family ownership. In this chapter, we will explain this power—which can be used to destroy your family business or sustain it for generations. We describe the five critical rights that allow you to harness the power of family ownership to achieve your desired goals. Understood and wielded properly, ownership is the most important tool to help your family business thrive in the long run.

The hidden pyramid

We're all familiar with the classic corporate pyramid, in which a CEO sits above everyone else. But in family businesses, an inverted, hidden pyramid sits on top of the classic one (figure 2-1). In this power structure, the CEO reports to a board, which is hired by the owners to pursue their objectives. *Owners* are on top of the entire pyramid structure.

The idea of owners at the top makes little sense at a widely held public company, given their limited influence beyond selling their shares. In the long-term potential of a public company, the owners aren't terribly important. The board and the CEO are the voices that matter.

But ownership is central to a family business. Think of the difference between renting and buying a house—a renter is transient, seldom investing in making the house a home. But when you own your own home, it becomes an important part of your identity. Think of how long you might have spent deliberating over investing in new windows or whether to update your kitchen. Being an owner of a family business is much the same. Ownership can be the source of resources, of identity, of responsibility. It can bring enormous pride in your family and its legacy, a deep connection to the communities in which you employ people and do business. And ownership can offer what may be the ultimate reward: getting to call your own shots. Whether positive or negative or a mixture of the

FIGURE 2-1

The inverted pyramid: the hidden power of owners

two, ownership of your family business probably means something significant to you. When we speak of ownership in this book, we are referring not only to direct holders of shares but also ownership that occurs through trusts, which will include trustees and beneficiaries.

The importance of ownership has often been overlooked, even by family business experts. Instead, they have focused on family unity and developing the next generation in the business. These efforts to organize and strive for consensus in the business family led to the creation of globally recognized, valuable approaches such as family councils, family meetings, family constitutions, and protocols (discussed later).

These are important ideas, but they skip over the critical role of family members in making decisions *as the owners of the company*. The exercise of ownership power is very different from efforts to unify and develop the family. Most families strive to be inclusive and harmonious. By contrast, ownership decisions need to ultimately trace back to the shareholders themselves, a practice that may be imbalanced and exclusive. Some families have tried to use their family governance to make ownership decisions. This approach mixes apples and oranges and typically doesn't work. Other families focus instead on containing the family so that it does not interfere with the business. While those boundaries can be useful, they can also create a vacuum in which the power of family ownership isn't exercised by anyone. So, despite all the good work done in the name of organizing the business family, the critical role of ownership has been a particular weakness.

Instead, ownership-related issues have been largely left to lawyers, whose primary job is to protect assets from the government (or other family members). Lawyers are hugely important to certain aspects of protecting family businesses through labyrinthine legal structures such as trusts, estates, and shareholder agreements. Because of these difficult structures, family members seldom fully understand how ownership works in their own family business. And of course, other dimensions of ownership beyond the legal—for example, financial, tax, psychological, cultural, strategic, and political—make ownership challenging to grasp. But the powers and responsibilities of ownership are far too important to simply leave to lawyers to map out in complex documents. Misunderstood and misdirected, the power of ownership can destroy what your family has spent generations trying to build.

The power to destroy

In any work setting, people disagree about strategy, money, status, authority, and so on. Family businesses, of course, are no exception. However, conflict can escalate in a family business in a much different way. In a public company, the rules and ruler are clear. The owners delegate most of their power to the board of directors. CEOs may have almost unlimited power to make decisions while they are in office, but even they can be replaced by the board. And when they are fired, that's the end of the story. A CEO may leave the business (often a lot richer than when they started) but the board's ability to make such significant decisions is rarely challenged. In a family business, it's much harder to keep conflict under control.

To see the destructive power of ownership in action, consider the story of Market Basket, a third-generation grocery chain based in Massachusetts and owned by the Demoulas family. During his tenure as CEO, Arthur T. Demoulas, grandson of the founder, grew sales to more than $5 billion in total and nearly doubled the company's number of employees. Market Basket opened new locations throughout New England at a time when other grocery stores were retrenching because of financial troubles and competition from Walmart and Costco. Affectionately dubbed "Artie T" by Market Basket staff, the CEO became known for his ability to remember employees' names and his personal connections to them, including attending their weddings and funerals. Artie T created a generous employee-benefits program and even put money back into the profit-sharing program after the 2008 recession so that employees would still get their bonuses. His leadership fostered deep loyalty among his employees and customers.

But Demoulas's run as CEO came to a crashing halt in 2014, after years of intrafamily fighting over the fate of the company, when he was fired by the Market Basket board. Though the board made the formal decision, the move was engineered by his cousin, and co-owner, Arthur S. Demoulas, whose branch had gained control after a small but important shift in the balance of ownership power. The firing of Artie T led to the resignation of six high-level managers and massive employee protests, including picket lines. Moved by the extraordinary employee loyalty to Artie T, Market Basket customers stayed away, eventually triggering a reported loss of more than $400 million in the process. After months of painful public and private wrangling, Arthur S. Demoulas agreed to sell his branch's half of the company to Artie T's branch. Artie T returned as CEO in late 2014 to the jubilant support of his loyal workforce. Market Basket survived the owner battle, but the business had to scramble to get back on the sound economic footing it had previously enjoyed for decades. The damage was real.

The Market Basket saga perfectly illustrates the destructive power of family ownership. Conflict among the owners spiraled into a bare-knuckle brawl that nearly destroyed the business in a matter of months. The two branches of the Demoulas family originally owned the business equally, but after a lawsuit in the second generation, Arthur S's branch had been granted control of 50.5 percent of the company and gained control of the board. After internal board maneuvering had allowed Artie T to impose his will on the company as CEO, family branch loyalties returned to side with Arthur S in firing his cousin—setting in motion the conflict that threatened the company's survival. Through their inability to agree on a path forward for the company, the owners almost destroyed one of the most respected, profitable businesses in their industry.

Because the owners of family-owned companies make the rules, they can also break them. Independent boards cannot resolve disputes, since owners can fire the board at will. Absent the involvement of the judicial system, owners have no higher power to appeal to. Unless they figure it out for themselves, conflict can continue to escalate. (For a full discussion of how conflict can spiral out of control in a family business—and how to prevent that fate—see chapter 12, "Conflict in the Family Business.") When that happens, the power of ownership to destroy what has been built over years and generations can be unleashed. Family businesses rarely survive a civil war among the owners. As one family we work with puts it, "The biggest danger to this company is *us*."

These kinds of destructive stories, often played out in public, can make failure seem to be the destiny for many family businesses. This sentiment is reinforced by an often-cited adage about family businesses: the so-called three-generation rule says that only 30 percent of family businesses make it through the second generation, 10 to 15 percent through the third, and 3 to 5 percent through the fourth. According to this rule, few family businesses survive beyond three generations, and the family fortune is lost in the process, too. These disheartening numbers generate anxiety in the third generation in any family business; the generation worries that it will have to beat the odds to survive.

But the adage is misleading. Although the majority of family businesses don't make it through three generations, this failure rate also applies to businesses of every kind. Making a company last for decades is a great achievement. And no evidence suggests that family businesses are more fragile than are other kinds of businesses. In fact, most lists of the longest-lasting companies in the world are dominated by family companies. The three-generation rule also ignores the possibility that some families may not have been trying to keep their companies for longer or that some families may have sold their businesses and then started something new. For more, see the box "Debunking the three-generation rule."

This three-generation rule is destructive because it creates an inferiority complex for family business owners, who believe their business, and family, are doomed to fail. That point of view, in turn, creates a self-fulfilling prophecy. Instead of focusing their energy on how to succeed, they worry themselves to failure. Or they are so concerned about the perils that they don't even try.

The pervasive fear that family businesses can't survive over generations almost derailed one family we advised. An independent board member had told the founding siblings of a successful business, "Family businesses never make it beyond three generations. If you want your business to survive, you should not pass it down to your children." The siblings indeed cared deeply about their business and the people who worked there.

Debunking the three-generation rule

A 1980s study of manufacturing companies in Illinois is the basis for most of the facts cited about the longevity of family businesses. The researchers took a sample of companies and then tried to figure out which of them were still around during the period they studied. They then grouped the companies into thirty-year periods based on their longevity to estimate generations.

A few observations about the study are worth noting. First, its core findings are often described incorrectly. Many people interpret the results to say that 30 percent of family businesses only make it *to* the second generation. But the study actually says that 30 percent make it *through* the end of the second generation, or sixty years. That's a thirty-year difference in business longevity, so choose your words carefully!

Second, the researchers found that 74 percent of family businesses made it for at least thirty years, 46 percent lasted for sixty years or more, and 33 percent survived for ninety years or longer. Finally, the study provides no insight on why some businesses disappeared. Although a family dispute or a business issue could have destroyed the company, perhaps the owners simply sold the business and started a new one.

Those caveats aside, the study still raises the question: Do family businesses have longer or shorter lives than do other types of businesses? A study of twenty-five thousand publicly traded companies from 1950 to 2009 found that on average, they lasted around fifteen years, or not even through one generation. In addition, tenures on the S&P 500 have been getting shorter. If the average company joined the index in 1958, it would stay there for sixty-one years. By 2012, the average tenure was down to eighteen years. A BCG analysis in 2015 found that public companies in the United States faced a five-year "exit risk" of 32 percent, meaning that almost a third would disappear in the next five years. That risk compares with a 5 percent risk public companies faced in 1965.

The data can be interpreted another way: making a business last for decades is hard and, at least for public companies, is getting harder. The studies do not indicate that family businesses are fundamentally flawed with grim survival rates. In fact, the data suggests that the average family business lasts far longer than a typical public company does.

They also very much valued the idea of leaving this business as a legacy for their family rather than cashing out and giving the next generation the sale money. So, when the siblings were ready to retire, they agonized over whether to sell the business to their long-standing nonfamily managers or pass ownership to the next generation. The board member's advice had them believing that they had to choose between making their company last and keeping it in the family. But after realizing that, as owners, they didn't have to assume that their business couldn't survive to the next generation, they decided to give family ownership a try. They are now well into a successful transition to the next generation, with a thriving business led by nonfamily managers who are bridging the gap between the retiring owners and their children.

The power to sustain

Owners no doubt have the power to destroy. But we have learned a different lesson in our work: the owners of family companies also have the power to build enterprises that can be sustained for generations.

Take, for example, the amazing story of Italian winemaker Marchesi Antinori, which was established in 1385 and has survived as a family business for more than six centuries. Among many other crises, Marchesi Antinori has survived default from the English royals as bankers, World War II, and the 1980s methanol crisis, which killed scores of people who had drunk certain wines from the Piedmont region in Italy and which threatened to shut down the then $900 million Italian wine export industry. By 2020, the business was in its twenty-sixth generation of ownership by the Antinori family.

While its longevity has certainly involved some good fortune, the owners have also made specific decisions to sustain the business from generation to generation. For example, the practice of passing control of the business to one male descendant had always ensured that the land and business remained united rather than divided up and that there was a family member who dedicated his career to winemaking. The twenty-sixth generation has no males, however. Instead, patriarch Piero Antinori has three daughters: Albiera, Allegra, and Alessia. This presented a dilemma: "I'm from a different generation, and women didn't participate in the business affairs of the family," he told us. But Piero's daughters began to show interest in managing and owning the business together. Rather than giving the business to one of his daughters, Piero ultimately decided to make them all owners. The connection between ownership and being active in the company remains, but now three voices will decide instead of one.

Part of continuing the legacy has been an explicit investment in developing the next generation. As Piero likes to say, "people are like vineyards. It is important to understand their qualities and potential, but also to sow seeds in the right kind of soil so that they can blossom and grow to the best of their abilities." Piero started teaching his daughters about his love of wine and the business when they were young girls, bringing them on business trips and enabling them to develop early relationships with the business, the employees, and the work.

The Antinoris have made other decisions that have enabled both generational development and financial stability. For example, they always remain fiscally conservative, incurring low debt levels, financing growth through retained earnings, and diversifying their holdings only within their concentrated focus on wine.

For companies like Marchesi Antinori, family ownership has become a source of advantage that helps them thrive in an increasingly competitive marketplace. Family businesses have greater employee retention and engagement, a longer-term orientation toward investments (as opposed to focusing on quarterly results), and more trusted relationships with customers (as confirmed by the Edelman Trust Barometer) than do public companies. And compared with public companies, family enterprises make big decisions faster and better align the interests of owners and managers.

For most of the last century, those benefits have been largely outweighed—at least in the advanced economies of North America and Europe—by the limits on growth that come from lack of access to outside capital, especially through selling ownership to the public. In the race to scale, family companies were at a marked disadvantage. But the game has changed. In the 2015 list of the *Fortune* 500, 84 percent of CEOs agreed with the statement "It would be easier to manage my company if it were a private company." These CEOs believed that "surviving the new technological revolution requires long-term thinking and smart investment. But public shareholders . . . are demanding short-term results. Public-company CEOs are caught in the crosshairs."

So, rather than believing that your family business is somehow doomed to failure, realize that it has the potential to build a sustainable competitive advantage in the twenty-first-century economy. (For more on this point, see "Why the 21st Century Will Belong to Family Businesses," cited in the "Further Reading" section.) Your decision to sustain the company can help it succeed beyond any others. And that's good not just for the owners of family businesses, but for society as well. Family companies have been shown to be better employers and more committed members of their communities. At their full potential, these businesses represent capitalism at its best.

The five rights of family owners

The power to destroy or sustain a family business comes from the owners' unique ability to make choices that influence virtually every aspect of their companies. Ownership can be considered a series of rights. Exercising these five rights gives owners the power to shape not only the business but also the business family:

1. **Design.** Owners have the right to decide what type of family business they will create. Only they can determine what they will own together, who is eligible to be an owner, and how ownership control is divvied up. Through those choices, the owners design their family business.

2. **Decide.** Owners have the right to make every decision involved in running the business, if they so desire. They choose which decisions to keep for themselves and which to delegate to others. They also determine how decisions will be made, whether by majority rules,

unanimity, or some other way. And they can choose to make each decision as situations arise or to establish policies that set precedents in advance. In doing so, owners exercise their right to decide.

3. **Value.** Owners have the right to define success as they see fit. They can maximize shareholder returns, much as public companies do, or sacrifice returns for nonfinancial objectives such as environmental sustainability. Owners can also determine how much of their annual profits they retain in the company or instead pay out in dividends. And they can decide whether to maintain total control over the company or relinquish some of it by bringing on equity partners or taking on external debt.

4. **Inform.** Owners have the right to access information about their business, in particular, how it's performing financially and who owns what. This access, in turn, gives the owners the right to determine what to share with others, including family members, employees, and the community. If a business goes public, owners give up much of this right as part of meeting disclosure requirements. When a business is private, the owners choose how much of their information to make available both to those inside the company and to those outside it.

5. **Transfer.** Finally, owners have the right to choose how and when to exit ownership. Owners can decide who will own the business after them, what form that ownership will take (e.g., shares or trust), and the timing of the transition. Transfer rights have varying levels of restrictions, depending on where the owners live. For example, in the United States, owners can essentially sell or give their companies to whomever they want, except if the shares are held in a trust, which sets out specific requirements. In Brazil, by contrast, inheritance laws require owners to distribute 50 percent of their assets equally among their children and spouse. The owners have flexibility for the other half. While the degree of discretion varies, the decision about

FIGURE 2-2

The five rights of family owners

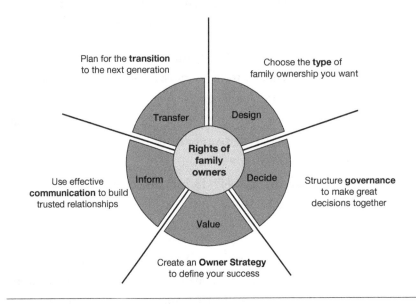

Plan for the **transition** to the next generation

Choose the **type** of family ownership you want

Transfer

Design

Rights of family owners

Use effective **communication** to build trusted relationships

Inform

Decide

Structure **governance** to make great decisions together

Value

Create an **Owner Strategy** to define your success

who receives ownership in the company and when they receive it is up to the current owners.

The key to longevity of a family business lies in how its owners exercise these five core rights (figure 2-2). Understanding and effectively exercising these five rights leads to the long-term success of a family business. But misunderstanding or misdirecting those rights can also destroy what a family has spent generations trying to build.

Owners need to work together as they make these choices (detailed in part 2). The specific choices made are often less important than whether all the owners are behind them. And these choices have to be revisited over time. What worked brilliantly in one generation may sow the seeds of collapse in the next.

We won't sugarcoat our point: without the hard (and smart) work of the owners, family, employees, and others, family businesses all too often naturally implode. It takes energy to keep the inevitably competing interests from destroying the company, and it takes work to sustain a family business across generations. But we clearly lay out the path in this book. You and the other owners of the business have the power to sustain the company if you cooperate. United you can stand, divided you will fall.

Take a moment to capture how you are wielding the power of ownership today. To see this information in an easy-to-visualize format, make two lists. In the first list, note the major actions you have taken to help sustain your family business. They might be tangible things, such as a shareholder agreement or a dividend policy, or less tangible things, such as a next generation that is committed to the business or annual vacations that strengthen family bonds. For the second list, write down the issues that you think create the biggest risk of a major rift in your family business—which issues, if unaddressed, could destroy your family business. They may be current conflicts or ones that you see coming down the line.

Review this initial inventory with others in your family business—next-generation owners, extended family members, and trusted advisers and employees. And come back to it after you finish reading the book. Doing so will help you develop greater insight into your powers as owners and the actions you can take to sustain your family business. You should ultimately see a path to building on the strengths of your family business and addressing its vulnerabilities.

Our message to you is this: you must understand ownership if you want your family business to last. You can hire an outside management team or bring in independent directors for the board. But ownership is the one thing in your family business you can't outsource. In the next part of the book, we will explore each of the five rights of family owners and help you understand how you can thoughtfully exercise them to create a platform for multigenerational success of your family business.

Summing up

- Ownership is what unites family businesses of all sizes around the world. Companies owned by people related to each other are fundamentally different from those owned by investors who have delegated most of their rights to the board.

- Family ownership brings with it a destructive power that is activated when the owners are divided. Nothing can ruin a great business faster than acrimony among the owners.

- Beware of the myth of the three-generation rule. Despite the challenge of ensuring longevity for any business, there is no evidence that family businesses are more vulnerable than other kinds of businesses. To the contrary, most of the longest-lasting companies in the world are family owned.

- Family owners have five key rights: design, decide, value, inform, and transfer. In part 2, we will discuss how to exercise these rights to create lasting success for your business.

PART TWO

The Five Rights of Family Owners

Design

Choose the Type of Family Ownership You Want

In college, Megan finally found her passion. An inspiring biology teacher had led Megan to dream of becoming a biology professor herself one day. But after graduation, Megan's mother, Lauren, convinced her only child instead to join the family pet care business, which her mother owned with her two brothers. Putting aside her own academic aspirations, Megan accepted a position in sales and marketing.

But try as she might, she never settled into the job. After many sleepless nights, she worked up the courage to tell her mother that she wanted to leave the business to pursue a PhD. Megan was unprepared for her mother's response.

"Megan," her mother said, "you can't leave the business. Our shareholder agreement stipulates that only employees of the company can be owners. If you leave the business, I won't have anyone to pass my shares on to when I retire. I'll be forced to sell them to my brothers, and I just can't bear the thought that my whole life's work will benefit your cousins rather than our family."

Megan and her mother, who are part of the Dillon family introduced in the genogram in chapter 1, found themselves in a heart-wrenching dilemma. Even though she was an equal owner, Megan's mother had fought for every bit of recognition her brothers begrudgingly gave her. If she was forced to sell her ownership to her nieces and nephews, she would see her life's work disappear and her brothers would somehow have won. At the same time, if Megan sacrificed her own dreams to support her mother's, Megan feared she would end up bitterly resenting her mother.

How did the Dillon family find itself at such a thorny crossroads? The type of family business they had created—one that restricted ownership to those active in the business—was the source of brewing conflicts that could potentially destroy their family business and their relationships. A decision to allow only those who work in the business to become owners had seemed like the best way to make sure the business was led by family members close to it. But they had not realized how this choice would put limits on the next generation.

Under the broader heading of *family business* is a range of companies that operate in fundamentally different ways. Although hybrids do exist, most family businesses can be described as one of four basic types of ownership that we will discuss in depth throughout this chapter:

- **Sole Owner:** A single family member in each generation holds all the ownership.

- **Partnership:** Only those actively participating in the business can be owners.

- **Distributed:** Any descendant is eligible to be an owner.

- **Concentrated:** Any descendant can be an owner, but a subset has ownership control.

You may never have stopped to consider how your family owns its business. The type of ownership may seem like a formality that was determined in a legal document long ago. But designing the type of family ownership you share is one of your core rights. Each of these types has advantages and disadvantages to the long-term health of both the business and the business family. So in this chapter we will help you with several steps in designing your business:

1. Understand the three main design choices for your family business

2. Identify your type of family ownership and understand its long-term implications

3. Think through whether the type of ownership you have still works for your family or if you need to consider a change

What type of family ownership do you want?

The foundation of your family business is built on three core design choices that you have made, either implicitly or explicitly. The three key choices are:

1. What is the scope of shared assets?

Imagine a spectrum of how your assets are shared with your family. On one end, you share virtually everything—for example, a family that not only reinvests almost all the company's profits for growth but also owns other assets such as car collections, vacation homes, investments, and philanthropic endowments together. Some families own everything collectively, including their personal savings and homes. On the other end of the spectrum are operating companies, whose owners reinvest just enough to keep the business running. For example, one family business that we worked with would annually distribute 100 percent of its profits to the owners, who took that money and either spent or invested it outside of the business family.[1] Most families sit somewhere in between these two extremes. Table 3-1 summarizes the most common reasons that business owners either keep their assets integrated or separate them.

TABLE 3-1

Trade-offs in your design choices

Why integrate?	Why separate?
• Provides a powerful motivation to keep the family unified • Allows family to gain the benefits of scale, both in business and in areas like investing and philanthropy • Avoids major differences in levels of wealth across the family—differences that could come from pursuing investments separately • Protects the family's businesses and wealth by keeping their assets together	• Decreases the risk of family conflict by reducing the number of decisions you have to make together • Creates more "emotional diversification" by reducing total reliance on shared assets • Avoids family members' dependence on the business; dependence can be risky as the family grows or as the business declines • Reduces business and family complexity, which can be difficult to manage

Why be inclusive? (operators, governors, investors)	Why be exclusive? (only operators and/or governors)
• Avoids creating strong incentives to join the company in order to be owners, even when family members are ill-suited ("golden handcuffs") • Maintains capital in the business, rather than using it to buy out family owners who no longer meet eligibility requirements • Broadens the family talent pool across generations • Expands the estate planning toolkit by separating ownership from role in the business (see chapter 7 for further discussion) • Avoids pitting relatives against each other if there are limited roles available • Avoids conflict over the definition and enforcement of ownership eligibility criteria	• Better aligns interests among the owners of the business (see the discussion of the three-circle model in chapter 1) • Reduces conflicts over why some are benefitting from the hard work of others • Allows for more focus on the business, less on dealing with questions or interference from people not actively involved • Establishes a clear exit path for family members who are not interested in the business • Ensures that all family shareholders have firsthand knowledge and understanding of the business

Why share control?	Why unify control?
• Balances power; prevents any one person from making decisions that could undermine the business • Avoids a situation where owners may want to sell if someone else is in control, which could divert capital from growth or threaten the viability of the business	• Streamlines decision-making and thereby enables the business to make big decisions more quickly • Places limits on conflicts by having a single authority who can resolve them

2. Who can be an owner?

The second main design choice concerns who is allowed to own your business. Most family businesses deliberately restrict ownership to bloodline descendants of the original owners. So, for example, the daughter of a founder may someday be entitled to ownership, as will her children, but her husband or stepchildren will not. In our analysis of one hundred family businesses, all but one had some family-line requirements for ownership. Some companies go further and allow only male descendants or those who carry the founder's family name to be owners. In some countries, such as those governed by Sharia law, the question of who will become an owner is set out in advance by law or custom. In other countries, parents are legally required to divide their inheritances equivalently. But even when equal distribution of wealth is not required by law, many parents want to treat their children the same. If the parents' main asset is the business, then it may make sense to split the business equally among the children. This approach creates family branches that extend across generations.

Beyond such bloodline restrictions, many family businesses have additional requirements based on participation in the company. Individual owners fall into three distinct roles:

- **Operators:** owners who work in the business, usually in some leadership role

- **Governors:** owners who meaningfully contribute to decision-making at the shareholder or board levels

- **Investors:** owners who do not participate in decisions in any meaningful way beyond attending annual meetings and reviewing proxy statements (as a public-company owner would)

Some family businesses, like the Dillons' enterprise, set a minimum threshold of engagement for ownership, believing that passive ownership (being an investor) threatens the business's survival. They therefore allow only those who participate actively in the family business to be owners. These family businesses vary in how they define active participation: some firms allow only operators or only governors; others permit either type of owner. The middle portion of table 3-1 compares the advantages of inclusive and exclusive rules of ownership in family businesses. An inclusive approach would allow all types of owners (operators, governors, and investors). An exclusive approach would allow only those who meet the standard of participation.

3. Which owners have control?

Ownership control is often connected to each person's overall share of the company. Under this approach, each individual's level of control over the business is based on the number of eligible heirs in their branch. In the Dillon family, for example, Megan was one of six (living) cousins in the third generation of the family business. But as an only child, she could potentially end up owning more of the business than would her cousins, each of whom would split their father's one-third ownership of the business with their siblings. One of the three fathers had three children; the other had two. So if Megan ended up staying in the family business, she might one day control a third of it, while her cousin Ana (one of three surviving children in her family) might end up with one-ninth (a third of one-third), or just over 11 percent. In cases like this, those who happened to be born into a smaller family will have the good fortune to eventually wield more control over the company. Those with more siblings are destined to have less power.

The alternative to sharing ownership control this way is to consolidate it in the hands of a subset of the owners. Sometimes, one family member

Creating a shared asset map for your family

Given what you know, create a shared asset map for your family. Table 3-2 shows the range of assets that families can share, and it breaks them out by typical categories. To the best of your knowledge, list the shared assets of your family, their rough value, who can own them, which people (or trusts) own them today, who can be owners in the next generation, and issues that the family may face as a result of the ownership design. We included an example of the Dillon's family business to get you started (table 3-2). This map will begin to give you a sense of how your family's ownership is designed and what the embedded issues are.

Asset class	Shared asset (rough value)	Who can own assets?	Who are the current owners (%)?	Who can be owners in the next generation?	Anticipated issues
Operating companies	Dillon Pet Care ($30M)	Operators only	Henry (33%), Nick (33%), Lauren (33%)	Only third-generation members who work in the business	Megan needs to work in business to be an owner. If she doesn't, Lauren would need to sell her shares to her brothers.
Active investments (e.g., companies your family controls but doesn't operate)	Controlling interest in probiotic chicken supplier (PCS) ($3M)	Owned by Dillon Family Trust	Dillon Family Trust (51%) with first and second generations as beneficiaries. Nonfamily company management.	Future beneficiaries of trust are all Dillon third-generation members (distributed)	Will there be conflicts of interest between the business owned by the whole family and that owned by the subset who work in Dillon Pet Care?
Passive investments, (e.g., jointly owned mutual funds)	None				
Real estate (e.g., vacation homes, land, operating real estate)	Beach vacation home ($1.5M)	Owned by Dillon Family Trust	Dillon Family Trust (100%)	Future beneficiaries of trust are all Dillon third-generation members	There are no current shared family property rules about use, upkeep, or expenses (see chapter 13).
Family-controlled philanthropy (e.g., foundations, donor-advised funds, affiliated nonprofits)	Dillon Dog Adoption Family Foundation Endowment ($0.5M)	Controlled by foundation	Owned by foundation	Owned by foundation	Third generation all sit on foundation board to make grants. Grant priorities of individuals vary widely.

is given a majority of the shares, with the explicit understanding that he or she will manage the business for the benefit of the entire family. In other cases, family businesses split their ownership into voting and nonvoting shares, with one or more owners holding the majority of the voting shares, or a *golden share* (and thus control over the business), even if the nonvoting shares that bring most of the financial benefits of ownership are divided equally. When ownership is held in trust, ownership can be consolidated through the trustee powers or the use of a voting trust. For example, in some family businesses, the value of the company is divided across the entire family according to the number of heirs. But one family member in each generation is selected as a trustee of the trust that holds all the voting shares of the company. In practice, this arrangement means that even though the family benefits evenly from the success of the business, one person has control of all major decisions. The bottom portion of table 3-1 captures the primary reasons why families will either unify control in a subset of the owners or share it among all of them.

So what type of ownership does your family business have? Let's start with the first design question, which is about the scope of shared assets (see the box "Creating a shared asset map for your family"). For those assets, is the ownership group consistent, or are some owned in different ways? For example, like the Dillons, you may have an operating business with one set of owners and real estate with a different set. To understand your type of business, you should think of these endeavors separately.

You now need to address the second and third design questions for the business, or businesses, you own in common. Putting them together in the two-by-two matrix in figure 3-1 points to the four most common types of family ownership.

The y-axis points to whether family members have to meet some participation criteria, like working in the business, to be an owner (exclusive) or whether any descendant can be an owner (inclusive). The x-axis differentiates family businesses by whether control is placed in the hands of

FIGURE 3-1

The four most common ownership types of family businesses

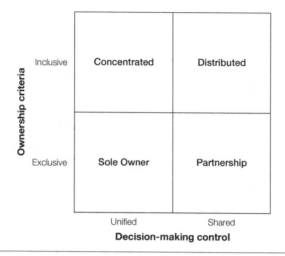

a subset of the owners (unified) or is spread among all owners (shared). In a survey we conducted of family businesses of a variety of sizes, industries, and geographic locations, we found that 13 percent have a single family member of each generation holding all the ownership (Sole Owner), 24 percent require owners to actively participate in the business (Partnership), 36 percent allow any descendant to be an owner (Distributed), and 27 percent allow any descendant to be an owner but a subset having voting control (Concentrated).[2]

Most family businesses start out in the lower left-hand box (Sole Owner). Ownership is exclusive to the founder, who retains full voting control over the business. Some family businesses stay in this mode, limiting ownership to only one person in each generation. This category includes what's known as *primogeniture*. Other businesses still have only one owner but select the next-generation owner on criteria other than birth order and gender. Cognac-maker House of Camus, based in France and founded in 1863, provides an example of the Sole Owner structure. In each generation, one family member leads the company. That person is then required to buy out the siblings' shares and become the Sole Owner. Cyril Camus, the fifth-generation owner, believes that the owner's proximity to the business has been essential to its longevity.

Some family businesses move from having a **Sole Owner** to a **Partnership** (the lower right-hand box in figure 3-1). They retain the connection between ownership and active participation but allow for more than one person to be an owner. Much like the situation in a law firm or a management consultancy, ownership in this type of family business usually requires some ability to contribute to the success of the business, and ownership ends when the partner leaves the company. The Dillon family chose a Partnership. This ownership arrangement can work for generations. The German-Dutch Brenninkmeijer family owns COFRA, a holding company that owns fast-fashion retailer C&A and other businesses. In the COFRA Partnership, the children of current owners, as described on its website, "undergo a rigorous process of selection, evaluation, and apprenticeship lasting around 15 years" before they can earn the right to ownership. There are currently around fifty family owners, part of a much larger family that is going into its sixth generation.

Other family businesses move to a more shared and inclusive model of ownership (the upper right-hand box in figure 3-1) after the founding generation. Since both ownership and control are widely shared, we have dubbed it the **Distributed** form of ownership. Distributed ownership has no participation requirements, and shares are passed down through the family lines. For example, Bacardi Limited has been owned by seven generations of Bacardí family members—descendants of the company founder Don Facundo Bacardí Massó. Because of the company's Distributed form of ownership, a major family shareholder in the Bacardi empire has around a 1 percent share.

Finally, some family businesses exit the Sole Owner mode and move to the upper left-hand box. They adopt an inclusive definition of ownership, usually all descendants of the founder. However, the unified control of the founder is maintained in a subset of the owners, often one person or a few people at most. We have named this form of business Concentrated because of the differential power of those who are given ownership control. For example, the family owners of Vitamix, a manufacturer and global leader in high-performance blenders and blending solutions, have adopted what they refer to as a "collaborative leadership model." While the economic value of the hundred-year-old company is passed down through descendant lines, in each generation the CEO is required to either own or control the majority of the voting shares. While the owners aim for consensus on major decisions, this approach allows the CEO to make the final call if they can't reach alignment.

Understanding the current and future implications of your ownership type

We have seen success stories in all the types of family ownership. As summarized in table 3-3 on the next page, each type has strengths and challenges for companies navigating across a changing business landscape.

In some cases, how owners act in practice can greatly differ from the legal form of ownership. For example, we worked with a group of siblings who technically owned their company equally, but the eldest exercised control on all decisions related to the business. This family business is legally a Distributed type but in practice acts like a Concentrated type. Operating under such an *enacted* type of ownership that differs from the legal structure may never be a problem if future generations understand and agree with the practice. But it could also lead to conflict and confusion if the next generation has a different perspective. If your actual practice differs from the legal structure of leadership in your family business, consider over time aligning your legal structure with your enacted type or vice versa.

Take a moment to reflect on the ownership of *your* family business. Using figure 3-1, answer the following questions:

- Which of the four ownership types most closely resembles *your* family business today?

- Has your type of family ownership changed over time? If so, trace the evolution across the two-by-two matrix.

TABLE 3-3

Benefits and challenges of different family ownership types

Definition	Benefits	Challenges
Sole Owner: A single family member in each generation holds all the ownership.	Works best when the business requires a single leader with decisive control and when there are other assets for those who do not become the Sole Owner or when the business creates enough liquidity to take care of nonowners.	You must address the question of who the successor will be and how they are selected becomes central. The Sole Owner must also wrestle with what benefits the rest of the family will receive. Parents will sometimes give other assets to their children who are not chosen. Others keep most of the assets in the business but expect that the Sole Owner will take care of everyone else. Sometimes this expectation is documented, but usually it is set by the family culture. If the Sole Owner is selected by a rule such as primogeniture, the individual's merit for the role is set by the rule, not by ability.
Partnership: Only those actively participating in the business can be owners.	Functions best when the business benefits from active participation by multiple family owners, and when there are other assets for those who do not become owners or when the business creates enough liquidity to take care of nonowners.	You must clarify the rules by which family members enter and exit the ownership group, as well as what happens to those who are not active participants. Some partnerships will limit the shared assets to operating companies, keeping investments or family properties outside the business and allowing all descendants to own them. Many partnerships require each generation to purchase their shares from the previous one. This practice, however, requires the company to recapitalize itself each generation (reducing investment in the business). Recapitalization can also preclude the use of valuable estate planning vehicles that can reduce taxes but require knowing who the owners will be many years in advance.
Distributed: Any descendant is eligible to be an owner.	Fits well when the majority of family wealth is held in a single asset and when either the family culture or the legal system requires shared ownership across all family descendants.	You will be challenged to align the interests of different owners, since owners may have different levels of engagement. And with no owner having a majority share, you will have to define ways of delegating and making decisions that build consensus. Because no one is required to be active in the company, the ownership group risks becoming too distant from the business and losing control. (For more on this situation, see chapter 14.)
Concentrated: Any descendant can be an owner, but a subset has ownership control.	Works well when the business requires decisive action even when there are multiple owners.	You solve many of the problems of the Distributed type of business but create others. As with a Sole Owner or a Partnership, the question of who gets to exercise control becomes more complicated with each generation. Is control passed down through the same branch? Or if it goes to the most qualified, how is that defined? How do those who have control keep the other owners from becoming disengaged, since the others' vote doesn't matter?

Changing your type of family ownership

Your type of family ownership can change across generations, sometimes evolving naturally in response to family or business dynamics. For example, the Antinoris, the Italian winemakers we discussed in chapter 2, have modified the ownership of their family business. Rather than giving the business to only one of his daughters, patriarch Piero ultimately decided to shift ownership to a Partnership, in which each of his daughters, Albiera, Allegra, and Alessia, would be both an owner and active in the company.

The Antinoris' ownership type may have to evolve again for the twenty-seventh generation. All six of the three daughters' children will be owners, but at this point it seems unlikely that all of them will end up working in the business. The family is defining the rules for how the next generation will manage the inherent challenges that come with a move away from the Sole Owner type. But the Antinoris' willingness to change their ownership type has been instrumental in keeping the company going across the generations.

In other circumstances, you might need to change your type of family ownership to address a conflict that threatens to destroy the business itself. When family businesses find themselves trapped in this kind of situation, the problem almost always runs deeper than "Who is qualified to be a successor?" or "What career path should the next generation take?" The challenges these families face generally reflect a mismatch between the ownership type that worked for the current generation and the one that best suits the needs of the next.

As we discussed at the start of this chapter, the Dillon family found itself with this sort of dilemma because of their Partnership structure, which no one had openly questioned before Megan's situation arose. Fortunately, Megan and her mother were not the only ones feeling the stresses caused by their ownership design choices. Of the six members of the next generation, only three were enthusiastic about working in the business.

After much discussion, the Dillon family decided to allow family members who were not working in the business to be owners. Accepting a different definition of ownership required a seismic shift in thinking for

Megan's mother and uncles. The expectation that all their children would be equally interested—and skilled—in working in the business was unrealistic. Lauren and her brothers concluded that despite their ultimate goal of maintaining the business as a family legacy, they also wanted to be true to the spirit of having a business controlled by those working in it. A Concentrated structure that allowed all family descendants to be owners but left control in the hands of those working in the business would make these two goals possible. Such a change required new governance structures, policies, and estate plans. These measures required a significant investment of time and energy. But they facilitated a smooth transition to the next generation. And more importantly, the next generation could pursue their professional passions, rather than living out those of their parents. Megan now teaches in a university and is actively engaged as a board member, committed to keeping her mother's legacy alive.

We hope that by describing these types of ownership, we have helped you open up that kind of conversation. As you review your design, ask whether it is appropriate for the future. The needs and interests of both the family and the business change over time. For example, owners can increase in number or diverge in their capabilities. Sometimes, owners need outside capital as the business grows. Define your objectives as owners, and explore whether the current approach is best suited to achieve them. You should consider reviewing and potentially changing your design under these circumstances:

- The next generation is coming into the business.

- The size and complexity of the business changes significantly.

- You are facing capital constraints from the need to buy out owners of the business.

- You are stuck in a conflict where the root cause relates to what you own, who can be an owner, or who has control.

- You're making the transition from family leadership to nonfamily leadership of the business.

At the foundation of every family business are choices that define its basic form. Although often taken for granted, these choices are essential for you to understand, and revisit, if you want your family business to be a part of your future.

Summing up

- Owners have the right to choose their type of family ownership. In particular, they have three main design choices:

  - What do you want to own together?

  - Who is eligible to be an owner?

  - Which owners have control?

- Each of the four main types of family ownership—Sole Owner, Partnership, Distributed, and Concentrated—brings its own strengths and weaknesses.

- Family businesses often change their type of ownership over time. Trace the history of your family business by looking at how its type has evolved over the decades.

- Your type of family ownership significantly influences your governance structures, strategic options, communication patterns, and succession methods.

- If your family business is experiencing a major challenge, consider whether you have the right ownership design in place. Revisit what assets are owned together. Can you benefit from adding new shared assets or separating existing ones? Will your family ownership type enable you to address the challenges of the future?

4.

Decide

Structure Governance to Make Great Decisions Together

The decision-making power of the owners of a family business is profound.[1] In some sizable businesses, not a dollar can be spent without the approval of the owners. But that doesn't mean owners *should* be making all those decisions. As the size and scale of both your family and your business increase, the role of owners is less about making decisions directly and more about exercising decision-making power effectively. When held too tightly, the power to control all decisions will stifle the business *and* the family.

That's where governance comes into play. Good governance helps owners balance the need to maintain control over what matters most with the need to delegate responsibility to others. It allows for better and faster decision-making.

If your business is small or has functioned well with an informal decision-making process, you may consider formal governance unnecessary. But with a company's success and growth, the number and difficulty of decisions soon become too great for any one person (or one group of people) to make all the decisions well. And with no power over decisions, other family members and employees can end up feeling powerless, disengaged, or in conflict with one another. Time and again, we have seen businesses underperform and slide into chaos when they have failed to learn how to make good decisions together. Too often, the blame is placed on the family members in leadership roles, rather than the collective failure to build good governance.

Take, for example, the case of Steve, the president of a third-generation family business. "I'm a cowboy," he told us proudly. "Ready, shoot, aim." Steve had good reason to boast about his cowboy instincts; they had been critical to his family business's rapid growth in the past two decades, from a small number of local shops to an admired regional chain. For nearly thirty years, Steve ran the company with his sister and cousin, each of them equal owners in the enterprise that their fathers had handed down to them. But Steve was earning no accolades from his co-owners for his business instincts. In fact, his solo cowboy decisions were the source of conflict that threatened to derail the business. When his sister and cousin asked him to slow aggressive growth and keep them better in the loop, Steve bridled at the constraint. "To hell with that! I built this place!" Steve confessed to us. The business was thriving, but relationships were strained to the point where all three owners wondered if it was time to go their separate ways.

At its core, Steve's struggle wasn't about a lack of good intentions; it was about a lack of good governance. Steve and his co-owners had no healthy process for making decisions together. Once they recognized this problem, however, they set up a formal governance structure that required Steve to seek approval from his sister and cousin for any business decision over a certain dollar value. This solution has had the dual effect of relieving his co-owners' concerns of being left out of the loop on major decisions and requiring Steve to plan and justify moves more carefully. The business—and the family—are now back on track.

The quality of your decisions will determine the future of your family business. So how do you sort out the myriad of decisions every family business faces and decide who should make them? In this chapter, we will help you understand good governance by presenting four tools:

1. The Four-Room model, a framework to help you organize decision-making in your family business

2. A roadmap for setting up the Four Rooms in your family business

3. A guide to creating processes that work well for the various people and rooms in your family business

4. A plan for overhauling your current governance to make more effective decisions

The Four-Room model

A simple framework for better decision-making starts with a metaphor. Imagine your family business system as a home with four rooms: an Owner Room, a Board Room, a Management Room, and a Family Room. Each room has clear rules about who is allowed inside, what decisions are made there, and how those decisions are made. We call this framework the **Four-Room model** (figure 4-1). It's a simple but useful way to map out who should make which decisions in your family business. Well-run family businesses funnel decisions to the appropriate room, and family members and others play different roles and behave differently in each room. A non-family CEO, for example, leads the Management Room (which focuses on the day-to-day business) but shouldn't decide how the owners will use their dividends. Similarly, family members can't just walk into any room and make decisions. The value of building your governance around the Four-Room model is that the rules and boundaries of decision-making are clear: everyone knows which rooms they are allowed to enter, and they understand how the rooms work together. The Four-Room model is an effective way to organize the people, the relationships, and the decision-making systems in your family business.

The Four Rooms are not randomly configured. Think back to the inverted pyramid in chapter 2. Management answers to a board that

FIGURE 4-1

The Four-Room Model

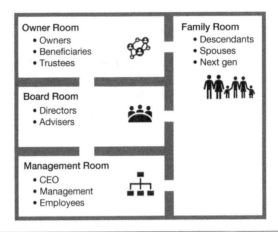

ultimately answers to the owner group. But the Family Room has an important place as well. As figure 4-1 shows, it is not perched atop the other rooms, because the other rooms don't report to the family. Rather, the Family Room runs *adjacent* to all other rooms in this model to indicate the importance of maintaining family influence and unity and developing the talent of family members, who, if qualified and interested, can eventually move into other rooms.

The atmosphere in each room should feel different, and this difference is by design. For example, we discussed earlier the importance of relationships in a family business. The right relationships and environment should be present in each room to be effective. In its ideal form, an Owner Room is about power and influence, about making the rules. A Board Room is about wisdom and judgment. A Management Room is about competence and execution. A Family Room is about love, unity, and development.

The decision and information flow among the rooms is key to the Four-Room model. Each room will make decisions or create policies that the other rooms will have to know about to do their work well. For example, the Owner Room might create a policy about how family members are compensated when they work in the company or for when dividends are paid. The policy must be communicated so that the people in other rooms, in turn, will understand how their own decisions need to support those policies.

Many family businesses are not large or complex enough to warrant a full Four-Room build-out. Nonetheless, you can put into practice many of the ideas in a more informal approach. You could, for example, have discussions in all the appropriate rooms in a single meeting. You just need to set a clear agenda ("We'll discuss Owner Room decisions from 12 to 2 p.m., Board Room decisions from 2 to 3 p.m." and so on), make sure the right people are in the right discussion, and *enforce the boundaries you have set up*. The fundamental decisions are the same for family businesses of any size.

To improve governance in your family business, you will need to focus on two areas:

1. **Structures:** Which rooms will you create, and which decisions should be made in each room? This is the blueprint of your house.

2. **Processes:** How will the rooms be integrated? This is the flow of your house—how the rooms are connected to, and communicate with, each other.

We explain each of the rooms in detail below.

Structures: form your Four Rooms

The first task is to define what decisions are made in each room and to establish the forums (decision bodies with the appropriate knowledge and authority) needed to do that work. Let's walk through how decisions are typically allocated across the Four Rooms. The Four-Room model we use in this chapter can be customized so that it works best for your family and family business.

Setting up your Owner Room

No matter what the specifics of your family business are, you should set up an Owner Room in which to make the decisions that will shape your business for years (and indeed for generations). The absence of an Owner Room, even in a family business with otherwise well-developed governance structures, is the single biggest gap we have seen in our work.

What decisions happen in the Owner Room?

When setting up an Owner Room, owners explicitly retain a few important decisions. Four decisions sit squarely in the Owner Room and should not be delegated:

- Defining how ownership interests can be bought, sold, and transferred, including to the next generation (often captured in a shareholder agreement, which is discussed later in this chapter)

- Making the final call on actions that change the nature of what it means to be an owner, such as going public, taking on significant debt, or selling the company

- Setting goals that define success for the company (for more on this topic, see chapter 5)

- Electing family or nonfamily board members to represent the owners' interests

Beyond these core decisions, owners also can reserve other decisions for themselves. For example, we know an eighty-year-old family business owner who decides the location of each of his company's retail outlets. Firmly believing that store location is the most important decision for the success of the firm, he reserves it for himself. Owner groups vary greatly on the list of reserved decisions. To be an effective owner, you need to decide which *few* decisions are so important that only owners should make them. Everything else can and should be delegated.

Who is in the Owner Room?

The current owners of the business are the core members of the Owner Room. If your business is owned by trusts, then the trustees and beneficiaries are involved in the room. (While trusts bring large tax benefits to owners, they make owner decision-making far more complicated; see chapter 7.)

Future owners are only invited into the room when the current generation sees them as fit to be part of owner discussions. These young people can typically join in discussions in their late twenties and beyond. Having great influence on both the current and the next generation of owners, the spouses of the owners are sometimes invited to participate in the Owner Room. (In our client base, about 20 percent have a formal role for spouses in the Owner Room. In some countries, spouses legally become owners and are naturally included.)

How does the Owner Room work?

Effective businesses must set the right tone in the Owner Room. Unlike in the Management Room, in which the CEO is the ultimate boss of the employees, owners have no boss. Though the person or group with 51 percent of the voting shares has legal control of the asset, minority shareholders also have their own rights and interests, both protected by law and often explicitly spelled out in a shareholder agreement. (For example, a shareholder agreement might stipulate that the business can't be sold without the consent of a super majority of shareholders.) Minority shareholders don't report to a majority shareholder. This lack of hierarchy makes the group dynamic in the Owner Room challenging. Without a boss, an Owner Room works on power and influence. Decisions in this room are affected both by vote (where voter weight matches the percentage of shares an individual or group controls) and by voice (where nonvoting input can play an important role in decision-making). Even in a Concentrated ownership structure, a controlling owner risks conflict if they fail to seek input from minority and next-generation owners. Well-run Owner Rooms ensure that all owners have a voice in the major decisions, even if they don't have a vote. And most operate by consensus, defined as a decision that may not be what each person would do if it were only up to them, but that everyone can live with. Even if you have the votes, we advise trying to work toward consensus first in order to maintain as much unity as possible.

An Owner Room typically has two structures: an owner council and a shareholder meeting. An **owner council** represents the ownership interests of a family in business. It provides several benefits:

- A forum for family shareholders to receive updates on the business and to express their views

- A working group to make recommendations about key ownership issues (shareholder agreements, dividend policies)[2]

- A liaison from the shareholders to decision-making groups: board, management, family office, family council

An owner council should convene somewhere between monthly and quarterly. If your company has ten or fewer owners, each owner typically attends all meetings. In larger families, the owner council often becomes a representative body that works on ownership issues on behalf of all owners. In that case, members are elected either by branches or by all the owners. In a Concentrated type of family business, where a subset of owners has control, the owner council may not have any decision-making power. Instead the council is a formal mechanism for the controlling owner or owners to hear from the other owners.

A **shareholder meeting** is the venue through which the legal rights of owners are typically exercised. In this meeting, board members are elected, bylaws are changed, and major decisions are approved. All holders of shares—either directly or indirectly as trustees or beneficiaries of trusts—are invited to attend the meeting. In smaller ownership groups, the meeting is usually a formality, often happening alongside an owner council meeting. In larger ownership groups, the shareholder meeting is often more formal, with votes cast in person or by proxy. Shareholder meetings typically happen annually unless a major decision, such as selling a business, arises sooner and requires ownership approval.

Setting up your Board Room

What decisions happen in the Board Room?

The role of the Board Room reflects its position between the Owner Room and the Management Room. A board should ensure that managers are operating the company in a way that accomplishes the objectives set by owners. You can identify which decisions are important enough to ask the board to focus on by a simple litmus test: Is the decision so significant that a bad choice could place the business at substantial risk?

Board-level decisions typically include these issues:

- Hiring or firing the CEO, which many board members consider to be their single most important decision

- Planning management succession, whether within the family or with nonfamily employees

- Setting appropriate executive compensation, including that for the CEO and the CEO's team (if the executive is an owner, the board should separate compensation for management from returns to the owner)

- Approving business strategy recommended by the CEO and "material" decisions such as acquisitions and loans

- Ensuring proper regulatory and legal compliance

- Setting annual dividends in light of the policy set in the Owner Room and that year's business performance

The board should *oversee* the business, not run it.

Most jurisdictions have a legal requirement to appoint a board, but sometimes it's just a formality for companies. There are good reasons to go beyond the basic legal requirements and to create a board that will actually help guide and advise your business. Various types of boards can be helpful in a family business; you don't need to automatically default to a

TABLE 4-1

Family business boards at a glance: What type do you need?

Description	Advantages
Informal advisory board: advisory group that provides informal advice to company executives and owners; has no legal authority	• Easy to implement • Flexible • Limited liability
Formal advisory board: advisory team that meets regularly to provide advice to shareholders and executives; has no legal authority	• Flexible • Limited liability • Structured advice • Institutional memory • Some outside directors will only take advisory roles
Fiduciary board: formal group of directors legally empowered to make board-level decisions about the business	• Institutional memory • Makes tough decisions • Can provide stopgap leadership • Members have legal responsibility to represent all shareholders • Some outside directors will only take fiduciary roles
Hybrid fiduciary/advisory board: mixture of fiduciary family directors with voting power and outside advisers without fiduciary responsibility	• Mix of advantages from the formal advisory board and fiduciary board

classic big company board setup. Table 4-1 outlines the different options you might want to consider.

Who is in the Board Room?

You may be tempted to limit your board to family members in an effort to keep the details of your business private. We recognize that bringing on an outsider is a big step for family businesses, but we urge you to consider adding at least some independent voices to your board. Independent directors can change the dynamic of a Board Room to make it more professional, help you manage the careers of family members in the business, and bring complementary expertise to board discussions, to name just a few benefits.

Who should be on your board then? When your business is sufficiently large and complex, adding independent directors or advisers is one of the few universal best practices that we will highlight for every family business. Remember, as owners, you'll always have the right to fire an independent if they fail to serve your interests. You're still in control. Whichever configuration you select, make sure your board is composed of people who understand the interests of owners and who can wisely guide and oversee the business in the board-level decisions.

"No buddies, no business" is a good rule of thumb. You shouldn't have your golfing buddy on your board. Nor should you have an adviser who sells services to your company. And a board with several members from management lacks an independent perspective. Management shouldn't oversee itself.

Setting up your Management Room

What decisions happen in the Management Room?

The Four-Room model pushes nearly all remaining business-related decisions to the Management Room. Of course, every business has a long list of management decisions—recommending strategy, operating the business, hiring or firing the management team, to name a few. While the owners have the right to make these decisions, with the Four-Room model, the owners who are not explicitly operators step away from management decisions. The Four-Room approach gives management the language to put back in its appropriate room any "helpful advice" from nonoperating owners or other family members, thereby enforcing important boundaries.

Who is in the Management Room?

In the early stages of a family business, you may only have family members acting as managers. As the business grows, you'll probably need to add nonfamily professionals to help run it. Some family businesses require their business to be run by family members; other firms prohibit family members from working in the company. Most businesses are somewhere in between, and successful family businesses exist across the entire spectrum. But you don't have to choose between being family-run and being professionally managed. With the right policies and processes, you can be both. (We will discuss the challenges of family and nonfamily working in the business in chapter 9.)

A nonfamily CEO can be central to the success of a family business. But it's important to recognize that by bringing one in, the owners are ceding some amount of decision-making power. To position both the owners and the new CEO for success, take the time to clarify the scope of the new CEO's authority, as well as how you will work together.

Setting up your Family Room

What decisions happen in the Family Room?

The primary purpose of the Family Room is to enhance family unity and build family talent. In this room, both love and other emotions come into play, though they are usually unwelcome in business decisions. A Family Room allows all family members—including spouses and next-generation members—to build and strengthen their bonds, to share experiences, and to stay connected with the business.

Distributed and Concentrated family businesses, which may have dozens or even hundreds of family members, clearly need strong Family Rooms, while Sole Owners and Partnerships may have less of a need.

We benchmarked Family Rooms across a wide range of sizes, industries, and geographies. They all work on similar challenges:

- What unites us as a family?

- How do we develop healthy communication within the family and between the family and the business?

- How do we develop the next generation?

- How do we organize our family to stay together?

- What family policies should we put in place to clarify expectations and manage conflict?

- How do we build connections and have fun together?

Who is in the Family Room?

All family members above a certain age can be part of the Family Room. But who exactly constitutes your business family? Typically, families include all descendants and spouses of their founder. That seems obvious, right? But if a branch sells its ownership in the family business, is that branch still part of the business family? What about divorced spouses whose children will someday be owners? Family businesses have different definitions of family—and there are many common permutations—but the most successful business families are inclusive.

How does a Family Room work?

Most Family Rooms have two common structures: a family council and a family assembly. **A family council** is a small group of family members (four to seven) who are elected by the full family to lead the work on the challenges listed earlier. Typically, a family council might have a few mandates, such as the responsibility for developing and educating the next generation (as shareholders, family members, citizens, and professionals). A family council might manage communication among the family members (e.g., many families we work with communicate updates via messaging platforms). Or the council might ensure integration across the family and preserve the family legacy through speakers, events, and other activities. Membership in the family council can offer people who don't work in the business or who are not active owners a wonderful opportunity to help contribute to the longevity of the family business.

A **family assembly** is like a family reunion for a business family. Typically, it occurs every year or two and is organized by the family council. The agenda covers both the family and the business. We have seen everything from an all-day picnic to an all-expenses-paid getaway to a five-star resort. Whatever their level of expense and formality, successful assemblies set aside time for family connections, fun, and education. One family we know celebrates any family wedding that has occurred since the last assembly. Another family asks each member over a certain age to contribute their biography (in whatever form they choose) to the family library. In another creative approach, one family prepares mini case studies for the younger generation to work through to understand the family's business history. Time is also set aside to communicate changes in the business, introduce new business leaders and board members, and new structures and policies that the family council is developing. As families grow larger and spread across different branches, family assemblies are crucial. Siblings grow up in the same house and share experiences and deep bonds. But once family members are part of different households, those bonds can't be assumed. Cousins are more likely to develop important cross-family bonds through regular, shared experiences available at family assemblies.

Table 4-2 provides a basic blueprint for how to organize the Four Rooms. But you have to think through what will work best for your family.

TABLE 4-2

Four Rooms at a glance

Room	Key decisions in room	Who occupies room and has decision authority?	Typical forums in room
Owner Room	• Decide who can be an owner • Make final call on decisions that change meaning of ownership • Set owner-level goals and standards • Elect board members	• Current owners • Next-generation owners • Beneficiaries • Trustees	• Owner council • Shareholder meeting
Board Room	• Hire and fire CEO • Plan management succession • Set executive compensation • Approve business strategy and material decisions • Ensure compliance • Set annual dividend	• Family directors • Independent directors (who have fiduciary duty) • Independent advisers (whose guidance and wisdom you value)	• Board of directors • Board of advisers
Management Room	• Recommend business strategy • Implement strategy • Run the day-to-day business	• CEO • Management • Employees	• Management meetings • Executive committee
Family Room	• Build family unity • Educate family members • Develop next generation	• Family members, including spouses and next generation	• Family council • Family assembly

Processes: integrate across rooms

Family businesses need well-designed rooms for effective governance. But remember that a family business is a system—what happens in one area affects other areas, often in unintended ways. Because major decisions are likely to affect the family, the business, and owner groups, they require coordination and cooperation. Not only do you have to have well-defined forums to make decisions, but you also need to figure out how those forums interact with each other. Without good integrating processes, even thoughtfully created structures lose their impact.

To work effectively, the Four Rooms must function well together. To ensure this integration, good governance includes four core elements: family businesses should map out the key decision processes across rooms; create formal connections between the rooms; establish policies to address cross-room hot spots, or conflicts; and put formal agreements in place. The following sections discuss how family businesses can accomplish this integration.

1. Map out the key decision processes that connect across rooms

Certain decisions, such as how you will select board members or make an acquisition, are sufficiently important and frequent to warrant a clear, already-decided system for making them. One helpful tool is a **decision-authority matrix**, a map that categorizes the different roles that groups play as part of a healthy decision-making process. Questions that the matrix answers include who has input into a decision, who assembles the input into a recommendation, who makes the final call, who (if anyone) can veto that decision, and who is informed about the decision even if they didn't participate in making it. (See Paul Rogers and Marcia Blenko's "Who Has the D?" in the Further Reading section for more details about a decision-authority matrix.)

A decision-authority matrix can lay out a clear process for how important decisions pass through various rooms (see table 4-3). For example, the CEO may recommend acquiring a small company to meet the company's strategic goals. That recommendation starts with management and then moves on to the board. The board members have the authority to decide

TABLE 4-3

Sample partial decision-authority matrix

Decisions	Owner council	Board	Management	Family council
Major acquisition or sale	A	D	R	I
Annual dividend payouts	A	D	R	
Raising major equity or debt capital	A	D	R	
Selecting/removing board members	D	R		I
Hiring/firing CEO	A	D		I
Hiring/firing employees			D	
	A = approve	D = decide	R = recommend	I = inform

on the recommendation, basing their decision on the investment required. But the owner council can veto such a major decision. And finally, the family council should be informed of the acquisition, perhaps in its annual meeting or through a special communication.

Take time to create a map of the important decisions your family business will face and how those decisions should be made through the Four Rooms. You can't map out every decision that cuts across rooms in elaborate detail, but we encourage you to identify those that are frequent and important enough to justify the effort.

2. Create formal connections across the rooms

More structured decision-making can become balkanized, with each of the Four Rooms unaware of what the others are doing. Building connections across the rooms can be a valuable way to keep decision-makers or stakeholders from becoming too insulated. For example, you might consider instituting two practices:

- **Overlapping memberships whenever possible:** Having an owner sit on the board, for example, helps create a natural flow of information from one room to the other.

- **Distinct points of interaction:** Some board and executive committee meetings have a regular spot on the agenda for an owner
representative to share the work of the owner council, for example,
and to raise any questions or concerns about the business. You can
build opportunities into the agendas of different groups to stay
connected.

3. Establish policies to address cross-room conflict

Family businesses can avoid recurring conflict by creating policies ahead of
time. If you can agree beforehand on issues that should always be treated
the same way, you'll minimize conflict down the line. For example, rather
than treating each next generation coming into the business as a one-off
decision, develop a policy that sets standards for entry into the business.
(For more on this, see chapter 10.) Setting policies this way helps increase
the communication and transparency among rooms. We have also seen
effective cross-room family business policies on dividends (chapter 11),
conflicts of interest, the use of company resources, and access to family
properties (chapter 13).

4. Put formal agreements in place

Once you have done all the work to define how your family business will
make decisions, you need to document these policies. Many family businesses operate through informal understandings and handshakes, which
tend to work just fine right up until the moment they don't. Consider two
main types of agreements.

A **family constitution**, or **protocol**, captures the core rules and regulations of your family business. For example, the document will often consist of the family business's purpose or values, key policies, ground rules,
and conflict resolution guidelines. These agreements are not usually legally
enforceable. We have seen families get too focused on the development of
the constitution itself, rushing to get it on paper or even hiring outsiders to
write it for them. The process is much more important than the printing
of a document. The goal is to get everyone to agree on the rules that you
believe will benefit the entire business family.

A **shareholder agreement** codifies the mechanics of ownership. It is a legally enforceable document. Having in place a shareholder agreement *that you have read and understand* is another best practice we advise for every family business. If you don't have a shareholder agreement, start working on it as soon as possible. Without one in effect, your shareholder agreement is whatever the laws in your jurisdiction prescribe, which may not be at all what you want. For example, some places give judges the right

When your house is not in order: identifying problems with decision-making

Sometimes, family businesses don't realize that their governance structure is lacking until they encounter significant problems with decision-making. For example, Steve's "cowboy" approach—investing in new businesses without consulting his sister and cousin, as described at the beginning of the chapter—had not been a problem until recently. When decision-making is not working in a family business, we usually find that the rooms are not designed or functioning correctly. David Ager, cochair of the Families in Business program at Harvard Business School, sees the problem frequently. "I am often invited into family businesses with little to no formal family governance," he told us. "Most of the time, it is the senior generation that is resistant to the idea of governance because they 'have managed just fine without it.' What they have a hard time acknowledging is that fostering unity, building meaningful relationships, and taking decisions in an eight- or even sixteen-person system is far less complicated than doing so in a forty-, sixty-, or eighty-person system. And so, part of the task in launching more formal governance in a family business is persuading the senior generation of its purpose and value."

to initiate the sale of a business if the owners are in a stalemate. If you have a shareholder agreement but have not read it lately, pick it up and make sure you understand its implications. A shareholder agreement typically does the following:

- Clarifies ownership's decision-making authority, that is, who makes what decisions, what the decision rules are (majority,

We have encountered four main patterns of problems in family business governance. Continuing with the Four-Room analogy, we describe them as lofts, silos, missing rooms, and messy rooms and summarize them in table 4-4.

TABLE 4-4

The most common problems in family business governance

Problem	Indicators you have an issue
Loft: An informal decision-making approach with few boundaries between decision makers. Rules and roles are unclear. For example, the business rarely has an organization chart.	• Boundaries are lacking; business decisions are made over the dinner table. • Exclusion is a problem. If you're not in the room when decisions are made, you may have no input, even if a decision affects you. • Fundamental decisions (e.g., shareholder agreements and estate plans) are avoided.
Silos: Replicates the decision-making approach of a loft but within individual areas, or silos. People avoid any important cross-business decisions.	• Owners tend to dig in on why their branch is in the right rather than learn to collaborate. • The business has difficulty passing ownership to the next generation, which is not prepared to collaborate across silos.
Missing rooms: A key forum is missing from governance. Often missing is the Owner Room.	• The business often fails to make important decisions because it's unclear who should make them. • The board is asking the owners what they want from the business.
Messy rooms: A room or two has lost its original purpose and function.	• New people, such as spouses, enter the system. • No one wants to join the family council because it seems irrelevant. • There's confusion between the board and the owner council.

supermajority, unanimity), and what ownership percentages constitute the majority

- Places restrictions on the transfer of ownership, such as prohibiting nondescendants from being owners

- Establishes the rules by which shares can be bought or sold, including who has the right of first refusal if someone wants to sell and whether owners have a right to "put" their shares to the company (i.e., to sell their shares under specified terms)

- Specifies any situations in which ownership must be redeemed, such as when an owner violates the terms of the shareholder agreement or is convicted of a crime

- Gives minority or majority shareholders certain rights, such as tag-along and drag-along rights, in a sale of the business[3]

- Determines share valuation methodology for various situations

By mapping key decisions, creating connection points, establishing policies, and putting formal agreements in place, you can build the processes required to integrate the rooms.

Overhaul your governance

There are common patterns of poor decision-making. See the box "When your house is not in order." If you have concluded that your decision-making processes need help, where do you start? Several steps can help you pinpoint the problem and take action to address it:

1. **Clarify the dissatisfaction.** Be on the lookout for a room in which you don't seem to be making sound decisions or in which the decisions are challenged by others in the system. When people feel excluded from decision-making, it's often a sign of a messy room. Form a working group to recommend changes, but make sure you get the proper decision-authority to do so. Working groups are often

composed of interested people with varying roles and points of view—both those satisfied with the current system and those dissatisfied. If your proposed changes cross rooms, then the working group should ideally include representatives from each one.

2. **Write a charter for new forums that the working groups plan to create.** These entities include groups such as family councils or boards of advisers. A **charter** defines how the forum will function and outlines the forum's criteria, including its mandate, size, qualifications, terms, leadership roles, decision-making rights and processes, meeting frequency, funding source, and compensation. A charter doesn't need to be a magnum opus; it can simply (and briefly) lay out the preceding criteria. Change often requires the implicit decision rules and processes to be made explicit.

3. **Obtain approval for the change from whoever has the current authority.** Ultimately, the owners will need to support the change, but don't neglect the soft power in your system. If, for example, you are changing your Family Room, you will want to get approval and support from influential family members. Remember, family businesses need to compromise. Your changes will never be exactly what you want but may be good enough to serve the full system.

In most cases, rooms should be worked on one at a time. Too much concurrent change in governance easily creates confusion in decision-making and roles.

Exercising your decision rights as owners is an important responsibility. A thoughtful governance structure may seem bureaucratic, especially to family businesses built around one entrepreneur's business acumen. But in the long run, strong governance can minimize conflict and, more importantly, help you make better decisions to achieve your goals.

Summing up

- The Four-Room model of governance divides the work of a family business into groups that are most appropriate for certain decisions. The model defines who and which decisions belong in the Owner Room, the Board Room, the Management Room, and the Family Room.

- For a family business to thrive, the owners should identify the key decisions to hold on to and delegate the rest to the right room.

- Owners should build a governance structure by establishing **forums** to do the work of each room. Even if the same people are involved in each room, how you make decisions will differ.

- Make sure you integrate the rooms. You should map key decisions, create formal connections, write policies on handling conflicts, and document what you have agreed to.

- Keep an eye out for lofts, silos, missing rooms, and messy rooms. When these problems begin to develop, it means you should consider renovating your governance structures and processes.

5.

Value

Create an Owner Strategy to Define Your Success

"What do you mean we can't pay dividends this year?" Leigh was incredulous. The board of the surfing brand company she and her sisters Sarah and Sharon had founded had just reviewed projected end-of-year performance. This meeting usually celebrated another incremental step forward, with moderate growth, no debt, and significant dividends, which Leigh, Sarah, and Sharon used to support their comfortable lifestyle and charitable donations. This year, however, revenue growth was way up, but profits were down, and Leigh learned that the covenants on the debt taken out by the company to achieve that growth did not allow for any dividends. For the first time, Leigh felt out of control of the company she had cofounded.

How could the founders of a successful company find themselves surprised by its inability to pay them annual dividends? Leigh and her sisters had done many things right in building their business, including eventually appointing an independent board and an outside CEO to help the company reach the next level. But in turning over day-to-day management to the CEO, they also forgot something critical. They assumed that the new CEO would guide the company well, but they failed to clearly articulate the tangible outcomes that they wanted to achieve—and avoid—as owners. That opened the door to the CEO to pursue a business strategy that ran counter to what mattered most to them.

While public companies' success is usually measured by growth in shareholder value, the same is not necessarily true for family businesses. And that's one of the best things about family ownership. You don't have to define success the way that other companies might. You can follow your own path in determining what matters most to you and your family.

This right to define success typically translates into three possible outcomes for the business. You can aim for *growth*, looking to maximize the financial value of the business. You can seek *liquidity*, distributing cash flow to the owners to use outside the business. And you can want to maintain *control*, keeping decision-making authority within the ownership group. You have the freedom to do what you want with your company. No outsider can force you to value revenue growth more highly than, say, offering family members employment in the business. Or choosing to treat employees like family. Or forgoing growth opportunities that don't sit right with your beliefs. The right to determine what you value is an incredible opportunity and responsibility for owners.

But ensuring that your business produces tangible outcomes that are aligned with your values won't happen on its own, as Leigh and her sisters discovered. Few family owners describe their sole objective as maximizing shareholder value in the way most business books assume. And for many family business owners, it is not even one of their primary objectives. Yet, the owners are often unclear about what they do want—or want different things. Unless you find alignment you will miss opportunities for growth, fail to retain talented employees, lose control as management fills the void with their own priorities, or sell the business out of frustration.

To avoid those outcomes, your family business needs an Owner Strategy that defines the rules of the game, how you keep score, what winning looks like, and what moves are not allowed. In this chapter, we will discuss how to:

1. Define value in terms of **growth, liquidity,** and **control**

2. Articulate a compelling **purpose**

3. Translate that purpose into specific **goals**

4. Define **guardrails** to keep your company from veering off course

5. Communicate your purpose, goals, and guardrails in an **Owner Strategy statement**

Your Owner Strategy is one of the purest expressions of who you are as individuals, as a family, and as a family business system. It's your course to chart.

The right to define value: growth, liquidity, and control

Why should you take the time to define clear objectives in your family business? If you fail to do so, you risk losing your raison d'être for being in business together, especially as the business grows and makes the transition to new generations. That path often leads toward the end of family ownership.

So how do you determine what your family values the most? Start by asking three questions that only owners of a business can answer.

Do you want to place any restrictions on the growth of the business?

This first question might seem counterintuitive. Most public companies single-mindedly focus on growing their financial value because that's what shareholders demand. As a society, we're used to measuring success that way. But as Bo Burlingham points out in *Small Giants*, a book that focuses on companies that choose to be great rather than big: "What's in the interest of the shareholders depends on who the shareholders are."

As an owner, you might wish to constrain growth by taking off the table any actions that would otherwise make you more money or broaden your global influence but that don't align with your values. Several companies we have worked with have deliberately avoided growth in favor of creating a strong culture and, like Frederick (the earlier-described man of routine in chapter 1), a sane work–life balance for the owners and management. "We could triple our sales in a year," one owner told us. "But that would dramatically change all our lives. There's a lot of stress that comes with growth."

How much liquidity do you want to take out of the company?

Owners of a business have the right to the *residual*, the profits left over after all the bills have been paid. It is up to you to decide whether to reinvest those profits or pay them out in dividends. Family businesses exercise this right in different ways, including payouts of 100 percent of the annual profits to the owners and no dividends for decades with all profits reinvested in the company. The right to make that decision rests with the owners, either directly when they are closely involved in decision-making or indirectly through the policies they set for the board of directors.

Are you willing to give up control over decisions?

Owners set the capital structure of the company, that is, the extent to which the company uses outside debt and equity. As owners, you can decide whether to have the company operate only with the resources it can generate internally or to access other people's money. Many family businesses resist accepting equity capital from outside investors because they want to maintain full control over their decisions. With such control, the owners can make decisions that benefit their family and that an outside investor would rarely allow. For example, the family business might pay its employees well over market compensation. Owners also tend to worry that debt will reduce their control over their own destiny, since borrowing usually comes with rules and restrictions. "It's one thing to negotiate with my brother and sister, who know how to push my buttons and annoy me," said the CEO and co-owner of an Australian retail chain, "but I'll take that any day over having to report back to the 'suits' at a bank, with their insane paperwork and bureaucracy." As a result, this CEO's company avoided taking on any debt—something many other family businesses do as well.

Through this influence over growth, liquidity, and control, owners shape the company's strategy. You can define the objectives of the company in purely financial terms (similar to a public company) or prioritize non-financial objectives like improving the environment or paying employees above-market compensation. Likewise, you can allow managers to use any (legal and ethical) means that maximize those objectives, or you can take actions off the table because they conflict with your core values. How you exercise this right puts you in the position to create a company that pursues what you most value.

Defining purpose in a business family

Why do you choose to own your business *together* with family members?

When we ask that question of families, superficial answers sometimes arise: "We need to maintain our grandfather's legacy." Others make a financial argument: "It makes better financial sense to pool our assets." But such answers are ultimately not compelling—they are what we call *surface purpose*. If your family business is bound together only by a surface purpose, it's unlikely to last in the long run. It's not enough to live someone else's dream or maximize undistributed profits.

You can find a better answer to that question by working with other owners to identify a compelling reason to own the business together. While we like the term *purpose*, some families prefer to talk about their mission, vision, or values. Whatever terms you use, you need to define your purpose in these ways:

- The purpose should build family unity by making the family proud of their ownership and of their family.

- It should be aspirational, inclusive, and attractive to all generations and the entire family.

- It should encourage family members to spend more time together.

- It should define how you will exercise your right to determine what you value.

If you don't have a clear—and shared—understanding of your family business purpose, you can start to identify it (or test it) through the lenses of growth, liquidity, and control:

1. **Do you own the business together to grow it?** You may value growth because it is a path to change your economic situation or it creates jobs and other opportunities for family members. You may see it as a way to broaden your influence over society. The larger the business, the more you can influence the world. Or you may not value growth at all—if it happens, you might think, that's great, but you might be more than happy with owning a business that stays more or less in place.

2. **Do you own the business together to take money out of it?** You may see liquidity as a way to provide for the next generation in a way that your parents could not provide for you. You may view it as a mechanism for funding charitable causes that are close to your heart. Or you may see wealth outside the business as something to be avoided, given its potential to corrupt the family.

3. **Do you own the business together to have autonomy over your lives?** You may want to control your own destiny. Maybe you started the company, or joined it, because you didn't want to pursue someone else's dream. Or perhaps you see control as critical to running the business however you see fit. You may value what the business can do for your family. Alternatively, you may not value control at all, as long as the business seems to be on the right track.

There is no right answer to the question of a business's purpose. Most families find that each generation has its own reasons to stay together as a business family. The subsequent generation then updates these reasons for their own situation, renewing and refreshing the purpose of the business. Through these lenses, family businesses can express their purpose in countless ways.

We admire several companies' clear sense of purpose. For example, one US-based family business that we work with lost family members in the Holocaust. It deeply values and appreciates that the United States welcomed the family in a time of terrible crisis. Part of the family business's purpose is to support countries committed to freedom. As a business, it has explicitly decided to invest only in countries with a high score from Freedom House, a US nonprofit nongovernmental organization that advocates democracy, political freedom, and human rights investment in the United States. The company guards its ownership control tightly, as the owners know that an outside investor may not share their political views when making investment decisions.

Mars, Incorporated has set aggressive goals and takes committed actions to improve the lives of people in its supply chain and reduce the environmental footprint of the company. As the company website explains, "Mars has been proudly family owned for over 100 years. It's this independence that gives us the gift of freedom to think in generations, not quarters, so we can invest in the long-term future of our business, our people and the planet—all guided by our enduring Principles. We believe the world we want tomorrow starts with how we do business today." That clarity of purpose has led Mars to commit to invest more than $1 billion over several years in the early 2020s to become sustainable in a generation, to focus on improving the well-being of families around the world, and to apply and share its research to create a better world for pets.

Families often capture their purpose in a statement. Here are two examples.

> *Our family loves and respects this company. It represents the vast majority of the family's wealth, it is an important source of our income, it holds us together as a family, and it gives us a chance to make some positive contributions to our troubled world. We want*

our children and our grandchildren to have these same opportuni-
ties to benefit from this company.

We deeply appreciate that a family company can contribute to the
personal success of the owners. For us, success includes engaging
in work that is meaningful and that could provide financial au-
tonomy. Since personal success is unique to each family member,
we want the company to support parents and adult "children" to
maximize opportunities for healthy development, while guarding
against any downsides of family wealth. We are more willing than
most investors to compromise current income to meet our goals of
helping family members find fulfillment. Nonfamily owners might
not share these views. For this reason, we want the family to retain
full control of the company.

Does your family business have a purpose? We encourage you to discuss with the other owners and the leaders of the family—including both
the current and the next generation and both bloodline and spouses—your
purpose in owning the business together. Doing so will not only help you
decide why you are in business together but also help you clarify how your
family business will define success.

Setting owner goals

Besides helping family members bond as a business family, a clear definition of purpose will also help you make concrete choices about, and see
the trade-offs in, how and where to create value. We call these choices
owner goals.

Owners must balance their goals when deciding how fast to grow, how
much liquidity to take out of the company, and how much control to retain. If you take money from the company's profits and distribute it, less is
available to invest in growth. If you maintain control by avoiding outside
debt or equity, you have less money available either to invest in growth or
to provide liquidity to the owners.

FIGURE 5-1

The Owner Strategy triangle

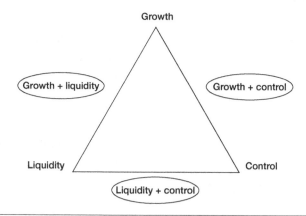

Owners might pursue only one of these three goals (growth, liquidity, and control) or some mix of the three. There are trade-offs to all the combinations. In the Owner Strategy triangle depicted in figure 5-1, we have found that most family businesses prioritize a two-goal approach (the circled goals) at the expense of the remaining goal. Which of these three dual choices best describes the goals of your family business? Let's look at them in detail.

Growth and control

If you value growth and control, you primarily grow through retained earnings, paying low (or no) dividends. You also have low (or no) external equity or debt, since answering either to outside investors or to borrowers requires surrendering some autonomy. When outside equity is taken on, it is often done on a limited basis or through dual-class shares to ensure that the initial owners maintain control.

The owners of a company we know in the construction industry in Asia reinvest the vast majority of their profits back into the company every year, growing through retained earnings. They pay minimal distributions beyond what is required for taxes and have little debt. This approach works for these owners, as they live relatively modestly and want the business to continue on its current path. The board—and especially the nonfamily directors—have sometimes pushed the owners to lever up the company and acquire other businesses in their sector. The owners have been willing to do that to some minimal degree, but they don't want to lose control by being beholden to banks. They're quite happy to limit growth to a level at which they retain control. "Slower and steadier" is their motto.

Growth and liquidity

If you value growth and liquidity, you are still focused on expanding but also on paying out money to the owners. You use other people's money (equity or debt or both) to keep the engine going, giving up some control as a result.

We worked with a business in the fuel industry in Latin America. Ever since its founding almost fifty years ago, the business had grown by reinvesting the majority of its profits into new facilities and stations (the growth-and-control strategy). The owners continued to see much growth potential but were concerned about the long-term threat of disruption in their industry by emission regulations, electric cars, and ride services like Uber. Recently they decided to sell 30 percent of their company to an outside investor. Beyond gaining the benefits of the partner's expertise, a primary rationale for this move was to take some money off the table to reinvest outside the company. To accomplish these goals of growth and liquidity, the owners sacrificed some control by bringing an outsider into their close-knit family. They have had to contend with a new reality in which their decisions are constrained by the rights they gave to the partner. But the family doesn't regret the decision, because it agrees that growth and liquidity are the priorities.

Liquidity and control

If you value liquidity and control, you are not as concerned with how rapidly you grow. Instead, you want to produce significant liquidity while maintaining control over decision-making. You probably have moderate to high dividends, low to no debt, and relatively low capital expenditures.

Leigh and her sisters fit this profile as owners of their surf business. They started the business several decades ago as a passion project. Growing the business had never been a priority for them. As long as it maintained the culture of innovation and allowed them to enjoy the financial fruits of their labors, Leigh and her sisters were happy.

We know highly successful family businesses that define their goals in each of these three ways. These are broad strategies, and companies can find a space in between. In defining your goals, you need to understand what you explicitly or implicitly value as owners. Though purpose will remain your high-level statement of intent, revisit how you achieve that purpose through these trade-offs as things change because of external factors like the economy, industry consolidation, and government policies or internal factors like a generational transition, family conflict, and a transition in senior management.

To start refining your owner goals, look at your previous decisions as an owner group. Which of the three approaches best describes how you have acted: growth and control, growth and liquidity, or liquidity and control? Embedded in the decisions that you have made is your current Owner Strategy, which may provide insights into whether you want to change your goals.

Each of the three approaches brings its own issues to be managed. You should make sure that these issues find a place on the agenda in the appropriate room:

- The owners of *growth-control* companies need to manage the expectations of family members about distributions, since the distributions can only be paid at a level that does not deprive the business of growth capital. We have also seen that these companies often fail to make good use of the owners' equity. Since most, or all, of the profits are retained in the business, some management teams will pursue new projects simply because capital is available, not because the ventures are a great investment.

- The owners of *growth-liquidity* companies need to manage the extent to which they are losing control of decision-making to equity partners or lenders. They can do that by paying careful attention to loan and deal terms and by designing governance structures to maximize the owners' remaining influence.

- The owners of *liquidity-control* companies need to manage the firm's rate of growth. If growth is too fast, it will require additional investment, which may not be available, to maintain its pace. If it is too slow, the business's momentum will be undermined, employees might leave, and the company's competitive position may erode.

Creating owner guardrails

Aligning your priorities through your purpose and owner goals is a good start, but it's all just lip service unless you translate them into specific measurements that the leaders of the business can use to make decisions. These **guardrails** are the final component of your Owner Strategy. Like the guardrails we rely on to keep us driving safely on highways and busy roads, owner guardrails won't tell you what to do. But they will provide boundaries around standard business strategy decisions (e.g., opening new stores and investing in new machines), allowing some actions and proscribing others.

Owner guardrails will help you ensure that those running the business day-to-day are directing their energy and resources to what you care about most. Clear guardrails enable more effective ownership. With guardrails in place to spell out how owners define success for the company, you can more confidently delegate decisions to directors and managers.

Guardrails are both financial and nonfinancial. *Financial guardrails* set specific standards of performance to align with owner goals. They identify the right metrics for evaluating performance and the minimum or maximum threshold for each metric. Imagine that your company has a growth-liquidity focus. You should define how you will measure success for both growth and liquidity—what metrics you will use and what threshold you expect the company to exceed. For example, you might define your financial guardrails as a minimum return on equity of 10 percent and a maximum debt-to-equity ratio of two times your earnings before interest, taxes, depreciation, and amortization.

Owners should home in on only a few financial metrics (usually four to six). Doing so provides clear guidance to the company's leadership while leaving them ample opportunity to determine the best business strategy. These metrics should connect with the three core owner goals. Table 5-1 describes the objectives of the metrics for each goal and provides examples of those metrics.

Nonfinancial guardrails define outcomes for which owners are willing to sacrifice financial performance. These guardrails assess more abstract aspects of the company, for example, the family's purpose for being in business together and the owner goals. Nonfinancial guardrails provide the rationale for maintaining control over decision-making. For some families, the nonfinancial goals are both part of the glue that holds them together and a means of making the world a better place.

These nonfinancial guardrails typically fall into four main categories:

- **Leadership:** Does the company need to be led by its owners, even if they are not objectively the most qualified? One family business we worked with believed strongly that only a family member should run the company, even if it meant that the business would grow less quickly. This belief enabled the family to nurture leadership in each successive generation while ensuring that only someone who truly understood and valued the family legacy would be leading the business into the future.

- **Business sectors and geographic locations:** Are there particular businesses (e.g., tobacco, firearms) or places (e.g., South Africa during apartheid) that the owners wish to avoid investing in or, conversely, are willing to sustain even if the businesses are unprofitable? For example, one family business that started in the steel industry expanded more profitably into new sectors over the

TABLE 5-1

Financial guardrails: how to measure success

Goal and objective	Examples of common guardrails or metrics
Growth: Show owners that their assets are earning an expected return relative to peer companies or to other investment opportunities	• Returns: ROIC, ROE, ROA, EVA • Asset appreciation: valuation, multiples, discounted cash flow • Top-line growth: revenue, volume (e.g., pounds, units) • Earnings growth: EBITDA, EBIT, net income • Investments: growth capex, M&A
Liquidity: Show owners that the business is producing the expected amount of liquidity for uses inside or outside the business	• Profitability: gross margin, net margin • Free cash flow: margin, yield, free cash flow to equity • Dividends: yield, payout ratio
Control: Help owners understand and manage significant risks that could threaten their control of the business	• Debt: total debt, debt-to-equity, debt-to-EBITDA • Viability: market share, market size • Volatility of earnings (net income, EBIT, EBITDA), cash flow • Stress testing: quick ratio, current ratio • Maintenance capex

Note: capex, capital expenditures; EBIT, earnings before interest and taxes; EBITDA, earnings before interest, taxes, depreciation, and amortization; EVA, economic value added; M&A, mergers and acquisitions; ROA, return on assets; ROE, return on equity; ROIC, return on invested capital.

years as the steel business waned in profitability. But the family was reluctant to get rid of the steel business, even as it became a drag on its portfolio of companies, because the members believed that steel was an important part of their legacy. It had sentimental value to them that they were willing to pay for.

- **Harmony:** Will any decisions be made or avoided to preserve family harmony? Some family firms will keep a division or an office open despite its poor financial performance, because it is led by an owner and closing it will upset the broader harmony of the group. Others have a rule that a family member should never report to another family member, even if this rule causes inefficiency.

- **Business practices:** To what extent are you willing to sacrifice financial performance to align business practices with your values (social, religious, environmental, etc.)? For example, some companies pay higher than market wages or commit themselves

to environmental sustainability standards that exceed industry expectations. See the box "Philanthropy and your family
business."

Identifying your nonfinancial guardrails can be one of the most meaningful parts of deciding what you value. By establishing financial and nonfinancial guardrails, you select metrics to help inform major decisions and
ensure that your family business continues to truly represent who you and
your family are.

Developing your Owner Strategy statement

Finally, to capture and express what you value, owners should create an
Owner Strategy statement, a document that articulates your purpose,
goals, and guardrails. This statement becomes a sort of credo for your family business. It should answer the three main questions we have worked
through in this chapter:

- **Purpose:** Why do you own your business together?

- **Goals:** What trade-offs will you make between growth, liquidity,
  and control to achieve your purpose?

- **Guardrails:** What metrics and boundary conditions do you need
  to provide to the board and management to help them understand
  and implement your goals?

These three questions are highly interrelated. You will find that working on one question will inform your answer to another.

Developing the purpose of your family business should be a shared
Owner Room and Family Room activity. Family members who are not
owners are affected by your purpose and play critical roles in sustaining
it, so involving them in the process will pay off even if it takes more time
and energy.

Translating that purpose to goals and guardrails is an activity led by
the Owner Room, though you should draw on the expertise and guidance

Philanthropy and your family business

Giving back is a priority for most of the family businesses we know. Primarily, they do so to make the world a better place. Besides that altruistic motivation, many family businesses see other benefits to their social contributions. Among the benefits are these:

- Deepening the family members' connection to each other

- Identifying and passing down shared values

- Creating a venue to learn about the meaning and responsibilities of wealth

- Developing talent and leadership in the next generation

- Shifting family assets as part of estate planning

- Building pride and purpose in the family business

- Improving goodwill and loyalty with customers, employees, and other stakeholders

- Assessing the capabilities of family members before they move into the business

- Creating an opportunity to contribute for those whose talents lie outside the business

In these ways, philanthropy can help you sustain a multigenerational enterprise. There's nothing wrong with having several sources of motivation for giving. We believe that society benefits most when the value that people see in giving back goes beyond pure altruism. If the perceived value is core to your objectives rather than peripheral to them, you will be more likely to sustain your philanthropy over time. Moreover, if the nonaltruistic benefits of philanthropy can only be achieved when you execute the benevolent action well, then your acknowledged self-interest is more likely to motivate you to conduct the philanthropy as effectively as possible.

Regardless of your motivation, there are three main avenues for accomplishing your giving goals:

- **Family philanthropy:** The vehicles that many family businesses set up for giving back are outside the core business. For example, families often form a family foundation, though there are other vehicles, depending on your country (e.g., donor-advised funds in the United States). Some foundations focus on giving grants; others on running programs. Some families endow their foundation by selling shares of the company, while others use dividends to fund their philanthropy. Although donating money is important, don't forget about the value of your time, expertise, and political capital.

- **Corporate social responsibility:** Increasingly, family businesses are integrating socially responsible business practices into their core operations. Some companies also have corporate foundations that serve hybrid business and social objectives. And many family businesses have established programs that facilitate employee involvement in the community.

- **Impact investing:** Many families are looking to harmonize their investment decisions with social goals. For example, if a company is focused on environmental sustainability with its giving, it doesn't want to invest in companies whose business model is to indiscriminately cut down rain forests. Some family businesses make more active investment decisions, investing in other companies that are explicitly addressing social needs.

Take the time to identify your philanthropic objectives, including how giving back can help you accomplish the goals you set in your Owner Strategy. Then ensure that the resources you are deploying through your family, business, and investments align with those objectives. But be careful. Because philanthropy involves core values, it can also touch on sensitive topics. When a CCC Alliance survey of the more than one hundred members of its network of family companies asked, "In the broad range of family activities where your family office engages, list three activities that create family harmony and three that create dissension," charitable foundations or philanthropy appeared on both lists.[a]

a. Barney Corning and Laird Pendleton of CCC Alliance.

of your board (if you have one) and your executive team. The board's job is to ensure that management develops and executes a business strategy in line with your Owner Strategy. Even if your family business has not yet developed the Four Rooms, you will still benefit from mapping out the roles and clarifying who to involve in each level of the design of your Owner Strategy.

The Owner Strategy statement should be specific enough to help the board and management make decisions that require trade-offs. For example, you might decide to set a 15 percent return on invested capital as a minimum threshold for retained earnings. When the business is expanding, you might then reinvest all the profits back into the business, but as the market matures, you might reduce that investment and increase distributions to shareholders. We have seen several family businesses with liquidity-control goals whose boards are focused on growing the business and cutting the dividends to invest in that growth—not the hallmarks of a liquidity-control strategy. Clarifying goals will help close the gap.

A good Owner Strategy statement should form the basis of a dialogue among owners, the board, and management. Acting as a dashboard that identifies the metrics used to gauge success, the statement helps the owners know whether the business is meeting the objectives they have set, and it spurs dialogue when the business goes outside the established guardrails. Because a good Owner Strategy statement is a living document that owners refer to regularly, it should be revisited whenever there are meaningful changes to the internal or external environment.

In the case of Leigh and her sisters' surfing business, their mistake was their failure to articulate their Owner Strategy first to themselves and then to the rest of the company. After realizing the gravity of their situation, they ultimately opted to fire the outsider CEO and elevate a veteran insider to the role instead. While the new CEO lacked the outsider's credentials, they knew that he would ensure a return to a prioritization of culture and creativity over hockey-stick growth. To avoid a repeat experience, they spelled out their Owner Strategy to the company and worked with the board to align the new CEO's compensation incentives with it.

Defining your Owner Strategy puts you in the position to create a company that accomplishes what *you* value most. Owning a family business creates an opportunity to choose your ownership adventure. That, after all, is part of the fun of building a family business and an enduring legacy.

Summing up

- As owners, you have the right to define what *value* you want the company to create, because only you can answer three core questions:

  - What restrictions, if any, should be placed on the company's *growth*?

  - How much *liquidity* should be taken out of the company?

  - Are you willing to give up *control* over decisions by accepting outside capital?

- An *Owner Strategy* defines the rules of the game for your business. It consists of three main elements:

  - A compelling *purpose*, which answers the question: Why do you own the business together?

  - The *goals* that you want to accomplish through your shared ownership. While a purpose is aspirational, owner goals are specific outcomes that speak to how you will navigate the trade-offs between growth, liquidity, and control.

  - The *guardrails* you want to place around the company's actions to ensure your goals are accomplished. Guardrails can be both financial and nonfinancial.

- Capture these three elements in an *Owner Strategy statement*, which will help ensure alignment between the family owners and the leaders of the company. The statement should be a living document that you revisit when there are major changes to the internal or external environment.

6.

Inform

Use Effective Communication to Build Trusted Relationships

Sophie was growing increasingly frustrated. As a professor at a leading business school, she was sought after by many companies for her expertise. But apparently not by her husband Matthew's fourth-generation media business in Asia. Concerned about what seemed like a blasé attitude toward the need for change in an industry that was undergoing serious disruption, she began to inquire about the company's long-term strategy. But she was offered vague responses, which frustrated her more. As she started asking more questions, the executive team began sharing less information at the annual shareholder meetings, to which spouses had long been welcome. Worse, Matthew's siblings instructed him not to share with her the financial reports they received, because she was rocking the boat too much.

Sophie's anxiety was not about the impact on her but about whether her children would own something of any value by the time it got to them. As a spouse who had married into the family, she wasn't expecting to make decisions about the company. But she thought that as a parent of fifth-generation owners, their daughters Ellie and Anna, she deserved to know what was going on and to have a chance to discuss her concerns. Ironic, she thought, that her expert opinion seemed to be valued the least by the company she cared about the most. Feeling frustrated, excluded, and disconnected from the family business, Sophie emotionally withdrew. She discouraged family dinnertime talk about the business. She scheduled vacations during the annual family assemblies, effectively keeping her children from their best opportunity to get to know their cousins— with whom they would one day own the business. Torn between his family and his wife, Matthew began to wonder if keeping everything so private was wise.

As owners, you have the right to inform. You decide who can know what about your business.[1] That right, in turn, gives you control over the communication function in your family business, since nothing of consequence can be shared without your permission. As you exercise this right, you have to decide how to balance the often-competing goals of privacy and transparency. The impulse to remain private is understandable: privacy can keep your business, and your family, safe from outsiders. At the same time, there is a real cost to too much secrecy. One of the most valuable attributes of family businesses is their ability to build trusted relationships, which in turn help create the capital they need to thrive. By withholding information, you risk depriving your family business of its ability to cultivate valuable relationships that can have a major effect on both the success of the business and the closeness of the family. We have seen family businesses in which the failure to communicate effectively is the single biggest reason why they don't last, and others whose communication excellence enables them to survive tough times.

In this chapter, we will explore three aspects of communication:

1. The importance of communication in building the capital your family business will need to thrive

2. The trade-off between privacy and transparency for the key audiences of your family business—current and next-generation owners,

spouses, employees, and the public—as well as how to decide how much information to share with them

3. The steps required to create effective communication in your family business

Done well, exercising the right to inform lets you create strong relationships that will serve your family business many years into the future.

Building trust

Trusted relationships are one of the most valuable assets in a family business. Trust can help you navigate the inevitable challenges that come with working together, and it can help you form lasting partnerships. Strong relationships sustain your family business across generations and help you compete with companies that may have more resources. The value of relationships is hard to understate since they make so many other things possible, or impossible. We're talking about the relationships not only between the owners and the family, but also with groups that become part of your broader family—employees, customers, suppliers, and other stakeholders.

Communication is critical to building that trust. Trust may seem like an amorphous idea, but according to A. K. Mishra, it has four measurable components: "Trust is one party's willingness to be vulnerable to another party based on the belief that the latter is competent, open, concerned, and reliable."[2] Is that person:

- **Competent:** Do they bring relevant and effective knowledge, skills, abilities, and judgment?

- **Open:** Are they transparent and honest in sharing information, plans, and decisions?

- **Concerned:** Do they demonstrate care about more than themselves?

- **Reliable:** Can they inspire confidence by consistently producing what others expect?

Each of these four components requires great communication. Going back to Sophie's situation, the business leaders may actually have had a clear strategy to deal with the disruption of their industry. But without open communication, they couldn't demonstrate their competence to her. In the process, they lost access not only to her expertise but also to her efforts to connect the next generation to the business.

Think of trust like a bank account that, with each interaction, you are either adding to or subtracting from through your behavior. When your account balances are sufficiently high, you are generating three forms of capital that a family business needs to thrive:

- **Financial capital:** committed owners who, with an emotional connection to the business, are long-term holders of their shares

- **Human capital:** engaged employees and family members, including spouses, who bring the full extent of their talents to their work and to the family

- **Social capital:** a positive reputation with customers, suppliers, the public, and other stakeholders, which can help your company differentiate itself in a crowded marketplace and build relationships with all generations

You can nurture each of these types of capital through what and how you communicate. That doesn't mean you suddenly have to open your bank account numbers to everyone, but you can share information to help you build and grow these various forms of capital.

The trade-off between transparency and privacy

For many family businesses, the instinct to hold information close is powerful. Owners are, understandably, afraid that sharing information about the business can create trouble—entitled children, meddling spouses, greedy employees, or a loss of competitive advantage. Why should anyone else be privy to the details of your business? Information is so tightly controlled in one family we have worked with that the owners would never dream of taking out a loan—even if it would help the business grow—because it would mean revealing the company's financial statements to bankers.

We appreciate those concerns. But we encourage you also to ask yourself the question: What are the consequences of *not* sharing information? If communication is necessary to build trust, what are you giving up by holding your cards too close to your vest? It's natural to struggle with the trade-offs between privacy and transparency in a privately held family business. But some forms of information can be shared without sacrificing privacy. Before you start thinking about how to approach different audiences, take an inventory of the information in the hands of the owners. Table 6-1 provides a starting list, organized by the other four rights.

Let's walk through the key stakeholder groups to examine what information you should consider sharing with them and how and why you should do so.

TABLE 6-1

What information can you share?

Design	• The assets you own together, including key products and manufacturing sites
	• How ownership of the business is held across the family today (e.g., voting or common shares versus nonvoting or preferred shares)
Decide	• The roles and responsibilities of the Owner Room, Board Room, Management Room, and Family Room, including eligibility criteria to participate in each
	• Key agreements (shareholder, buy-sell, family constitution) and policies (family employment, dividend, use of company resources)
	• Background and capabilities of your business leaders and board members
Value	• Your family history, sometimes already captured in a written form
	• Ownership goals for growth, liquidity, and control
	• Financial performance of the company (e.g., valuation)
	• Key operating metrics of your business, such as market share and price realization
	• Impact of your family or company in the community
	• Current state of the industry and the business's strategy within it
Transfer	• How assets will be transferred to the next generation
	• The timing for the handoff of leadership roles
	• What capabilities the next generation will need to be successful

Current owners

In some families, owners have different levels of involvement. As we mentioned earlier, individual owners often fall into three distinct roles: operators, governors, and investors. Those who work in the company (operators) or who are involved in Board Room or Owner Room decision-making (governors) will naturally be party to more information. The understandable instinct may be to be guarded with those who are not as deeply involved in the business (investors).

One family business we know went to great lengths to keep financials away from the one owner who was not on the board. She was, of course, legally entitled to that information, but the board made the information difficult for her to get. When she simply asked about the value of the business at an annual shareholder meeting, the board members perceived the question as a precursor to asking for the company to be sold, which was in turn seen as disloyal to the family and company. What may have started as a genuine desire to understand the family business eventually ended up in court. Nobody wins when conflict devolves in this way.

You should be careful about the long-term consequences of leaving investors out of the loop. Businesses thrive when they are backed by owners with a willingness to commit their capital over the long term. In fact, if investors plan to pass their shares down to the next generation, your cost of capital is only the dividends you distribute every year. If you keep dividends moderate, you can have a real advantage over your competitors. Family businesses often underappreciate passive shareholders, as long as they support the multigenerational objectives of the business. Nurture this committed capital by keeping these investors informed and engaged, or destroy it by having to buy out disconnected, and therefore often disinterested, shareholders.

Next-generation owners

One of the biggest fears of family business owners is that somehow their success will create a new generation of entitled brats (chapter 11 discusses this fear in detail). So the owners go to extraordinary lengths not only to avoid communication about the business with their children but also to actively hide the information. They are afraid that if they divulge financial information with the next generation, the knowledge will foster the children's sense of entitlement. This concern, of course, can be valid in some situations, but you can share other valuable information besides financials with the next generation. You can gradually bring younger people into the loop with information about your ownership structure, your decision-making processes, your family values and Owner Strategy, and, in time, your plans for transferring the business.

A successful industrial company we know had a dominant founder who kept all business and ownership information away from his children, well into their forties. The only source of information was what they could glean from the tax returns that the company's chief financial officer (CFO) placed in front of them to sign each year. Consequently, the next generation understood little about the business, which was in an industry undergoing disruption, and was never encouraged to learn about what it meant to be good owners. When the owner passed away suddenly, the children were not in any position to take over as owners. Instead, they sold the company at a low-ball price as soon as they could find a buyer.

Successful family businesses foster a sense of stewardship of the business among all members of the family. We have seen families expose the next generation to every aspect of their business—from appreciating where the raw materials come from to how their customers use their products. The members' engagement helps sustain the business (and the family) through difficult times and generational transitions. If you shield the next generation from knowing about the business, you are failing to prepare them to be owners and good stewards. You're also missing an opportunity to build their emotional connection to the business (and each other), and you risk limiting how much of their passion and talent they will invest.

Spouses

Spouses, too, can provide talent and expertise to the family business. In many family businesses we work with, an in-law runs the business—and is doing it well. (Roughly 10 to 20 percent of our client base has an in-law

CEO.) Beyond offering their own talent, in-laws play a critical role in raising the next generation and greatly influence their children's interest in the family business.

Many other families we know struggle with how much information to share with spouses who marry into the family. Relationships may be strong, but many family businesses still have the nagging fear that sharing, say, financial information with spouses creates vulnerability. The worry is that when a spouse fully understands the value of the family business, they could use that information someday in a divorce proceeding. Even routine pillow talk that gives a spouse insight into the company and the family may unintentionally fuel grudges. (*You* may be able to smooth over whatever gripe you had about your fellow owners, but a spouse's protective instincts often kick in and intensify feuds.)

Don't assume that just because you exclude spouses from some communications they won't hear it. In one family business we know, the spouses were formally kept out of the loop, but they met frequently with each other and tried to piece the picture together using what each had heard. Unsurprisingly, they didn't get the story right, and their frustrations at being excluded were passed down to the next generation. Some of our clients hold spouse-only sessions at their family assemblies so that the spouses can share experiences. One client called it his "family business support group." In contrast to an excluded spouse, a spouse who understands the Owner Strategy, the family's legacy and values, decision-making in the business and family, individual family members' roles, future transition plans, and so on, can feel invested in the business's success and provide valuable behind-the-scenes support.

Employees

Some owners share information with employees only on a need-to-know basis. Often, family members occupy the key financial roles or the owners have only one trusted nonfamily executive (sometimes called a "consigliere") serve in that position. These owners see holding a virtual monopoly of financial information as a critical means to maintain control over the company.

But if you are too guarded with what you disclose, you risk losing your employees' engagement with, and loyalty to, your business. When employees are lacking insight into the overall health of the business, they start filling in the void with rumors, conjectures, and their own anxieties. A substantial body of research suggests that employees who feel connected to the mission and success of a business are far more engaged, loyal, and productive. If they understand how the business is performing and believe in its mission, the research says, employees will care about contributing to its success.[3] They start to behave more like owners than like hired hands.

Many family businesses see the benefits in the engagement and alignment that come from openness with employees. For example, Hilcorp is the largest privately held independent oil company in the United States. The founder, Jeffery Hildebrand, has created an organization that thrives on openness. Each year, the annual bonus for all employees is tied to companywide goals. The company also sets five-year "BHAGs" (big hairy audacious goals) that result in a bonus for all employees when the goals are hit. In 2015, every employee received $100,000 when Hilcorp doubled a series of performance metrics over the previous five years.

Public

If you are a privately held business, you decide what to share with the public. Advocates for minimal disclosure point to the risks that publicity can bring to family safety and the survival of the business. Families that live in countries where kidnapping is a significant danger tend to be most attuned to this issue, but most successful families have security concerns. We know one family that structured its business holdings in a way that made it nearly impossible to untangle the web of who owned what. The owners missed opportunities to leverage the synergies across the companies, but they were more than willing to pay that price to avoid having anyone outside the inner circle knowing the extent of their empire.

Even if the family's safety is not threatened, its business could be. In an age of virtual protests, the actions of owners can harm their companies. When Linda Bean, granddaughter of L. L. Bean, came out in support of

Donald Trump in the 2016 US presidential election, her stand spurred a movement to boycott the retailer. Executive chairman (and fellow owner) Shawn Gorman had to quickly quell the outrage, countering that Linda didn't speak for the family. "Like most large families," Gorman wrote on a Facebook post, "the more than 50 family member-owners of the business hold views and embrace causes across the political spectrum, just as our employees and customers do. And as every member of the family would agree, no individual alone speaks on behalf of the business or represents the values of the company that L. L. built."[4] Gorman's point was reasonable (and probably true in most families), but consumers are unlikely to make those kinds of distinctions. Fairly or unfairly, any owner who speaks out can be seen as representing the business. This assumed connection between owners' personal beliefs and company policy reinforces the value of privacy.

But family businesses that prioritize remaining below the radar should consider the costs and practicalities of doing so. Family brands are increasingly valuable. An annual study by the public relations firm Edelman has repeatedly shown that family businesses hold a significant trust advantage in every country it studied, other than China.[5] Some family businesses are so desperate for privacy that they go to great lengths to hide the fact that they are family owned. But if the public doesn't identify you as a family business, you are leaving that goodwill on the table. Besides, many families will struggle to control an outlier owner who has a different point of view about sharing with the public. In our experience, it's far better to have a thoughtful communication policy with the public to reap the benefits of the goodwill that family ownership creates rather than scramble to control the message when it comes out through unofficial channels.

Drafting your communication plan

Effective communication is one of the most vital tools to sustain a business that endures over the years. While few people will disagree with that sentiment, they are often uncertain about how to actually do it. Excellence in this area requires you to construct a deliberate communication strategy. Here are the key questions to answer as you build your strategy.

With whom do you need to communicate?

The first step in communication is to clarify your main audiences. We have focused in this chapter on five important stakeholder groups: the current ownership group, the next generation of owners, the broader family (especially in-laws), the company, and the public.

These audiences are a generic set—yours may also include other internal groups, such as the family office or the foundation, or external ones like suppliers, regulators, and key customers. Identify the most important stakeholders with whom you need to communicate—and which are lower priorities. You must be clear about whom you need to communicate with.

What is the extent of that communication?

Once you have mapped out the audiences that will receive some information on your family business system, decide what you want to share with each audience, or at least with those in the higher-priority tiers. The answer is likely to vary across audiences.

Sharing information doesn't mean you have to open your financial statements to public scrutiny or divulge the details of who owns what percentage of the company.[6] But in our experience, owners are often so worried about protecting the details of their wealth from others that they fail to think through the litany of other information they *can* disclose—information that will help those stakeholders feel connected to the long-term success of the business. Think of the owner rights we have discussed in this part of the book: you can share your owner values and strategy, how decisions will be made, how you are thinking about succession, your passion for the business, and so on.

Table 6-2 depicts one owner group's approach to working through how to share the type of information described in table 6-1. As the table shows, the owners applied different levels of transparency for each audience. While the company remained careful not to reveal financial information widely—either inside or outside the family—the business became

TABLE 6-2

One family's communication approach

Information	Owners	Next gen	Spouses	Employees	Community
Design					
• The assets owned together	Open	Open	Open	Not	Not
• How ownership of the business is held across the family today	Open	Open	Open	Not	Not
Decide					
• The roles and responsibilities in each room	Open	Open	Open	Metered	Not
• Shareholder agreements	Open	Open	Metered	Not	Not
• Family employment policy	Open	Open	Open	Metered	Not
• Background business leaders and board members	Open	Open	Open	Open	Metered
Value					
• Family history	Open	Open	Open	Metered	Metered
• Ownership goals for growth, liquidity, and control	Open	Open	Open	Metered	Not
• Financial performance of the company	Open	Open	Open	Metered	Not
• Impact of the company in the community	Open	Open	Open	Open	Open
Transfer					
• How assets will be transferred to the next generation	Open	Open	Metered	Not	Not
• The timing for the handoff of leadership roles	Open	Metered	Metered	Metered	Not
• What capabilities the next generation will need for success	Open	Open	Metered	Not	Not

Open communication   Metered communication   Not communicated

known as highly transparent. In turn, it increased the loyalty of its owner group, family, and employees.

Another family business has a thoughtful stage-gate process in which the next-generation owners are first given a quarterly update on the business once they turn eighteen. Over the next few years, they are offered training relevant to understanding their role as future owners, such as how to read a financial statement, the elements of a shareholder agreement, and how trusts work. When they're deemed ready, they're allowed into the owner council discussion to both listen and exercise their voice on owner issues. All this work has not only helped prepare the next generation for their roles as owners in the future but also helped build relationships among them.

What will you not share?

You must be clear on what you will *not* share. Sometimes lines must be drawn and you'll need to find the right lines for your family business.

For example, one family we worked with decided that in-laws should have access to information as long as their spouse supported this disclosure and the in-laws went through an agreed-on process through the family office. Another made a significant effort to educate the spouses about the business but didn't share financial information.

We know a third family that aims to have full openness within the ownership group but is careful in how the business communicates with employees. In particular, the family members want to avoid a culture of gossiping about the family, instead presenting a united front to their team. To help them do that, the owners created a code of conduct that spelled out how owners should behave in different situations. For example, they decided that if an employee ever asked personal questions about another owner, the answer would always be, "It is our policy not to comment on matters related to owners. If you have a question, we encourage you to ask them directly."

If you're not going to be transparent with information, be transparent about why. Many of the negative feelings associated with exclusion can be mitigated by explaining the rationale behind your need for confidentiality.

Are you communicating eye-to-eye?

A forty-five-year-old next-generation owner once told us, "Everywhere else, we are treated like the adults we are; here in the business, we will always be treated as the kids." When communication takes place in a way that feels condescending, it can do more harm than good.

Transactional analysis is a subbranch of psychology that looks at how people interact with each other.[7] Every person has three "states": child, adult, and parent. The child is playful and impulsive. The adult focuses on the rational and problem solving. The parent is judgmental. Each of us, as we interact with others, moves up and down these three states, as does

FIGURE 6-1

Who is talking to whom? Parent, adult, and child

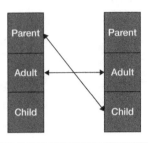

the person we are talking with (figure 6-1). In our communications with others, if we interact horizontally on the diagram, that is, adult to adult or child to child, we are in an appropriate relationship. However, if in a business setting we interact diagonally, say, parent to child, one person is communicating inappropriately with the other.

This framing is particularly powerful because family business transitions are fraught with numerous potential diagonal interactions, such as a father treating his fifty-year-old daughter as a child in front of the board of directors. You may find that having a language to call out such behavior helps improve relationships in your family business. For example, you can redirect a conversation by simply noting that the conversation wasn't "eye-to-eye" with another family member or "you're talking to me now as my father, not my business partner." Small cues can help reframe your respective roles. And if you're working in the business, you should be careful to never refer to "Mom" or "Uncle Vlad." At work, you have to maintain professional roles and boundaries. Your mother is always "Aline." Your uncle should just be "Vlad."

Not everyone has natural communication skills, but everyone can learn to communicate better, if they're willing to put in the work. We have seen families understand one another better by employing a personality assessment tool called DiSC (for its assessment of a person's dominance, influence, steadiness, and conscientiousness) or other psychology-based tools that help identify people's natural tendencies.[8] Some people, for example, can't focus on what you're saying until you give them the bottom line. Others need to fully grasp how you came to a decision before they can accept it. Such insights can be helpful in learning that people give and receive information in different ways. Once you recognize these differences, you can tailor your communication so that the person you're interacting with will receive the information in a way they can appreciate and process. When faced with such complex challenges, use any resources you have available to learn to better communicate, disagree, and resolve issues. See "Further Reading" for several suggestions.

Do you express your appreciation to each other?

"It's my greatest joy to be in business with you," a sixty-three-year-old owner tearfully told his brothers, with whom he fights daily. The effect of those simple words on their relationship was powerful. We too often get trapped in the credit game, in which everyone focuses on what they did personally for the success of the business, denying the contributions of others. (Research tells us, by the way, that it's human nature to overestimate our personal contribution and underestimate what others contribute.) The credit game is zero-sum: for one person to win, another has to lose. Placing too much emphasis on individual accomplishments saps everyone's willingness to sacrifice for the collective goals. Appreciation builds trust through a person's concern. As described at the beginning of the chapter, being concerned is one of the essential four elements of trust. A large body of recent research in the social sciences demonstrates that expressing appreciation is also beneficial for the giver, who feels more positive and more satisfied with social relationships.

With so much going on in a family business, it can be hard to slow down and say thank you to those you are collaborating with. The book *The Power of Bad* describes the "power of four," which means you should plan on at least four compliments to make up for one bit of criticism. We urge you to pause at the end of each big meeting and tell at least one other person something you appreciate about them, as the sixty-three-year-old did with his brothers. It can be as simple as saying, "Thanks for that idea. I've never thought of it that way before." We have witnessed truly transformative moments when people pause to thank one another for something. Such comments create relationship capital, and you would be wise to make appreciation a habit.

What forms of communication do you need?

In addition to agreeing on what to share with different audiences, owners should consider the type of communication they want to have. In particular, is this a one-way message to provide an update? Or is there an opportunity for a two-way dialogue that gives people a voice even if they won't get a vote? Owners' lack of clarity on the form of their communication can undermine good-faith efforts to inform others. In one family business that had a history of total secrecy, the owners decided after much back-and-forth to share some financial information with the spouses. They expected to be lauded for their efforts. Instead, they were rebuffed. The spouses said, in effect, "We don't care about the data, because we have no say in the decisions."

Once you've mapped out your information strategy, you can begin to decide how and when you will inform the relevant stakeholders. In the early stages of a family business, communication can happen in a more ad hoc manner. Quite frequently, it takes place informally, such as over family meals or on the ride to or from the office. As the family and business grow, there is usually a need to have more formal ways of ensuring effective communication. That infrastructure can take several different forms:

- **Forums:** Ideally, each of the Four Rooms provides an appropriate forum for discussing relevant issues. But when there are no dedicated venues to discuss important issues, the problems can crop up at inopportune times. To avoid this from happening, the business should set up time in family assemblies (e.g., designate an hour on the agenda) or in other forums to address the issue. In her book, *War at the Wall Street Journal*, Sarah Ellison describes how the Bancroft family, former owners of Dow Jones and the *Wall Street Journal*, had aired its dirty laundry in the press. This exposure was one of the main factors that undermined the Bancrofts' unity as a group, contributing to their willingness to sell the company to Rupert Murdoch. Ellison says that one family member told *Fortune* magazine, "There is no mechanism within the family to discuss openly the business issues surrounding Dow Jones."[9]

- **Policies:** Having clear rules about what can and cannot be communicated is extremely helpful in defining shared expectations. Those rules are typically decided in the Owner Room, but other rooms can be involved with their execution as well. According to a study by the WHU–Otto Beisheim School of Management and PricewaterhouseCoopers, a third of German entrepreneurial families have rules requiring family members to limit their access to media. Globally, a number of business families are creating written policies for media exposure. For example, one family has prohibited family members from appearing on social media wearing anything with the company's name. Families may draft and approve relevant policies in the Family Room and then keep them on a shared platform for all family members to access. Sometimes the policies will be part of the Owner Strategy statement.

- **Functions:** Most public companies have a shareholder relations team, whose job is to manage communication between the company and its owners. As a family business grows beyond a loft, that is, as it grows beyond an informal, loose governance style, the company often needs resources dedicated to managing the different levels of communication. While owners reserve the right to decide what to disclose, and with whom, the actual sharing can be done within the Four-Room structure. For example, the family council might create a monthly newsletter with updates on family members. This sort of communication is a Family Room activity. Family offices are increasingly playing this central communication role (see chapter 13). Or the Board Room members might distribute their books to current and future owners to present an update on the state of the business.

- **Platforms:** Instead of relying on more traditional communication methods, family businesses can use technology to share information. For example, some families use surveys to get input on a major decision or to allow for anonymous feedback. When paired with the more standard newsletter, a survey can concurrently give people an update and an opportunity to voice their opinions. Other families take advantage of platforms designed to make information easier to disseminate and store, such as board management software or designated family portals like Trusted Family or Summitas. Yet others use the family office to provide a secure yet accessible information platform for business families to communicate.

Summing up

- The right to inform sits with the owners of a family business. Be explicit about how you will use this right.

- You must have good communication to build the trusted relationships your family business needs to thrive. While the impulse toward secrecy is understandable, consider the cost you will pay in reduced financial, human, and social capital.

- As your family and family business grow, effective communication requires a plan. As you create your plan, remember to employ these important steps:

  - Map out the key audiences you need to connect with. For example, your audience could be the current owners, the next generation, the owners' spouses, your employees, and the public.

  - Agree on what you will and won't communicate with each audience. Remember that you can share much more than financial information. If you're going to keep information private, explain why.

— Invest some time in getting better at talking to each other as business partners. Work on speaking eye-to-eye, tailoring your message to how the listener processes information, and showing appreciation for others' contributions.

— Put in place the infrastructure to facilitate effective communication as your family grows. In the early stages of your business, information flow is organic, often taking place over shared meals. As your family grows, consider what meetings, policies, functions, or technological platforms can help improve dialogue across your family business. Communication can vary in its frequency (e.g., monthly or annually) and its formality (newsletter, family texting group, etc.). You have to decide what pace and level of formality are right for your family.

7.

Transfer

Plan for the Transition to the Next Generation

In the beautiful opening scene of *The Lion King*, newborn Simba, the presumptive heir to the throne, is held aloft to all the animals of the African savanna, and they bow in reverence. "A king's time as ruler rises and falls like the sun," Simba's father, Mufasa, later explains. "One day, Simba, the sun will set on my time here, and will rise with you as the new king." The idea that the father can transfer power to Simba is a premise the tale explores.

Many family business owners seem to have this idea in mind as they consider exercising their right to transfer their ownership to the next generation. One clear successor will head the business, the ownership group, and the family; others will defer unquestionably to the heir; and respect across the generations and family branches will be freely given. The "circle of life" will continue. But as Simba finds out when his father unexpectedly dies and his uncle steps in to rule, transitions are usually far more complex.

With this right comes the burden of many complex and difficult decisions. What do you want to do with the assets you worked so hard to build? How do you let go? What roles should the next generation play? How should you develop the members of the next generation into those roles? Are their relationships strong enough to work through decisions together?

In this chapter, we will consider the decision of how (and whether) to transfer your business. We will advise you on creating a continuity plan that integrates how your family business will pass down assets, hand off roles, and develop capabilities in the next generation. Though the current owners will make the final calls, the process requires cross-generational collaboration. Everyone needs to understand how this transition will work. Family empires are consolidated or squandered in the transfer of power to younger generations. We can't state this strongly enough: a planned transition is far better for both the business and the family.

The right to transfer: 2G or not 2G?

The transfer of power has long been seen as one of the most emotionally fascinating challenges faced by family businesses. For generations, classic literature (think Shakespeare) and popular television shows have been built around the intrigue of backstabbing, power grabbing, and jockeying for heir-apparent positioning. Most family businesses are born out of the crucible of this decision. At some point, the founder faces a critical choice—whether to pass down the business to the children, thereby transforming the enterprise from a founder-led company to a family business. Or, to paraphrase Shakespeare (using the shorthand for the next generation), "2G or not 2G, that is the question."

As an owner, whether part of the first or twenty-first generation, you get to decide who owns it after you. You can exercise your transfer right in three main ways: **sell** the business, **divide** it, or **transition** it as a whole to the next generation. The importance of this decision continues well beyond the founder. Actions taken by each generation shape the family and business for decades.

Sell to an outsider

In many ways, when you are ready to let go of your business the easiest decision is to sell it to an outside investor. You may have good reasons to sell. Perhaps your firm's competitive position makes the future look bleak as a stand-alone business. You may have received a once-in-a-lifetime offer that's too good to refuse. You may have too much conflict in the owner group. Your next generation may have no interest in owning the business together. Or maybe you are just tired of the work. If so, you should seriously consider a sale.

If you opt to go down the sale path, be aware that many advisers—bankers, lawyers, others—are not neutral. They may encourage you to sell and some may understate its downsides, because the sale event is when many advisers make most of their fees. Also, since many sales fail to happen, you should continue running the business as if you will always own it. Keep your sales discussions restricted to the Owner and Board Rooms. And don't distract the management team unnecessarily. You want the business to stay healthy in the process of a sale, especially if it ends up falling through.

But the promise of the postsale life may not match the reality. You might imagine a rewarding but quiet retirement with few if any financial stresses after being paid for a lifetime of hard work. The reality, however, is often more nuanced. We know numerous owners who rue what the buyer did to their life's work—fired valued employees, changed the business strategy, altered its culture, and even closed it down. Sellers often struggle with their identity and what they are going to do with their time. "I sold my identity with my company" is a common refrain we hear. The wealth, once out of the company and in a more liquid form such as cash, tradable stocks, and bonds, is easier to spend and possibly waste. There are good reasons to take this path, but do so with your eyes wide open.

Divide among next-generation members

The second form of transfer is to divide the business itself among the members of the next generation. There are many ways to do this. But however you do it, dividing ownership among your children ensures that there is no shared family business to pass down. Instead, each branch charts its own course.

Take Robert "Bob" Jenkins, who purchased ABC Pest Control in Texas in 1965. When it was time to retire, he contemplated selling it. His three twenty-something sons, Bobby, Raleigh, and Dennis, changed his mind and offered to buy it from him, providing him the income he needed in retirement and giving themselves the chance to build on the platform he had created. Rather than having them own the company together, he decided to split it up, parsing the state of Texas into three regions. Each brother created his own company and sold services under the ABC brand, but only in their territory. An actual map (kept by their mother) demarcates the turf of the three brothers, and one of the core family values is "Thou shalt not cross into thy brother's territory." Splitting the company has worked out well for the brothers, each of whom has grown his own business but supported his brothers and shared some resources along the way. They have incredibly close relationships, which they attribute in part to their separation from each other.

Partitioning a business can be a good way to minimize conflict, but it is not without downsides. For one, the effort and resources expended to split the business could otherwise be used to grow the company. Additionally, this approach is hard to replicate when ownership changes. For example, if Bobby and his brothers do pass the company down to their children the way Bob Senior did, even a state as big as Texas can only be divided so many times before a company lacks the scale to be viable—if not in the next generation, then in the one that follows. Finally, even if the division is equal at the start and the family works well together across divisions, problems can eventually creep in as divisions grow in different ways: "You've got the good territory," "Dad gave *you* the growth business," and so on.

Transfer the entire business

The last option is to transfer the entire business down to the next generation. You may have already decided to make this transition as a matter of course, but the decision should be deliberate, taking the alternatives into account.

As the owners, you control not only the decision whether to transfer (and to whom) but also the process. Most obviously, you choose where the assets go, what vehicles are used (trusts, sales, gifts, and so on), and when they are passed down. But because ownership also brings with it the power to select the leadership of the Four Rooms (directly or indirectly), you also can shape how various roles are handed off. And given your influence not only as an owner, but as a parent, an aunt, an uncle, or a grandparent, how you handle this transition will also determine how well the next generation develops the capabilities required to succeed you, both as individuals and while working together as a group.

The essential elements of successful continuity planning

Even with good intentions, many owners find it difficult to plan their own eventual transition from the business that has become part of their identity (see the box "Five paths to a failed transition"). But delaying or poorly planning your transition can wreak havoc on the business in the long run. A BCG study of more than two hundred Indian family businesses found a "28-percentage-point differential in market capitalization growth between companies that had planned transitions and those that had not." The study concludes, "An enormous amount of value is destroyed by unplanned transitions, with potentially catastrophic consequences for the business."[1] And when businesses fail to transition, families often lose their cohesion as well.

Maintaining family ownership requires making decisions that will reverberate for years to come and that are based on imperfect information about the future (e.g., which of the next generation will be the most

Five paths to a failed transition

While there is no correct way to make the transition from one generation to the next, we have seen five main approaches that are likely to fail. If you identify with one—or more—of these scenarios, you are likely to be headed off the continuity cliff.

A problem patriarch or matriarch

This type of leader can't let go. They rule all aspects of their family business with an iron fist. Their hardball behavior, which led to their business success, is applied to the next generation, which finds it impossible to thrive under an iron-fisted senior leader.

Because of this oppressive behavior, the members of the next generation are incapable of leading the business or are so hurt by their previous experiences that they have no interest in continuing the business. Often, after the domineering leader leaves, they sell the business.

The one-size-fits-all fallacy

Governance, roles, and processes that worked brilliantly in one generation can be a disaster in the next. Even with good intentions, the senior generation can set the younger generation up for failure by maintaining rigid leadership roles without allowing the younger group to consider their own approach to leadership. Each generation brings different interests and skills to leadership—and the business itself may need different leadership skills. It's a mistake to assume that what worked for one generation will be right for the next generation, too.

Ruling from the grave

Owners can set the rules by which the next generation will work and own the business together, often through formal vehicles like trusts or through handed-down cultural expectations. The goal is often to protect what you have created and to help the next generation avoid mistakes. However, these formal approaches often backfire. Ruling from the grave removes the autonomy of the next generation to chart its own course and to respond to changing circumstances. Trusts are very difficult to undo, and even cultural expectations are hard to shift.

The chosen one

Many families have a cultural tradition that even when ownership is shared, the eldest male is put in charge of the family business. Sometimes, this person is given a greater ownership stake in the company (or all of it), and sometimes the power comes from being tapped on the shoulder by the previous generation. This tradition can help avoid battles over succession, since everyone knows their role at a young age. But more often than not, we have found that designating a successor at birth causes more problems than benefits. Even if it's not spoken aloud, everyone will recognize that the chosen successor may not be the best candidate for the job—that this person simply has the luck of being born first. This approach also places great pressure on the chosen one. Meanwhile, the rest of the family often feels disengaged and resentful.

All for none, none for all

When the current owners disagree on priorities, the individuals often want to compete with each other rather than collaborate. One way this competition happens is succession by attrition. For example, a "last one standing" provision in a shareholder agreement states that if, say, a company has three shareholders and one dies, then the two remaining shareholders must buy the shares from the surviving spouse at a discounted price. If a second shareholder dies, then, again the remaining shareholder is the buyer. The last person standing now probably owns all of the business, but because the business is likely to be heavily indebted, the last person will probably need to sell, too.

qualified to lead the business?). These decisions are steeped in meaning, connecting to issues of fairness (do I treat my children equally?) and identity (what do I do after I have exited from my life's work?).

To make a good transition, you need a **continuity plan** that maps out the path from the current generation of ownership to the next. Picture each generation on opposite sides of a canyon. If you just keep going along as you were, you will go right off the cliff. You need to build a bridge across. That bridge consists of three main elements: transferring *assets*, shifting *roles*, and developing *capabilities*. Let's examine each element in detail.

Assets

As you make your asset transfer plans, you need to revisit your family business type, align ownership with each person's interests, and make effective use of tax-planning tools.

Reaffirm or revisit your ownership type

We have already introduced the four main types of family ownership. Your type is at the center of continuity planning, because it defines much of what is permitted in a transfer. The owners can decide to move from one family business type to another. Such flexibility makes sense when personal interests or business context require something different. But the switch from one business type to another is not always so smooth. There are two common issues that can hamper generational transitions: a set and a stuck type.

THE SET TYPES. Some forms of ownership have strong inertia or legal conditions that are extremely difficult to change and thus cannot be adapted to meet different needs or wishes of the next generation. For example, franchisees such as Caterpillar and Toyota dealerships are often directed by the franchisor to, in effect, have a Sole Owner or a Concentrated type of ownership. The franchisor company wants to know that one person is in charge and accountable for important business decisions. A move away from that structure would risk the loss of the franchise. Alternatively, your trust structure may create a Distributed type, with the trust dictating that all family members become equal owners (more on the implications of trusts later).

Even when the family ownership type is set, you can optimize for it, emphasizing the importance of role handoff and capability development. For example, some Caterpillar dealerships, eventually needing to find the single successor, start working to identify and foster leadership talent in their family when the next-generation members are early teenagers. Family businesses set in a Distributed type, on the other hand, can work to build a strong Family Room, as the unity of a growing family will be key for their generational transitions.

THE STUCK TYPES. Though there may not be the same kind of formal restrictions that a set type has, a family ownership type can become stuck when owners disagree and therefore can't prepare for a generational transition. A stuck type is analogous to a tug-of-war with equal strength on both sides of the rope—nothing moves. In a family business we work with, one owner advocated for keeping its Partnership type into the next generation. Another owner viewed a Distributed type as a necessary ethical decision so that all eight of his children could benefit equally as owners, and a third owner refused to address the topic until the patriarch had passed away. While the three owners clung to their disparate views, the next generation began pursuing careers and interests outside the family business. This stalemate is likely to mean that the business will not pass to the next generation—an ending that none of the current owners want. If you find yourself in that situation, explore the alternatives and their implications with your co-owners.

Even when your type seems set or stuck, you can usually shift it with the agreement of all owners. You may find common ground through conversations—as Megan's family in chapter 3 eventually did by shifting from a Partnership to a Concentrated type—or you may decide that you need to go your separate ways.

Align ownership with interests

We described earlier how owners can divide up their assets among their children according to the recipients' degree of interest in the business, with some children inheriting shares and others receiving outside assets. The same approach can be applied to the business ownership: you can base how you divide ownership of the company on the different interests of the next generation.

Many owners want to maintain power until late in life, but there are benefits to distributing the economic value of your assets before you formally hand over the reins. You might start this distribution either to begin engaging the next generation in ownership or to gain tax benefits (more on that in a moment). One way to initiate this distribution is to pass down economic interests to the next generation while still retaining voting control. Some family businesses split their ownership into voting and nonvoting shares, then pass down to the next generation more of the financial benefits of ownership (via nonvoting shares) while keeping control in the current generation through voting shares until later.

Others take the opposite approach. When the current owners are ready to pass the risk and equity appreciation down to the next generation but want to maintain a source of income to fund retirement, ensure a spouse is taken care of, or donate to charity, you can adopt a "cash up, equity down," approach. The current owners structure the transfer so that they receive money over time while passing down ownership. The transfer is accomplished in a variety of ways, such as pulling out the real estate from the company, arranging directors' fees for being on the board, or having preferred shares behave more like bonds. In some countries, such as Argentina and Chile, this idea is legally defined as *usufructo* (in English, usufruct), the legal right of owners to enjoy the financial benefits of ownership while ceding control.

Cash up, equity down approaches are especially useful when the owners have prioritized growth and control over liquidity. They will have created a lot of value on paper without having taken much money out of the business over the years. When they're near the time to consider retiring, they may value liquidity more than they value illiquid assets. Meanwhile, the next generation may have a longer-term view, focusing on capital appreciation rather than current income.

Many other scenarios are found in practice. Owners should move away from the idea of an asset transfer as all-or-nothing and instead look for ways to meet the variety of interests within and across generations.

Understand tax-planning tools

The details of tax planning lie outside the scope of this book. But note that for a successful transfer of assets, you will need to understand the full suite of transfer tools, which include trusts, wills, gifts, life insurance, director's compensation, and dividend policy. Taxes are, of course, a significant issue for all businesses, but the role that taxes play in a transfer cannot be underestimated. As one of our clients once quipped, "Please don't sit in *that* seat. Our biggest partner, Uncle Sam, always sits there." The joke alludes to a very real issue: taxes—estate taxes, gift taxes, income taxes, and dividend taxes—greatly affect asset transfer. Unfortunately, the two certainties in life—death and taxes—often happen together. Without proper planning, your heirs may not have the liquidity to pay the taxes that come with the transfer. A number of family businesses have had to go public, liquidate assets, or sell the enterprise entirely, because they neglected to do effective tax planning.

Laws governing such transfer taxes vary greatly by country, and they change over time. In 2020, for example, Brazil had an 8 percent ceiling on inheritance and gift taxes and zero dividend taxes. The country doesn't recognize trusts. In the same year, the United States, on the other hand, levied an estate tax of around 40 percent at the federal level (above that year's approximately $11 million exemption per person), a tax on dividends that can be lower than the tax on ordinary income, and a sophisticated set of options for trusts. While estate planning is essential in both countries, the plans themselves couldn't be more different.

In jurisdictions that permit trusts, a core transfer decision is whether to own the assets directly or in trusts. Most large family businesses in these countries are owned by trusts. If you move an asset to a trust, you no longer own it; the trust is the owner. Trusts and direct ownership have significant pros and cons.

Direct ownership has three main advantages:

- Simplicity of ownership structure

- Clarity of control (as opposed to trustees, beneficiaries, etc.)

- Sense of "psychological ownership" created by a direct connection between owners and assets

Trusts also have three main advantages:

- Tax efficiency

- Privacy

- Protection of assets from family members, creditors, and others

Trusts come in dozens of complex forms. You will hear specialists talk in such technical and jargon-laden terms as *grantor retained annuity trusts*, *intentionally defective grantor trusts*, and *generation-skipping trusts*. Moving your assets to ownership by trusts will have a profound impact on your transfer taxes *and* how you can practice your ownership rights. Talk with your legal counsel about your options and the implications. Tax planning is vital but should not drive the bus. We have seen too many ownership structures that are tax-efficient but nearly impossible to govern or change. One family we worked with set up a generation-skipping trust designed to protect the third generation from tax consequences of a transfer of the business. The trust did indeed help with that goal. But it also triggered a strange dynamic between the third and fourth generations of this family. The third generation didn't directly own the family business; the children did. Avoid the temptation to set up rigid rules that will end up preventing the next generation from nurturing and growing the business you care so much about. It's possible to break a trust, but doing so can both be prohibitively expensive and trigger unwanted attention from the tax authorities. Tread carefully. The box "The Pritzker family: the unintended

The Pritzker family: the unintended consequences of an overstructured transition

To see the unintended consequences of overstructuring a transition, consider the Pritzker family, which built one of America's largest business empires, including the Hyatt hotel chain. Jay Pritzker, leader of the third generation, and his brother Robert gathered their family together in 1995. During that meeting, Jay and Robert handed out a two-page document that described their plans for the next generation. It detailed the intricate web of trusts that had been created to hold the family's assets, which were "not intended for and should not be viewed as a source of individual wealth."[a] The document spelled out when family members would receive distributions, with an annual stipend after college graduation, and specified that "lump-sum distributions were to be made on the occasion of major life events." Otherwise, the rest of the assets were to be used to reinvest in the family's companies and continue the family's tradition of philanthropy. In the letter, the next generation was told that this plan was to continue into the future, as "the family trusts were not to be broken up until the law governing trust perpetuities required it, which one source suggested might not be until 2042." The letter also clarified the succession plan for the companies, placing leadership in the hands of a "triumvirate" of three family members. It was undoubtedly a thorough and tax-efficient plan.

But the plan didn't last for long. Mere months after Jay's passing in 1999, the conflict began. Six fourth-generation cousins who were not part of the triumvirate questioned whether the "structure of our family enterprise needs to be updated," as the "growing clan developed divergent interests."[b] When that suggestion was rebuffed, legal proceedings began. Among them was a lawsuit filed against the triumvirate, claiming that "those running the business and controlling the family's vast network of trusts took 'disproportionate compensation or investment

(continued)

opportunities' for their work; improperly allocated trust investments and managed them imprudently; diverted assets away from beneficiaries; and failed to disclose material information." Several years later, the family settled on a plan to liquidate its holdings over the next decade, agreeing to "split their $15 billion business empire evenly among 11 cousins." Regardless of how you assess the final outcome, the tribulations to reach it were painful.

The estate-planning rules in the United States are making this type of transfer easier, allowing for the formation of *dynasty trusts* that provide the grantor exceptional and long-lasting power, removing nearly all decision rights from the living family members in perpetuity. Carefully consider the long-term negative consequences of such estate-planning tools. Ruling from the grave removes the autonomy of the next generation to chart its own course and to respond to changing circumstances. In our experience, too much specificity in transition planning jeopardizes family ownership over the long haul.

a. John C. Bogle, ed., *The Best Business Stories of the Year*, 2004 edition (Vintage, 2014).

b. Jodi Wilgoren and Jeff Bailey, "Records Expose Schism in Chicago Family," *New York Times*, January 11, 2006, www.nytimes.com/2006/01/11/us/records-expose-schism-in-chicago-family .html

consequences of an overstructured transition" illustrates some of the challenges that can arise from even good intentions.

Roles

A brilliant asset transfer plan is worth little if you don't carefully manage the handoff of roles from one generation to the next. A good succession is often described as the passing of the baton in a relay race. This helpful metaphor points to three aspects of the process—preparing the person currently holding the baton, selecting who will take it, and orchestrating the handoff.

We will focus on succession for family business CEOs and other senior business leaders. These roles are often the most challenging ones to transition, because of their position in the center of family, business, and owner relationships. However, the same approaches can be applied to passing the baton in leadership roles across the Four Rooms (e.g., owner council, family council, board of directors). Avoid the temptation to focus solely on who gets to take over running the company. In a family business, there are many possible and important leadership roles for the next generation to assume.

Preparing the current leader

Gracefully shifting your powerful roles is a profound act of leadership, but the transition isn't easy. As a current-generation leader, you may know that the transition to the next generation is the right thing to do, but you just can't seem to let go. Handing over power is also an act of deep loss at a time when your life is surrounded by loss. You wonder how to let go, how your identity is (too) closely tied to the business, and how to face your own mortality. You may be feeling pushed by an impatient younger generation.

But you can handle a transition with grace if it's thoughtfully planned and supported. Amid the sacrifice of stepping away, the senior generation needs to build an attractive place to land. As a wise client once told us, "You must retire to, not from, something."

Well-prepared leaders create a *glide path*, a five- to ten-year plan to move away from the business. Table 7-1 notes some elements of a successful glide path.

Don't expect to execute your glide path on your own. This is a major life change. You will need the support of peers such as an advisory board, a single trusted adviser, or a coach. And your spouse's involvement and encouragement are essential. When a founder was struggling to limit his glide path to less than fifteen years, his spouse said in no uncertain terms: "You *will* retire in five years, so we have some time together. You have had two spouses for forty years—the company and me. I want you alone before it's too late." That helped spur him to take his retirement planning seriously, and he and his spouse created a happy postretirement life together.

TABLE 7-1

A senior leader's glide path: how to successfully make the transition away from the business

Glide path element	Advice
Job responsibilities you will keep	Hold on to the parts of your job you are most passionate about. One of our real estate clients liked the title Chief Deal Junkie because it described his passion and what he hoped to do for a long time while handing over management responsibilities to others.
Job responsibilities you will let go	Most people peel off the parts they don't like doing. Discuss with other owners how your responsibilities and title will change during the transition, and communicate these changes across the Four Rooms.
Office status	For most executives, an office is a deeply emotional topic. Stripping away an office from a senior-generation leader can be devastating. We saw one tough eighty-year-old burst into tears when his son mentioned that he was remodeling his dad's office to take it over for himself. If the office is important to you, keep it. But don't use the location to interfere in job responsibilities that you have relinquished.
Compensation package and perks	Make sure your compensation package is large enough for you to be able to step back from the business. Ensure that between your ownership interest and other compensation, you don't feel the need to reengage in the business for more compensation. Write down the agreement, and have all interested parties sign it.
Activities to pursue outside the business	In our experience, it takes someone whose life has revolved around the family business up to five years to develop new communities of interest. Start early.

Selecting successors

One of the most challenging, and potentially contentious, aspects of a leadership transition is deciding who is most qualified to take the reins. Choosing your successor—without damaging the family—may be even more difficult than planning your own transition. There is no one right way to pick your successor, but we offer some suggestions to help you navigate this decision:

- **Make them earn it.** Taking over from a successful predecessor is hard enough. It's nearly impossible when the company sees the next-generation leader as the "COO," or child of owner. The successors who have demonstrated their capabilities *before* being tapped on the shoulder fare far better. That doesn't mean they have to follow the standard path each step of the way, but a successful track record goes a long way to demonstrate that your successor has earned the title. One family business we know had the business successor work his way up through each level of the hierarchy until he reached the executive team. Once there, he was put on the express path to take over the business, but by that point, he was already seen as qualified by both other family members and valued company employees.

- **Establish a clear and transparent process.** A horse race among next-generation leaders can generate much conflict, especially if there is a perception that it is rigged or otherwise unfair. The odds of a smooth handoff increase significantly when people in the family and the company see that the process has integrity. You can ensure integrity by setting out in advance the process you will use to select successors and gaining buy-in along the way. Start by developing clear job descriptions. Often, for example, the broad responsibilities of the current CEO need to be broken into several roles reflecting the growth of the company. It then helps to have a rigorous selection process that ideally considers multiple candidates. You don't need to publicly announce who they are; you need only to share that there is more than one candidate. It is helpful to communicate how candidates are being evaluated.

- **Ensure alignment with your Owner Strategy.** New business leaders will have their own ideas, which should be encouraged. But their efforts need to align with the goals of the owners. Don't, for example, switch to a growth-oriented CEO if the owners primarily want liquidity. If you don't have an Owner Strategy statement, now is a critical time to create it. If you have one in place, confirm that it captures what you want in the future, and use it during the selection process.

- **Get outside help.** You can greatly enhance the credibility of your successor by having objective input into their selection. If you have a board with independent members, this is a great time to use them. If you don't, consider forming a search committee with trusted advisers or using an executive search firm to guide you through the process.

- **Avoid the temptation to clone.** The leadership challenge in each generation is different. It is natural to look for someone who fits the profile of the current leader (think of Mufasa and Simba), but doing so can be counterproductive. We have found it helpful to differentiate between what we call *conquerors* and *rulers* in family businesses. Conquerors are business builders and have a deep focus on operational details and decision-making, often with an autocratic style. Rulers, by contrast, think strategically about both the business and the family ownership group from a broad emotional and developmental standpoint. They continue to build the business, but they also have to keep the branches engaged and working together, connecting it all through good governance. Assess whether your business needs someone who is more of a conqueror or a ruler.

- **Consider outside board and business leadership if no family member is qualified.** With the appropriate governance and guardrails in place, you will be less dependent on a pool of family members who may not be qualified or interested. There are still opportunities for family members to play important leadership roles in their capacity as engaged owners, board members, or leaders of the family council. Opting for a nonfamily leader does not mean that the family is ceding control of what matters most.

Orchestrating the handoff

The last aspect of the succession process is to make the passing of the baton as smooth as possible. Many resources are already available on this topic, so we will only highlight a few points that are critical to a family business.

First, *prepare the organization* for the transition. It's easy to underestimate the extent to which the entire company is built around a particular leader. When the next leader takes over, it can be difficult to fit into the surroundings. In one family business we worked with, the next-generation leader struggled to take over from his father. The father was the classic conqueror, engaged directly in nearly every decision. The son's style was different—he was more of a leader through delegating and managing. The organization was not set up for that kind of leadership. Several of the executive team members, for example, were trusted longtime employees who had failed to grow and keep up with the skills needed for the business now. The previous leader valued their loyalty and had filled in their deficiencies by going around them to their subordinates. Also, the previous leader had such a strong instinct for the business that he operated by gut feel. Consequently, there was little data available to monitor performance. The founder approved every major outlay of money and based measures of financial success on whether the company checking account increased at the end of the year. With no financial metrics, the son struggled to get a handle on how to improve company performance.

Many of the successor's initial struggles could have been avoided if the company had paid more attention to getting the organization ready for this change. For example, the founder could have helped to gracefully exit employees who could no longer meet their job requirements before his son took over. Hiring a CFO to produce comprehensive financial statements would also have made a real difference.

The handoff is also an important time to revisit your Four Rooms to make sure none are missing or messy. We worked with one leader who, knowing that power would soon be shifting to the next generation, created a heavy-hitting board that included two of his daughters while he also prepared and gradually transferred responsibility to his son. Family owners often construct their first board to anticipate their CEO transition. Owners should select board members or advisers who can talk eye-to-eye with the powerful family CEO about the need for an orderly transition. Especially when considering a family successor, the board needs to assess whether the organization would welcome a new family CEO or whether the appointment would be viewed as nepotism gone bad. The full system has to work in concert.

Second, set up *structured communication* around the handover of leadership. In a public-company transition, the retiring CEO often leaves the company entirely after a year as chairperson. In a family business, the departure is much more likely to be a multistep process than a single event. Typically such transitions happen over several years, in deliberate stages. Both generations of leaders (departing and succeeding) should plan for routine communication about the business, even if the departing leader has no official role. Since the departing leader will certainly want to know how the business is doing and most likely will still have sources of information about the business, the next generation probably can't shut them out even if it wanted to. Departing leaders can still play active roles in the Owner Room or Board Room, for example. And of course, they're still part of the family and will no doubt have opinions and expertise to share over family dinners and holidays. A better approach than ad hoc involvement is to establish a regular schedule of meetings during and after the transition. This way, you can keep the departing leader updated and get the benefit of their wisdom. Those sessions can gradually become less frequent and fade away as they are no longer needed.

Third, plan for the transition of *key relationships*. Part of what makes a family business valuable is the trusted relationships you build over time with customers, suppliers, industry associations, and so on. With all the moving parts of a succession, businesses can easily lose sight of the importance of ensuring that those relationships remain solid. We have seen many family businesses focus on the value of preserving key relationships years before the transition takes place, for example, by fostering a connection between the next generations of their family and their business partners' family.

Fourth, *start the transition early*. The time for psychological preparation is critical. The CEO is likely to need many years to adjust to the idea that they will not be the main actor. The company and the family will, too. Although every company should always have its CEO's successor clearly established, companies often fail to do so. If your family CEO is older than seventy with no transition plan, you are playing with fire. One seasoned board member's first question to a recently promoted CEO is, "Congratulations on your promotion to CEO! Now, who's your successor?"

Finally, *celebrate* the transition. The handoff of roles is an emotional moment. Make sure you take the time to thank those who have been critical to the success of the business. At one family business, the eighty-year-old consigliere, who had helped both the current and the next generation succeed, was thrown a surprise birthday party with all the owners attending and toasting his contributions to the family and the business. Smaller acts of appreciation are also helpful.

Capabilities

In planning your generational transition, you should remind yourself (and the next generation) that family businesses require all kinds of leadership to have continuity of ownership in the long term. Many family members can have meaningful leadership roles, even if they don't become the next CEO. Within the Four Rooms are many crucial roles, such as owner council member or head of the family council. Except in very small first-generation family businesses, there are typically more roles than qualified and interested family members. For your business to thrive, you will need to become a family talent development machine. That also means being as inclusive as you can, especially when it comes to gender. Family businesses that exclude women from leadership roles are not only missing out on talent, they are putting their survival at risk if there are no qualified male successors. We have seen a number of family businesses that have fallen apart due to their decision to exclude women from the succession conversation.

Leading organizations often "hire for attitude; train for skills."[2] We offer a variation on this advice for how great business families prepare their next generation for an eventual transition: "Raise with good attitude; train for skills." If you've done the work to raise your children well and educate them about the business, their future wealth, and family values, you have given them a solid foundation on which to build their skills and become strong leaders in the future.

Shape the next generation of leadership with an early effort to engage them and prepare them for their future roles in all Four Rooms. Three core elements help build capabilities in your successors.

Strive to create professional owners

Requiring conscientious work, family ownership should be anything but passive. Even family members who go to business school will learn little about what it means to be a family owner. Approach family ownership as a profession—a paid occupation that, to do it well, requires lifelong training and development across a range of knowledge and skills. While most development programs focus on their next generation, current generation owners will also need to build an entirely new set of skills to transfer the business to the next generation. We've seen many structured programs to help develop family members into family owners. Topics typically include:

- Business ownership skills and concepts (e.g., financial statements, legal structures such as trusts, tax laws)

- Family business principles and practices (e.g., Four-Room governance)

- Knowledge of the family assets (e.g., shareholder agreements, key managers, business strategy, industry dynamics)

- Family history and values (e.g., family constitution or protocol)

- Personal leadership competencies (e.g., conflict management, group dynamics, personal finance)

One way to get started on this path is to attend a family business executive education program together, such as Families in Business at Harvard Business School, Leading the Family Business at IMD, Enterprising Families at Columbia Business School, and Governing Family Enterprises at Kellogg Business School.

Construct pathways into the rooms

Family businesses will often put in place policies for working in the business (see chapter 10) but stop there. That leaves unaddressed the pathways into other leadership roles, such as board members and family or owner council roles. Owners should clarify the path toward those roles and provide support along the way. For example, we work with several family businesses that have created board trainee programs. Next-generation family members are invited to participate, and those who are interested receive training on what it means to be a good board member. They also have the opportunity to observe board meetings for some period. A similar concept can apply to businesses without such formal governance. Consider using internships or family meetings to build knowledge of the business. Look for opportunities outside the business, such as joining a nonprofit board, to build the skills the next generation will need.

Create opportunities for collaboration

In addition to building their skills as individuals, members of the next generation need to develop their ability to work with each other. These important relationships should not be left to chance. Just as you can build the assets of a business or create trusts to transfer them, you should have a strategy to build the next generation's relationships in your continuity plan. Create spaces where they practice making decisions together early on and with lower stakes. For example, some families have set aside some portion of their philanthropic budget and ask the next generation to collectively decide where to donate it. We have seen similar efforts aimed at having the younger family members make investment decisions. Whatever mistakes they make will generally be more than compensated for by the benefit of their learning how to collaborate.

How to set continuity planning in motion

In many cases, the biggest hurdle to continuity planning is getting started. Between pressures of the critical issues of today, the need to confront highly sensitive subjects connected to mortality and identity, and the requirement to engage a kind of cross-generational conversation, starting continuity planning may feel wholly uncomfortable. Here's how to give your planning the momentum it needs:

Treat your transition like the multiparty negotiation that it is.
The tendency, often out of respect, is to make this all about the
current owners. If you are part of the senior generation, you may
have the formal power, but you cannot achieve your objective
of continuity without the buy-in of others. If you are in the next
generation, don't forget your power to walk away or wait it out.
If you are a nonfamily employee, remember that you have influence through the trust you have accumulated and the ability to
vote with your feet. The more that the continuity plan becomes a
discussion and less like an ultimatum, the more successful it will
be. Make sure that your plan addresses the core concerns of each
party. Look for consensus solutions that everyone can live with,
even if it is not their first choice.

Put it on the agenda with a deadline. Discussions about continuity
planning will usually get delayed unless they have dedicated time.
If you have established an owner council, set aside time to have
updates and discussions on your plan. Or consider forming a continuity planning taskforce that meets once a quarter or twice a year.
Boards often play similar roles, as they have an explicit mandate
regarding CEO succession. Some sophisticated family boards have
also urged owner groups to prepare for owner succession.

Consider working backward. Many current owners are comfortable with the existing setup and are resistant to change. If that's
the case, we have found it valuable to avoid making immediate
changes. Instead, start by asking members of the next generation
to define how they will work together *when it's their turn.* That
way, they are preparing themselves to work together without immediately changing (or threatening) the status quo. They should
discuss how will they make decisions, structure the business,
define success, and so on. If nothing else, doing so creates clarity
for what will happen in the future. In parallel, ask the senior generation how they envision the future, say, fifteen years out, when
they have stepped back. Then work backward to think through

what needs to happen to get there. This approach can make the transition seem less threatening than would starting with what the senior generation has to give up today. These processes, especially when the senior generation is included in them, can open up incremental changes toward the next generation's plan.

Remember that transition is a process, not an event. In addition to steps forward, you will also take steps backward or to the side. As you develop and implement your plan, look for concrete markers of progress, such as a revised shareholder agreement or a new governance structure. And adapt to the changes around you. As events unfold—for example, a next-generation member shows unexpected leadership capabilities, or some tax laws change—new possibilities arise.

A healthy transition is much more comprehensive than a Simba succession plan. It takes a lot of work to make a thoughtful and successful transfer of your kingdom.

Summing up

- The right to transfer gives you the freedom to determine the future of the family business. You can choose to sell it, divide it, or transfer it to the next generation. Make this choice explicitly, thinking through the alternatives and their implications.

- If you want to transfer the business, you need a continuity plan to manage the complexity of the change. That plan consists of three main elements:

  - *Passing down your assets:* Will you keep the same type of ownership or change it? Will you transfer ownership all at once or in pieces? What tools will you use to minimize taxes?

  - *Handing off roles:* How will you create the glide path necessary for the current leaders to be ready to let go? How will you select successors in a way that feels fair? How will you ensure a smooth passing of the baton?

    — *Developing next-generation capabilities:* What skills does each person need, whether they work in the business or not? How will you help them to find the role or roles for which they are best suited? How will you create opportunities for them to learn how to collaborate with each other?

■ Although the final decisions usually lie with the current owners, a transition can't happen without cross-generational collaboration. If you get stuck, consider working backward by starting with what things will look like when the next generation is in charge.

■ Remember that an unplanned transition is extremely risky. Although it's not easy to talk about, find a way to get the process started early, and maintain momentum.

PART THREE

Challenges You Will Face

8.

The Business Family

Four Disruptions You Will Face and What To Do about Them

As gravel spun from under his wheels, thirty-four-year-old Jack Johnson turned his Ford F-150 out of the company's sugar beet processing plant just east of Fort Collins, Colorado. Jack's father and uncle were co-owners of the family's third-generation food manufacturing company. Possibly distracted by the argument he had had with his uncle moments ago, Jack looked to the right only before pulling out onto the main road. Tragically, an unseen semitrailer hit Jack's truck and killed him instantly.

Jack's death was painful for the entire family, not least because he was so young. But the family's grieving extended far beyond that. Unspoken blame for the circumstances of Jack's death permeated family relations, and infighting broke out among the remaining owners (and their children) about who should run the business in the future. Jack's sister, Fernanda, who became the largest single future shareholder after Jack's death, struggled to fill Jack's role in both the family and the business. Without her brother's leadership and companionship, Fernanda felt trapped working in the family business and, within a few years, was arrested for drug possession. The family was unravelling, threatening the business in the process.

We hope your business family never faces the trials of the Johnson family. But disruptions happen to even healthy business families. At such times, working together as a family becomes more difficult or in some cases impossible. Decisions can become entwined with emotions that you haven't had to navigate.

These disruptions, though painful, are normal. Most business families experience, at some time, four major disruptions: death in the family, new entrants into the business family, inequality, and behavioral health issues. Without some preparation for such disruptions, both your business and family could fall apart under the strain.

This chapter will raise your awareness of these business family disruptions and will help you anticipate, plan for, and navigate them when the time comes. We prepared you in the first chapter to look at your family business through the lens of the individuals, the relationships, and the system dynamics, as well as reflecting on how you are exercising your five essential owner rights. We offer concrete guidance from experts in each of these areas.[1]

Death in the family

Expected or unexpected, death is difficult for any family. But for business families, there are added considerations. If a family business leader dies, for example, her son might simultaneously mourn the loss of his often-absent mother, his demanding boss who once fired him but also mentored him, a trustee who took care of him financially, a great philanthropist, and a loving grandmother to his children.

Family members may experience a range of feelings, including profound loss, guilt about things left unsaid or undone, freedom from controlling behavior, shame that they are wondering about the financial consequences of the death, and confusion on what may change in the future. These are all normal feelings in a business family.

Even if you have developed sophisticated Four-Room governance, the emotions from a death may revert you and your family into a loft as you mourn. Your carefully constructed boundaries can be at least temporarily overrun ("I haven't seen Aunt Marcella since she fired me, but she's at the wake!"). In some ways, the breakdown of barriers is appropriate so that you can remember and mourn the person's life in its entirety. In other ways, the breakdown can be jarring at a time when you face major decisions.

During your grieving period for a loved one who has passed, when you are most vulnerable, you will face many unpleasant burdens. Funeral and burial arrangements are just the start. An Internal Revenue Service estate audit, new financial worries, loneliness, altered relationships, and other changes can swirl around you and the family business. Try to avoid making important decisions quickly during this time of mourning and change. You can easily make mistakes in your haze of grief. When Joe Robbie, then owner of the Miami Dolphins football franchise and Joe Robbie Stadium in Miami, died in 1990, his widow, Elizabeth Robbie, was unsatisfied with her annual income of $300,000 from the trust that held the family assets. To access more wealth quickly, she filed a petition of the trust that ultimately triggered a $47 million estate tax, which forced the family to sell its share of the Dolphins and the stadium at fire-sale prices. Elizabeth died within two years after triggering the sale. When the new owner resold these assets eighteen years later, it was widely reported that they were valued at more than seventeen times what the Robbie family had received.

Of course, preparing for death is disagreeable. Many business families avoid such preparation altogether. "When I'm dead," one client bluntly told us, "I won't care about the problems I leave behind." We met a founder of an Asian financial services business in his late sixties who recently had experienced a significant health scare. He had no will, no estate plan, and no clarity on ownership after he passed. If he made no changes, within two years of his death, his heirs would need to pay the tax authorities more than $400 million in inheritance tax, necessitating a fire sale of their business. That sale, especially during a time of grief, would probably have caused his children to lose both their business and their family relationships.

It's tempting to avoid planning for your own (or your family patriarch's or matriarch's) death, but if you forgo this planning, you are quite likely dooming the business to failure in the long run. Is that what you really want? "None of us want to recognize our mortality," Dave McCabe, a highly regarded trusts and estates lawyer with Willkie Farr & Gallagher, told us. But failing to prepare creates the potential for chaos. McCabe advises four basic steps to prepare for death in the family:

1. **Educate your family about the estate plan.** One of the most common fears in the immediate aftermath of a family member's death is that there won't be enough money for the surviving spouse and family members to live on. "The anxiety around death and what happens next is enormous," McCabe observes, "particularly if the surviving spouse has not really engaged with the finances of the family." Make sure family members are aware of the specifics of your estate plan well in advance. McCabe, personally, has a binder with all his estate-planning documents prepared for his wife and children. The first three pages list each of the accounts (by the last four numbers) and a contact person at each institution. As the father of four daughters, McCabe makes sure that each of his children personally understands the details of the family estate. "They don't need to know the dollars in every single account, but they do need to understand the scope of what's there and how to access it." Consider writing a *letter of wishes*, which is a nonbinding indication of how you hope your trustees will administer your estate. Such preparation may be costly and emotionally difficult, but your heirs will praise your foresight as a lasting gift to them.

2. **Review and update your plan every two or three years.** Big events in your life should cause you to reflect on the potential impact on

your estate plan: you get married, get divorced, have children, or remarry; your children get married; someone in your family dies; and so on. Life events can change everything. Imagine, for example, that the last time you updated your estate plan, you were single and decided to leave everything to a charity. But you now have a spouse and two children whom, of course, you want to provide for. It's easy to neglect these necessary updates to your estate plan, but the consequences can be significant.

3. **Make sure everyone understands the process and how it unfolds before they are immersed in it.** Navigating the administrative process after death can be frightening. When are funds going to be available to the surviving family members? Finalizing an estate with tax authorities can take years. But that doesn't mean surviving family won't have access to funds until then. Explaining the process in advance reduces anxiety. McCabe's firm provides clients with a one-page flow chart of how estate-planning documents work to make it easy for everyone to understand. Ask your estate-planning attorney to do something similar for you.

4. **Plan for the consequences on the business, too.** Having an estate plan is not enough. You'll want to plan for the transfer of the business, too. Make sure you have a well-considered ownership agreement that anticipates transfer of ownership at death. And have—and communicate—a succession plan. "You may leave everything to your spouse because that is tax-efficient," McCabe explains, "but that doesn't explain what to do about running the business. A very detailed plan is also important."

New people entering the business family

One new person can disrupt a long-established business family. It happens more easily than you might think. Whenever anyone joins the business family—for example, new children and spouses—the members of the family need to find a new equilibrium for their relationships with each other.

But most often, new spouses often disrupt the business family culture. That's because the entry of a spouse (1) creates a new nuclear family, (2) alters every relationship the newlywed has in the family—with parents, siblings, and others, and (3) creates several new important relationships such as the spouse's relationship with a father-in-law and mother-in-law. Communication patterns, loyalties, family customs and beliefs, and relationships all change, even in close-knit families. The impact is magnified because, unlike most families, business families can't choose to limit their interactions to social gatherings.

How a spouse enters the family makes a huge difference. Are they welcomed into the family and encouraged to bond with the extended clan? Or are they seen as outsiders and treated as such? You may not like your new brother-in-law, but he is likely to have enormous influence—constructive or destructive—over the culture and chemistry of your existing extended family.

Consider a family we know with an oil business in Houston. The second generation included a brother and sister who had a history of mistrust but who would one day be equal owners of their family business. Their strong-willed father kept a lid on the conflict but worried about what would happen when he was no longer around. In a twist of fate, when the sister married her brother's longtime best friend, things took a turn for the better. The friend-turned-spouse turned out to be just the relationship balm the siblings needed. Loved (and trusted) by both his wife and his brother-in-law, he helped the siblings rebuild trust, dramatically improving the family dynamic.

How you treat a new spouse will greatly influence how they enter and ultimately influence your system. As we have discussed, many business families try to "protect" their family from new spouses. As one spouse explained to us, "I learned a few rules of the road during my first year after marrying into this business family. You marry not only your spouse but also your spouse's business family." You quickly learn, this spouse told us, that though you are *in* the family, you are *out* of ownership. Prenuptial agreements and other legal documents ensure that you will never be an owner but that your children will. The spouse told us, "What they don't say is, 'Our family, that we *let* you join, is special. Your family is not quite as special as ours, but we would never say that out loud. We'll just make sure you feel that.'" Such messages, whether explicit or implicit, are usually received loud and clear. If poorly treated, spouses have the power to bias the next generation against the family business. Why would they want their children involved in a business family that has not welcomed them?

There are a few best practices to integrate new family members more smoothly.

1. **Decide who gets to be family.** Don't wait until there is the prospect of a new family member to decide how they will be legally and emotionally incorporated into the business family, advises Fredda Herz Brown, senior partner at Relative Solutions. "If you wait until you have the prospect of a new in-law," she told us "then the issue becomes focused around that person. It will feel personal and has the potential for all kinds of hurt feelings." Herz Brown advises instead to start discussing how your family wants to define who is family early on, perhaps when your children are still young teenagers. Discuss all permutations that might occur—adopted children, biological children, in-laws, stepchildren, and so on. "You're discussing the issue of membership in the family before it becomes about a particular person," she says. Your family may define family—and all the attendant benefits and emotional implications—in any number of ways, and that's okay. But family businesses need to raise the issue as a philosophical question for discussion before anyone in particular is in the picture.

2. **Protect the family assets.** Business families naturally want to protect their wealth and the business from new family members. Most families fear the worst-case scenario—where a nasty divorce damages both the family and the business. Shareholder agreements that specify who is allowed to own shares in the company can help avoid heated emotions down the line. (That doesn't mean spouses can't

benefit from the shares; it just means that they can't take ownership from outside the marriage.) It's also reasonable to ask a new family member to sign a prenuptial agreement—but the how you ask them is critical. The intended spouse should not hear about a prenup for the first time seated in the family lawyer's office or with the parents hovering nearby providing pressure to sign. The family member they are marrying should introduce the idea in private conversations, Herz Brown advises, as part of both sides discussing what they bring to the marriage and establishing their own boundaries and ground rules about their shared and independent wealth. Then a prenup can be discussed, negotiated, and signed with goodwill on both sides.

3. **Establish appropriate boundaries and roles.** As discussed earlier, spouses are not necessarily included in Owner Room discussions or privy to all financial information about the family business. Some families make explicit efforts to include spouses in the Owner Room. For example, one large business family offers new spouses the opportunity to buy a few shares so they can access the Owner Room. But even if spouses are not in the Owner Room, that doesn't mean you can't find opportunities for inclusion that will make spouses feel part of the family. Spouses play an important role in the Family Room and in establishing goodwill toward the extended family in the next generation. Take the case of Killian, a lawyer who married into a successful business family. Killian wanted to make sure he was supporting his wife (a future owner of the business) and earning the respect of other family members. So before he attended his first family assembly, he educated himself in preparation for weighing in on the business strategy. He soon realized, however, that as a spouse, he would never have a chance to vote on business strategy but that he was still welcome to have a voice in other areas. Resetting his expectations, Killian quickly found a constructive role helping create a family education policy to support the next generation with the costs of higher education. And perhaps importantly, his improved understanding of both the business and the

business family brought enormous respect for what his father-in-law had built and helped cement their relationship.

4. **Celebrate the culture of new family members, too.** Rather than signal that new spouses should consider themselves lucky to join your family, our colleague Marion McCollom Hampton, coauthor of the seminal book *Generation to Generation*, suggests that new spouses be welcomed into the family in ways that celebrate their background and culture as well. Acknowledge, for example, that the newlyweds will probably alternate important holidays with their respective families. Be open to including the new spouse's family traditions and rituals in your family, too. If the new spouse gets the message that they are expected to quietly adapt to the new family's culture while forgetting their own, that impression can set up conflict down the line. Find ways for new family members to feel part of your family while celebrating the one they come from, too.

5. **Set expectations for spouses in the family business.** Spouses entering a business family often face a peculiar career challenge. As one family in-law explained to us, "I married a fabulous woman from a rich business family. I love my career and like to work. Soon, however, some family members would ask me, 'Why do you work so hard? You will never make enough money to matter.' Yet my fellow spouses who don't have careers are considered freeloaders who take advantage of the family's wealth." In such systems, talking openly about the unusual circumstances and expectations is enough to resolve the mixed signals and encourage the spouses to pursue their career interests.

Family can be one of the most stable institutions in life. Your relationships with your brothers and sisters, for example, are likely to be the longest in your life. At the same time, families are constantly changing. When a generation is in its thirties and early forties—getting married and having children—you can expect lots of new family members. If, say, you are a first-generation member and your three children marry and each has two children, your family has gone from five members to fourteen members. And the number of unique relationships in your business family has gone from ten to ninety-one![2] As one matriarch told us, "As our family grows, it's hard work to stay together. But it's worth it!"

Inequality

Inequality in families happens as a slow-motion change to the business family. Children enter the world all "created equal," and most parents strive to provide equal opportunities. Siblings start out under the same roof and share many experiences. But as their lives unfold, they make thousands of decisions that lead to individual success, or not. Strong cultural influences, such as gender bias, amplify inequalities regardless of individual capabilities and choices. Luck also plays a major role in either opening up opportunities and success or closing them down. By their fifties, siblings will often recognize that the summation of all the choices and experience creates pronounced differences in siblings' capabilities, accomplishments, beliefs, wealth, and happiness. Some siblings will inevitably become more successful and influential in the family than others.

This disparity crops up not only in siblings but also in family branches. Some branches fall behind the others in wealth, power, and accomplishments. Those who are feeling inferior are often the first to sell to their cousins or to outsiders. One third-generation business family we worked with had two primary branches. One branch had the voting control over the company, amassed 90 percent of the family's wealth, and held all the family executive roles in the business. The other was labeled the "bad branch." The two branches will never be equal in power, wealth, or position.

Sociologists explain that humans tend to focus less on absolute differences between groups and more on relative differences within a group. In most business families, the "all created equal" thinking creates back pressure against the disparity. You will hear from family members comments like "You can't expect our son to work for his brother!" Or "Don't my children deserve a chance to work in our company?" Or "It's not fair that she got company stock and I didn't!"

Family branches have often made different choices through several lifetimes. Such outcomes are hard to unwind, to equalize. And would it be fair to equalize? Often, fair is not equal. And eventually, equal is no longer fair. Although some multigenerational business families try to equalize wealth, such policies can be harmful in the long run. Ellen Weber Libby, author of *The Favorite Child*, advises that families learn to be comfortable with some inequality developing over generations because it's inevitable. So how do you get comfortable? Here are five ways to navigate this path well:

1. **Focus on purpose.** As a family, working on defining and refining your purpose will help all of you keep your eyes on your collective objectives and what you are individually willing to sacrifice for the greater good. When families spend considerable time talking about inequality, that's a sign that they lack a clear and compelling purpose as a business family. Renew your conversation about why you own this business together. Such discussions can bring you all to higher common ground.

2. **Define your family culture.** Families can choose and build their culture over time. Some families focus on meritocracy—you benefit more from the business by working in it, for example. Others have a more "socialist" culture, in which taking care of the extended business family is an important shared goal. Either version (and many in between) is okay as long as you have built trust and communication among the family members so that everyone understands the culture. Feelings of inequality are often a symptom of an ambiguous family culture.

3. **Have a forum or another process for dispute resolution in the Family Room.** By having an appropriate family forum for handling disputes, you can help prevent conflicts from escalating. In many cases, you just need a forum that encourages civility, that is, the ability to be in the same room and make decisions together without the conflict disrupting the business or the entire family. The ability

to sit down in the same room and make objective decisions together, despite the inevitable disagreements, helps family members avoid the pitfalls of emotionally charged arguments that breed and spread when the involved parties don't communicate.

4. **If you're one of the haves, make sure you are sensitive to the have-nots.** Some inequality is inevitable, but that doesn't mean the family members who end up in positions of power should lord it over those who aren't so fortunate. Make sure your family culture prizes the family—and not just the finances. Those in a more comfortable financial position should be sensitive to those who aren't. When planning extended family activities, such as a family reunion or holiday gathering, make choices that everyone can afford. Don't plan to stay in four-star hotels if only some family members can afford it.

5. **Find common ground through gratitude.** Even if you are a have-not in your family, you're still likely to be better off than the average person in the world, Libby says. Keep your sense of inequality in perspective. Much research confirms that those who express gratitude for what they have and for what others do for them are far better off emotionally.[3] Take time to express gratitude in your family.

Behavioral health issues

Some issues can't effectively be handled through better governance, communication, or good intentions. An array of problems, including addiction, mental health disorders, eating disorders, and learning and other developmental challenges, are found in many families.

Business families aren't exempt from the range of behavioral health issues that any family faces, says Arden O'Connor, founder of the O'Connor Professional Group, which addresses the needs of families and individuals struggling with these concerns. Business families are families. But in their tightly connected world of business and family, often with blurry boundaries, family problems can be amplified. Crisis events—including family members' embarrassing themselves in public (where the family's reputation is at risk) or a medical crisis (where a family member ends up in the hospital) can jar a family into action.

More challenging, O'Connor told us, is when there are warning signs and symptoms but no clear-cut case that the family member has a problem. Families are very good at ignoring or minimizing what might to an outsider seem to be obvious signs of trouble. "You might question your own judgment about what is normal behavior," O'Connor observes, particularly in the case of substance abuse, which can be hidden for a long time. "You'll accept all kinds of excuses and explanations for strange behavior. You'll give your loved one the benefit of the doubt over and over again."

Successful families are used to being in control. They can pay for lawyers to help make charges disappear, and they can pay for someone to live in an apartment in another city for a while to avoid scrutiny. They can create jobs in their companies and build a veneer of respectability even when a family member is struggling with addiction or other serious behavioral health issues. And these capabilities, O'Connor says, can exacerbate the problem. Families can afford to try one solution after another, never really holding the family member in question accountable. One father whom O'Connor worked with actually paid a competitor to create a fake job for his son who struggled with substance abuse so that the son would not feel like a failure.

These efforts often make things worse. The family member can say, "How bad can this be? I've got a job, and I'm turning up at work!" when in almost any other scenario outside a family business, the person surely would have been fired or required to seek professional help. The longer a family covers (or pretends not to notice) a significant behavioral health problem, the more that critical family relationships are in jeopardy. "There's an adage in my business that for every one year of broken trust, it takes *five* years to repair," O'Connor says. So the longer it takes for a family member to get help, the greater the likelihood that the family relationships will be damaged beyond repair.

O'Connor, who is not only a professional in the field but also someone who has faced addiction in her own family, shared with us her tips to help you start to deal with a behavioral health problem in your own family:

1. Openly discuss any genetic predisposition toward mental illness or addiction—be honest about your family's strengths and vulnerabilities.

2. Identify and address signs of a behavioral health issue swiftly. One sign in isolation may be meaningless, O'Connor says, but a combination of smaller problems or a more serious problem might warrant attention. Issues like overspending, legal trouble, and some medical situations (e.g., a young adult's having to their the stomach pumped while at college) may suggest a deeper problem, including a mental health challenge, substance abuse, or an eating disorder.

3. If a loved one resists care, set small boundaries and stick to them until the person becomes more receptive. Consider an intervention.

4. Find a team of qualified professionals to make diagnoses, to outline a care plan, to recommend inpatient or outpatient treatment, and to monitor progress.

5. Assume that your loved one will need therapeutic support and accountability over the long term (one to five years).

6. Advocate for your loved one. Question the care providers when you're uncertain about the course of action, and get a second opinion.

7. Proactively manage privacy releases—HIPAA (the medical privacy law), healthcare proxy, college grades—so that family members can't hide brewing problems. Ask your family member for permission to see these critical records as a way of keeping track of how they're doing. "We recommend that parents introduce the release of information concept early on, to all of their children (not just individuals with preestablished challenges)," O'Connor says. "The language could be something like, 'We love you and want to make sure that we can access information if you wind up in a hospital or incapacitated. Because we are investing in your education, we also want to get a sense of your progress.'"

8. Identify a professional to work with family members (parents, siblings, children, etc.) on how to productively support someone with an addiction issue. Important topics include understanding the diagnosis, setting healthy boundaries, and maintaining individual self-care routines even during crises.

9. Working with professionals, create a reasonable plan for financial support. In the most complicated cases, the beneficiary received (or will receive) a lump-sum payment at a specific age, regardless of their mental wellness. For individuals who have behavioral health issues, the estate-planning document should include contingencies that allow the distributions to be discretionary, or dependent on specific criteria. Ideally, the professionals who draft and implement the actions in the document have access to mental health education and professionals.

10. Grieve the loss of your dreams for your loved one. Try to accept that your loved one may live a different life than the one you envisioned, but it won't necessarily be a lesser one.

Sweeping a problem under the rug does not help the family member you dearly love. With mental health or addiction issues, trying to handle a family problem on your own can hurt key relationships, sometimes irreparably. Allowing a behavioral health problem to go unaddressed threatens not only your family member's health and your family relationships but also ultimately the health and reputation of the business you've worked so hard to build.

How to stabilize after a disruption

Many members of family businesses seem surprised when they experience conflict, jealously, and different levels of commitment in the family business. They are also often surprised by how scared they feel after a parent's death. The truth is that virtually every one of the hundreds of business families we know shares many of these dynamics.

Disruptions to your business family are normal. And *normal* means that when these tough disruptions hit your business families, the members will have emotional and sometimes extreme reactions. Your business family won't be perfect. When a powerful disruption hits, the "crocodile brain" takes over—people will say hurtful or selfish things without even thinking through the impact of their reactions on others. They may descend into a conflict spiral (see chapter 12). Most often, the reactions are human and, indeed, expected, when people experience involved and unpredictable change.

Business families frequently resist accessing outside advice, especially if it is considered therapy. Some people worry about sharing their family problems with outsiders. One well-known family matriarch told us her family motto was "Never air our dirty laundry in public, no matter what." If your family is used to privacy, you hesitate to ask friends or experts for advice, because it's an admission of a family problem. Many business families pride themselves on being able to fix their own problems. Absolute self-sufficiency seldom works in the long run. Angry feelings fester, issues are covered up, and cracks develop later on. Seek help early on.

You can find a wide range of outside advisers available to help your business family. The range of disciplines that offer specialized support to business families includes family business advisers (this is the role we play), family system therapists, relationship therapists (e.g., marriage counselors), individual therapists (who come in many subspecialties), mediators, conflict resolution experts, life coaches, communication specialists, and group dynamics experts. Acknowledge that there are problems that you can't solve on your own, and reach out for the resources you need.

You'll want to carefully select the right type of adviser. If you reach out to a mediator, for example, they will see your problem through the lens of mediation. But that might not be what you need. If you are new to the field of advice you're seeking, talk to advisers in at least a couple of fields to see who really understands your problem in a way that you are confident will address the heart of the matter. Additionally, talk to at least two providers in whatever specialty field seems most applicable to your situation. The practices of individual providers vary significantly. Personal chemistry also matters greatly. When choosing an adviser, include the input of the family members likely to be affected by the change. Business families face tough dynamics. To ask for outside help is ultimately a sign of strength.

We believe that work can often be the best therapy. Working together—in the Owner Room, in the Family Room, or in the company itself—can build trust, commitment to others and to the business, and an appreciation for the difficulties faced by your business family. A key message of this handbook is that business families have much work to do together—defining what they value, working through difficult decisions together, building trust and communication, preparing the next generation to be owners, and so on. Through this work, families can build relationships.

The work that you've already put in with other family members can provide a shock absorber for when you're hit by an unpleasant disruption. By working together, you and the rest of your family prepare your business to react constructively. If all of you have collaborated in the past, you're more likely to work well together when it is most needed. Having good governance structures such as a family council in place ahead of time can help later, when difficulties arise, because you'll already have a place to discuss and decide on issues.

The Johnson family that, as described at the start of this chapter, fell apart after the unexpected death of the son has made significant steps looking to the future. Individually and collectively, and using some of the tools discussed in this chapter, the Johnsons have worked hard on mending relationships. And in the process, the members have managed to keep both the business and, more importantly, the family together.

In the following chapters, we will identify additional challenges that most family businesses face—no matter what size, what industry, or what generation. If together you and the rest of the family get these challenges right, you will add to your business's power to sustain. The best advice we can give you is, be prepared for curveballs. Counterintuitively, they're normal. You can't always control the disruptions that life sends your way, but you *can* control how you respond to them. That resilience can make the difference between families that survive and thrive generation to generation and those that fall apart.

Summing up

- ■ You will usually encounter four main types of disruptions:

  - **Death** is hard for any family to deal with, but in a business family, it can bring practical complications that magnify the emotional pain. To reduce the impact on your family business, make sure to have an estate plan that is understood and revisited as circumstances change, as well as an emergency succession plan for the business.

  - **New entrants** to your business family, especially spouses, will change existing relationships. How you treat new family members as they enter will have long-lasting implications, so be thoughtful about the messages you are sending as you ask for prenuptial agreements or establish boundaries for spouse participation. And celebrate what new members bring to the family.

  - **Inequality** is inevitable in business families. Sometimes what's fair is equal, but quite often trying to make everything equal is not fair. Rather than trying to avoid inequality, do your best to manage it. Be sensitive to the reality of haves and have-nots as you plan family events. And try to focus on your common purpose as well as the reasons to be grateful to be part of your family.

  - **Behavioral health** issues are common in all families but have an even bigger impact in business families because of the need for family members to work together. Keep an eye out for behavioral health problems that are simmering below crisis level, as many problems do for a long while. And exercise caution when you intervene. Many actions taken with the best of intentions can make the situation worse.

- When handling a disruption, a first step is to recognize that it is normal. There's nothing wrong with your family if you are struggling with any of these challenges. Sometimes, working together as a family can be the best remedy. In other situations, you will need to look for outside expertise to help you get through it.

9.

Working in a Family Business

Some people thrive after choosing a career in their family business. But others wither, bitterly regretting their choices. "I'm going to lose my business—and my family," one client lamented to us after his decision to join the family business immediately after college had turned out badly in the long run. His situation happens too frequently—and it's the worst-case scenario of what can go wrong when you jump wholeheartedly into your family business too early in your career.

Working in a family business, whether it's your immediate family, a family that you've married into, or someone else's family, brings its own forms of challenges and rewards. The decision to accept *any* full-time job offer can be stressful. But with family businesses, the choices can be far more complicated: it's as much an unspoken social contract as an employment one—and the consequences can last far longer. Even the most highly qualified family members have a hard time navigating the emotional mix of expectation, obligation, uncertainty, and desire for professional success when faced with the decision.

In this chapter, we will discuss how to thrive in a family business. We will consider several situations:

1. Deciding whether joining the business is right for you

2. Succeeding in the business if you are an in-law

3. Preparing yourself for life under a microscope within the company

4. Thriving in a family business when you are not part of the family

Deciding to work in your family business

When bright, ambitious young people talk about career prospects with a prospective employer, they are typically full of questions about how that company will support their professional growth. But remarkably, the same young people will confess that the prospect of joining their own family business leaves them tongue-tied. In families whose culture has been one of deep respect for those who are in the day-to-day trenches of the business, young family members often worry that asking too many questions might make them seem presumptuous or pushy. We get it. Asking too many questions can seem entitled. But we have seen many family relationships fractured from poor communication at the start of a family business job. This is *your* career. And *your* family. Making the wrong decision because you're afraid to ask good questions can lead to heartache for everyone. You can, however, avoid that fate by working through our basic guidelines for setting yourself up to succeed in your family business.

What is motivating you to join?

You might be interested in your family business for many reasons. We often hear statements like "It's my best shot at the top," "It's a great joy to work with my mother and sister every day," and "I'm passionate about our family business." On the other hand, we also hear "Dad expects me to," or like Megan earlier in the book, you need to join to keep ownership in your branch. How does what you can contribute to your family business compare with what you might bring to any other potential career option?

Often, a variety of motivations are in play, but what's important is that you articulate your own reasons—and ensure that they are compelling enough to make perhaps your single largest career decision.

Are you ready for the commitment?

More than almost any other career choice, joining your family business requires you to be all in. It will not be a nine-to-five job. Your family life and business life will be intertwined. Your personal identity will be more tied to your work than it would be if you go elsewhere. People don't leave family business jobs easily; the commitment feels more personal. You will probably remain with the company for many years more than if you join another company.

Do you already have significant outside experience?

In most cases, we advise family members to get a college degree and then work in another company for at least three years. Demonstrating to your family business leaders, managers, and employees (and yourself) that you are capable of earning a genuine promotion for your work outside the company helps ensure that you are appropriately valued in (and prepared for) your own family business.

Are the personal relationships among the family leaders healthy enough?

Do you see evidence that the leaders can make good decisions together about the future of the company? Can your own relationships in the family withstand the pressures of working together in the future? If your relationship with your father or mother (or whichever relative owns and runs the business) is not in a good place, joining the business is unlikely to make things better—and, in fact, it could make things much worse.

Is this a real job?

When you come into the family business, make sure it's for a real job, not one that has been made up for you. You will find your work more valued and your career path clearer if you do.

After you've assessed your own motivation, make a point to ask the family business leader what lies in store for you if you do join the business. You have to break the unspoken taboo against "daring" to ask these questions. In chapter 10, we'll explain in detail how to think about family members' employment in the business, but here we will stress that you are entitled to know about the business you are joining and where you will fit in. The current owners may not wish to answer every question you have, but many topics are likely to be addressed. Use the five rights of family owners to think through what you need to understand about your family business before joining.

- Is there a path to ownership? (design)

- Who will make decisions about my career? Who decides how much I get paid? (decide)

- What are your goals or priorities as owners over the next ten years? (value)

- What's your philosophy about sharing information about family ownership and company performance data with family employees? (inform)

- How are you are thinking about succession? Do I have a shot at the top? (transfer)

If you feel uncomfortable asking these questions of the current family leadership, that feeling is a red flag that you might not be ready to join your family business. You can take a dry run by talking with either of your parent's trusted advisers or the parent who doesn't work in the business. Ask them directly, "Would you join this business if you were I?" Often, their answers can provide telling clues about both the health of the business and your career prospects under the current leadership. If, after gaining this additional insight, you still can't approach the family business leaders directly, your reluctance may signal that joining is not the right choice for you.

You are entitled to know the structure, rules, and processes that will enable you to be successful in the family business—*before* you join. Perhaps most important of all is to understand that you will not be able to control everything about your career path in the family business. You can't always predict how the family will view your work in the long run, whether you'll thrive in the business, and whether you'll eventually be offered a top leadership position. The one thing you can control is your own choice of career path. Gather the right information to help you make a wise one.

Joining the business as an in-law

In-laws in many business families often find themselves at a disadvantage. As nearly every married (or formerly married) person recognizes, tensions with in-laws are common, whether you work together or not. When working in the family's business, in-laws (who sometimes call themselves "outlaws") have two strikes against them. They have to live up to the standards and expectations set down for nonfamily employees; at the same time, they are viewed by nonfamily employees as having all the perks that come with being part of the family. Essentially, they have the worst of both worlds.

And yet some in-laws do avoid a third strike; some even manage to hit a home run. In many family businesses we have worked with, an in-law makes a meaningful and enduring contribution to the business, often successfully leading it to the next generation.

What does it take for an in-law to survive and thrive? Successful involvement in the business depends on several factors, including the person's competence, personality, expectations, and opportunities in the business, as well as the family's philosophy about whether to allow in-laws in the company. Different in-laws can have different experiences within the same family business. Among our client families, the successful in-laws often follow several smart practices in navigating this challenging situation.

Play for another team first

As is true for younger family members joining the business, work experience for in-laws outside the family is often a prerequisite for being—and feeling—successful in a family business and for maintaining a sense of personal identity. This experience not only develops competence and skill but also builds a reputation, self-confidence, and credibility with both the family and nonfamily employees. As one in-law CEO put it, "I came in as an accountant, and I felt pretty good about that because I didn't feel like they were making a place for me." The importance of work experience was emphasized time and again—even by in-laws who had made it to the top of the heap but who had not worked outside the family business.

Negotiate like an agent

Given the porous boundaries between the family and the business in a family-controlled enterprise, successful in-laws draw an invisible but firm line between their personal and work lives. Just as is true for other family members, be prepared to negotiate for compensation and to clarify your goals, role, benefits, and career plan. Be honest and candid. As one in-law senior executive we know advises, "Don't treat it like a family decision on where to go for vacation. Act just as if you were negotiating with Oracle." The more transparency, professionalism, and clarity that you bring, the better placed you will be to shape your career in the family business.

Be clear about structure and policies

Several in-law executives attributed their success to the fact that they did not report to a family member. But if you must do so, then be sure that the family has an employment policy (see chapter 10) and that the policy is supported by the owners. It needs to identify your direct supervisor, your responsibilities, and what recourse you have if a family member is undermining your efforts in the business. Remember, structure is your friend!

Be smart about geography

The adage that familiarity breeds contempt offers sound advice. A number of in-laws we spoke to, and their spouses, attributed their success to the in-law's working physically far away from the home office. Distance not only makes the heart grow fonder but also allows for personal and professional growth and maturity in a way that is not always possible when you are at headquarters, under the magnifying glass of the patriarch or matriarch.

Don't view the job as a life sentence

Just because you joined your family business it doesn't mean that you need to work there forever. One in-law employee we know was surprised that when he left his job after fifteen years, many family members, who had never worked in the business or supported him while he was there, questioned his loyalty to the family. Looking back, he wished he had explicitly built into his employment contract re-ups every three years, so that leaving was always an explicit and supported option.

Be patient

Take a hard look at the makeup of the family whose business you are thinking of entering. If there is already a favorite son or daughter, there may be no room for an in-law executive. "If there are other 'real' family members working in the business," warned one in-law who spoke with us, "you may get sidelined. At the very least, you won't be deeply involved in the succession process." But sometimes, the heir apparent is neither good enough nor smart enough nor interested enough to wait around to take over the business. One CEO told us, "I tell every employee, including in-laws, to be patient and to do the job better than anyone else could do it. You will be paid handsomely, and if this doesn't work out, you'll be in a good position and will have the confidence to go work somewhere else."

Find a confidant outside the family

When you work for a family business, you just can't bring the job home with you. Forcing a spouse to take sides between you and the business family can put them in a sensitive position. "Maybe it's because your partner has grown up thinking that her father knows everything and is the smartest guy in the world," one in-law CEO told us. "But when you run up against that, you're in trouble. You really need a good friend that you can talk to if you hope to make it in a family business."

If all else fails, follow the practice of an in-law of one client family: keep a signed copy of your resignation letter sitting in your desk.

"Whenever it's clear to anyone that I'm not the right guy for the job, I'll just walk into the patriarch's office and hand over my letter," this executive said. But beyond having a letter drafted, prepare for a day when you might need to exit the business, whether it is by saving your own money, building an outside business, or cultivating employable skills. The additional security gives in-laws—and their spouses—the distance they need to be able to walk away from an unhealthy situation.

As an in-law, you may be given wonderful opportunities to stretch and grow and help the family business thrive for future generations. The key is to avoid letting your career in the family business simply happen; instead, you should actively shape your future in the business.

Preparing for life under the microscope

Working in your family's business—whether you are part of the family or you married into it—can bring enormous rewards, but it also carries great responsibility. Even when you and your family have done the right groundwork, you will never be seen as just one of the gang by fellow employees. When your family's name is on the door, everything you do could be fodder for the office rumor mill. Family business leaders we work with have learned that their actions—positive and negative—are amplified because of their status as owners (or owners-to-be) of the company. Even seemingly small gestures—driving a fancy car to the office, putting photos of themselves with celebrities on social media, or calling themselves an owner in front of colleagues—can unintentionally generate ill will.

Nonfamily employees tend to watch family members closely. How you behave will reflect on the full family, for better or worse. You will be "special"; that status is not always an easy thing. And the microscope doesn't shut down when you leave the business at night. The standard barriers between your work life and your personal life will be blurred, and the scrutiny on how well you are doing will be strong from both sides. Even if you're on your best behavior, it's easy to fall victim to some common traps.

Expecting promotions without putting in the work

When family members start at a level that is beyond their qualifications or are promoted much faster than they deserve, other employees are more likely to focus on patronage rather than performance as they look to climb the ladder. Ask for routine feedback on your performance so you have a fair idea of how you are doing—and how you can improve to earn your promotions (see chapter 10 for more details).

Working outside the chain of command to get special treatment

How do you seek approval for your ideas? Do you follow the rules and work as hard as everyone else does? Too often, family members take advantage of their access to senior members of the firm, seeing the rules as malleable and looking for ways around them. Instead, work through the chain of command. Don't ask for special treatment by relatives in senior positions, and abide by policies for vacation days, expenses, and office hours.

Blurring the boundaries between home and work environments

Office politics in family businesses are further complicated when members bring their family dynamics into the business, potentially enabling employees to pit family members against each other. Family members must set clear boundaries in the workplace, for example, referring to people by name rather than relationship (at work, your mother is "Mary" to you, never "Mom") and not discussing family drama at the office. These boundaries help set a professional tone. Keep family language there.

For family members, boundaries between work and life are more blurred than they might be for any other employee. However much they love and support one another, even the closest family members find it difficult to live and work together all their lives. As one of our clients, the gifted CFO of a large manufacturing company, said when he quit the business, "I can't continue going through life always being the younger brother."

His identity as a family member undermined his professional growth and effectiveness as CFO. When people cannot be their own person in a family business, the tragedy is that both the family and the business lose out.

Failing to create an identity outside the family business

Business families often have strong ties to the community, and their identity and status are deeply bound up with it. Yet your own identity can be subsumed under the family's prestige and stature in the outside world. While status confers many advantages, family members need to find a place in society where they can create an identity unrelated to the family. Look for ways to contribute to your community or pursue a personal passion in areas where your family name has nothing to do with what you can contribute. You want an outlet where you can be just Charlie or Eloise, rather than the owner's son or daughter all the time.

Thriving as an outsider in a family business

As a nonfamily executive, you may wonder whether you can thrive in a family business. You're right to be wary: no matter how good you are, you'll never truly be in the inner circle. And because families can be intensely political organizations, nonfamily executives must know how to play politics both in the business itself and in the dangerous borderland between the business and the family. Despite these obstacles, you can find enormous benefits to working in a family business, even as an outsider. We have seen nonfamily executives not only survive but also flourish, where they have come to be truly trusted. To enjoy this level of success, you have to understand the rules of the road.

Play in your room only

As someone who is not a family member, you're not always welcome to be in all Four Rooms of the family business. Successful nonfamily executives either know intuitively or learn through experience how to stick to the Management Room. They understand that when it comes to the Family

Room, the family plays by its own rules; it's never going to be a fair fight. Yet family disputes do spill over into the Management Room, and nonfamily executives must separate the business from the family when family members can't see past their own internal squabbling.

Ironically, it is often harder for the manager to stay out of the Family Room than you might think. Many business families either deliberately or naively try to involve the nonfamily executive in family affairs. We worked with a client whose patriarch was continuously trying to engage the talented nonfamily CEO in a bitter fight with his son. To enter such a fray would be a losing proposition for the CEO, who, to his credit, refused to take sides in family disputes. He was empathetic, but he firmly pushed back against being used as a pawn in a game that he could never win. He repeatedly told the patriarch, "That is a Family Room issue; please take it there." This strategy has served the nonfamily executive well.

Be discreet and competent

Restricting your influence to the Management Room does not mean that you are powerless as a nonfamily executive. Far from it. Given your position in the company, you typically have access to an enormous amount of privileged information, and information is power. As noted earlier, the problem for many nonfamily·executives is not that the family tries to keep vital information from them but rather that they are deluged by potentially explosive information. Woe to the manager who cannot keep confidences! Lose the trust of family members, and your career will tank, no matter how good you may otherwise be at playing the game of office politics.

This is not to say that family members always keep nonfamily executives informed of important business decisions that are in the offing. They don't. But the best way to avoid being left out of critical conversations is to demonstrate your competence. For example, one family made major business decisions outside the office, when the family got together on Sunday afternoons. Nonfamily executives can't force the family to involve them in these extra-office discussions, but in this case at least, one financial analyst was so good that the family invited her to all these meetings. She had demonstrated her talent, her dedication, her discretion, and her commitment. She doesn't attend these events as if she's a family member; she attends as a trusted employee. She knows how to be professional in a family environment, and the entire family has come to respect her.

Avoid proxy wars

Alignment with one family member or branch is dangerous because families can act out their rivalries by "taking out" a relative's favorite nonfamily executive. While proxy wars are hardly limited to family businesses, they can often be more intense in families because of the volatile group dynamics. For example, one client family member has vociferously signaled his intent to break up the team of employees who are fiercely devoted to his sister, with whom he has a particularly contentious relationship. Our advice to nonfamily executives faced with this dilemma: never hitch your wagon to just one star. Aligning yourself with a particular sibling or branch is always risky. Look for ways to gain exposure to more than one family member over time.

Give credit, and invoke the family's higher angels

The nonfamily executives who survive the longest know instinctively how to deflect credit from themselves and aim it back at the family. While your gracious acknowledgment of others' contributions in every accomplishment of yours is important in all office environments, in family environments this practice takes on far greater significance. You should never be disingenuous, but when you can legitimately, for example, make a son's value clear to his father—a battle that the son may have been waging all his life—you will win the loyalty of that son forever. Family members need mentors and cheerleaders in the workplace as much as the rest of us do.

What's more, most family owners are intensely proud of their companies. When negative family politics break out, you can nudge the family members to remember their family's greatness. Do this with genuine respect for the family's legacy, and you can go a long way toward helping the members bridge their immediate differences.

Use impartial outsiders

Supervising or providing feedback to a family member who reports to you can be tricky in a family business, where the person you are evaluating may someday be the boss. Your instinct may be to step back and tell the truth but to tell it with kid gloves. Indeed, caution is the appropriate response; you must deal with the reality of the power dynamics at play. Look for opportunities to make your feedback truly independent of you and truly confidential. Encourage your business to conduct 360-degree reviews using an outside provider. Or find an honest broker—for example, a trusted external board member—who can give constructive criticism to family members in the business without risking their career.

One of the most difficult political situations arises when a nonfamily employee has a genuine grievance against a family member who receives de facto protection because of the lack of any formal (or informal) channels to address the situation. Imagine for a moment what happens when a nonfamily employee with a complaint turns to the head of the business, who just happens to be the father of the son who committed some egregious offense. This situation occurred at one client family whose son was making inappropriate sexual comments to several female employees. In this case, the power of the nonfamily executive to put an end to the situation was limited; it took an outside adviser (approached privately by nonfamily staff) to step in, expose the issue, and stop the harassment. Another group of nonfamily executives we worked with came together to inform the boss of a family member's poor behavior. In extreme cases, some groups of nonfamily executives have threatened to leave en masse if the family member was not dealt with. Collectively, trusted nonfamily executives have real power.

Know your genetic limits

Finally, to succeed in a family business, you must have a realistic sense of your career path. Even the most masterful player of office politics is not going to get the top job if the leadership pipeline includes a family member who is destined to assume the mantle of CEO. Don't take it personally; it's not about you. In this situation you are not a member of the "lucky gene club" and have to be wise enough to recognize this fact. Always be thinking about the family tree and family dynamics when considering your own path up the career ladder.

In a family business, playing office politics successfully means having the humility—and the political shrewdness—to put the family first. That said, being a trusted employee in a family business can provide an extremely satisfying career. For example, the culture in the business may well prioritize loyal employees and customers over short-term growth pressures. And rather than working for a company that is laser-focused on squeezing out more profits each quarter, you may find yourself enjoying working for a business guided by family values. That philosophy can, in turn, offer you more meaning in your own work. Long-serving employees can have rewarding careers in a family business—as long as you understand the unspoken rules.

Summing up

- Whether you are a family member, an in-law, or an outsider to the family, working in a family business brings distinct rewards and challenges. When you are set up for success, this association brings you an incredible opportunity for a gratifying career with an outsized impact on the company. When it goes badly, both your professional and your personal lives may suffer.

- As a family member, make sure you do your due diligence before joining a family business. Think of it as a career move rather than a job application, since it is not easy to leave once you sign up. You can't change your family. You can only control your choice of career, so choose carefully, and gather enough information and outside experience to enter the company with confidence.

- As an in-law, you'll need to accept that you are neither fully part of the family nor totally separate from it. So, manage your career with care. Make sure you have a real job that builds on your previous experience before you commit. Be strategic about what type of role you take on and who you report to. And be prepared to leave if it's not working out. Maintain a good network outside the company, both for your own development and to keep your options open.

- As a family member or an in-law, you will always be closely watched. Anything you say or do—or neglect to say or do—will be magnified because of your proximity to the owners. Because of this connection, it will be much harder to get candid feedback. Look for ways, such as through anonymized 360 reviews, to get it.

- If you are an outsider to the family, remember that trustworthiness is one of the most valuable attributes inside a family business. Demonstrate your competence as well as your discretion. And pick your battles carefully. When in doubt, stay in the Management Room and out of the crosshairs of family disagreements.

10.

Family Employment Policy

Omar agonized about whether to join his family's fifty-employee ladder and scaffolding business. In high school and college during breaks, he had worked at the company his grandfather had founded, but Omar had felt no pressure to build his own career there. So he followed his own dreams for years, working as a newspaper editor. But after his own son was born, he decided it was time to settle into his family legacy. Not only did it mean saner hours and better pay, but he was also excited about helping his father and aunt run the business.

Four painful years later, Omar recognized that he had made a mistake. In hindsight, the family never really figured out how to bring its members into the business, and certainly not in any way that set them up for success. "Even when I was working there in the summers," Omar told us, "my grandfather would introduce me to people by saying 'This is my grandson. He works here now. I have no idea what he does.'"

When he joined full time, the employees in the business assumed he was both a future owner and the presumptive number two in the company.

But Omar couldn't get anyone to agree on his title, his responsibilities, or his decision-making authority. He never even got a business card, because of the disagreement over his title. Omar's salary was better than he had been earning as a newspaper editor but not the kind of family-insider salary he had imagined.

"I produced a lot of sales," he said, "but I never really got raises. I think the assumption was, 'You're a future owner. You will benefit in the long run.' But I felt like saying, 'I'll benefit in the long run whether I work here or not. This isn't fair!'"

After a series of work-related battles, both Omar and the rest of the family in the company felt disappointed that his job had not worked out. Family arguments turned into a downward conflict spiral.

"I kept thinking, they're not gonna fire me, right? But that didn't mean we didn't argue over and over. It was stressful." Eventually, feeling underappreciated, Omar quit. "The work was never my passion," he told us. "I worked hard but always sort of knew in the back of my head that I was not where I was supposed to be." It has taken years for him to patch up the damage to his family relationships.

For many family business owners, having a child (or another relative) thriving in the family business is one of the biggest payoffs of all. After all, who will care more about the company's success than a family member who may someday be the owner?

But having relatives work in the family business is complicated. Is every family member entitled to a job? Under what terms? Do they have to be qualified, or do family members get special consideration? Will anyone supervise and nurture their career path? Should spouses be welcome to work in the family business? What if some family members pour their heart and soul into the family business job while others take advantage of their position and barely check in? What happens if it doesn't work out? Family employment can trigger many issues—fairness, legacy, favoritism—and the parents' overriding desire to help their children, or at the same, time prevent them from becoming entitled.

But the risks don't have to stop your family from trying to make it work. By creating and implementing a family employment policy, family leaders can foster a healthy relationship between the business and family employees.

As we discussed in chapter 4, established policies allow families to "pre-decide" issues that could eventually end up being contentious and irreparably damaging to the business, the family, or both. A thoughtful family employment policy not only helps avoid that fate but also positions family members to succeed. What's more, the policy can help ensure successful generational transitions down the line. Your company's size doesn't matter. Family businesses—whether they have ten employees or tens of thousands—have benefitted from such a policy.

Many family businesses will establish some kind of family employment guidelines, which usually focus exclusively on how and when family members can be brought into the business. But such guidelines often stop there. Instead a good family employment policy should address six key decisions throughout the employment life cycle:

1. How you attract great family talent to be employees of the family business if you want them

2. The experience, achievement, and capabilities required for a family member to enter the business

3. The career path for the family member once the person has entered the business

4. How a family member receives feedback and development as an employee

5. How compensation for family members is determined in their role as employees—not as owners or directors

6. How family members, including the aging patriarch or matriarch, exit the business

For each of the six previously mentioned key components of a comprehensive family employment policy, we will discuss the range of options we have seen in family businesses around the world, and we will summarize the pros and cons of each. Skim through each of the lists to get a quick feel for which issues your family should be considering in creating the right policy to match your values and priorities. At the end of this chapter, we offer a summary chart that can help you identify which choices you have already made and which elements you should be considering.

Decide how to attract the talent in your family

The first issue is your family's position on how actively to attract family members to work in the business. In Omar's example, family members were neither encouraged nor discouraged from joining the business. He himself first raised the idea when he needed to earn a better living, with more stable hours, as a new father. Families should decide whether they want to deliberately attract talented family members into the business. Otherwise, beyond possibly creating false expectations, they could be overlooking what might be their best long-term source of talent and commitment. Your decision about how much to encourage family members to seek jobs in the company should align with the other policies and priorities you've set in your family business.

Some families deliberately discourage or stay silent on the issue of attracting family members to the business—and you don't want to attract family members if you don't have openings for them. On the other hand, some families create formal internship opportunities during high school and college as a way to expose the next generation to the business. If such an approach supports your family's priorities, you are in a position to appeal to the best and brightest of the next generation as a way to cultivate their interest and talent early on. Additionally, explicit rule-based and recruitment strategies have the benefit of shining the light of transparency on any implicit recruiting biases (e.g., gender biases) your system may have. Discussions about the *attract* decision often produce more inclusive policies for qualified family members. The following list outlines the ways some families attract or discourage family talent from joining the business:

- **Discourage:** The senior generation actively discourages the next generation of family members from working in the family business.

- **Stay silent:** Family members don't talk to the next generation about family employment. They instead strongly encourage them to find their passion yet avoid mentioning the family business as a place to find that passion. The family makes no guarantees for employment in the business.

- **Handpick:** Without using any overall policy, senior-generation owners handpick family members to join the parts of business they control.

- **Publish rules:** The family publishes some basic rules about family employment but do not actively recruit the next generation.

- **Recruit:** The family identifies and recruits family members into the business. It creates experiences such as summer internships to build interest, often with a coordinated family program.

Create entry rules for family employees

Omar's family had no existing rules about what experience he needed before joining the business. This lack of guidelines, in part, led to confusion about Omar's role. In our work with families around the globe, we have seen a wide variety of entry rules, including these:

- **None in:** No family member can work in the business. This rule avoids the conflict that can come from having family members in the business. But it also tends to discourage family members' emotional connection to the business and can lead to disengaged owners in the long run.

- **Glass ceiling:** Family members can work in the business but can't rise into the highest executive ranks, which are reserved for non-family personnel. This rule is often applied to avoid conflict in the

Management Room that can spill over into the Family and Owner Rooms. It is frequently instituted as a reaction to a past situation in which one person had too much power.

- **Level playing field:** Family members can seek employment as their own skills and talents and accomplishments merit, in the same way that any other employee would seek it. People from the family are hired into real jobs and are given no special opportunities or accommodations.

- **Higher bar:** Family members are allowed to work in the family business, but they will be held to a higher standard than are nonfamily to qualify for a position in the company.

- **All in:** Any family member who wants a job in the family business is entitled to one (or, in some cases, every family member is expected to work in the family business).

These policies represent a spectrum of what families do, but either extreme—none in or all in—can be fraught. For example, seldom do people thrive when their roles have been created simply to provide them with a paycheck. These completely open arrangements are often susceptible to all kinds of potential abuses as well. The family member who doesn't put in an honest day's work can build resentment among both the family members who do work hard and the valued nonfamily employees. Or some families don't allow the younger generation to even contemplate other career options. The young people are required to join the family business: "If you're good at math, we'll stick you in accounting. If you're good with people, you'll join sales," and so on.

On the other extreme, families with strict none-in policies designed to avoid family stress can ultimately miss out on bringing in talented and highly motivated employees. Some families specifically prohibit in-laws from joining the family business, while allowing bloodline descendants to do so. In some cases, while there is no explicit policy against women entering the family business, there are cultural norms or unspoken expectations that create a gender barrier.

The most successful entry policies have clear rules and boundaries that encourage *talented and interested* family members to engage and grow with the business. Time and again, we have seen family members who choose to join their family business thrive. And perhaps equally important, the business has clearly benefitted from their talents. Many family employees bring a lifelong connection to the company and the kind of commitment that only comes with ownership. While we have certainly seen unqualified nepotism play out poorly, nothing is quite as powerful as a business led by a skilled family member.

Plan family employee career paths

One of Omar's continued frustrations with his position in the family business was the lack of clarity on what job he held (hence the standoff on giving him business cards) and where that path would lead. Otherwise smart business leaders often fall short in thoughtfully planning career paths for family members. They think the family employee can wing it once the person has joined. Ironically, family members are often given *less* guidance or support than are other employees.

The most common mistake in family businesses, however, is bringing a family member into a level that is far beyond the person's competency. Parachuting someone right into, say, head of marketing because they're good at social media or appointing them director of technology because they "always loved computers" when they otherwise have no real-world experience—these moves can set that family member up to fail right from the start.

How will your company nurture and groom the career paths of family members? These five common career-path models are followed by many family businesses:

- **Undefined:** You can join the business, but there is no stated career path for you. "We'll figure it out. Maybe."

- **Branch silo:** Family members will be hired into the division that their parent (or their branch of the family) controls, and they remain there. If Dad runs manufacturing, for example, that is where they will find opportunities. They will never move out of their family silo, and promotions will depend entirely on Dad's seeing fit to grant them.

- **Company's career path:** Family members will be treated like any other new hire, brought into appropriate positions, and promoted according to the same guidelines applied to all other employees. There are no guarantees they'll be offered anything outside the standard company path.

- **Custom family path:** Family members will be given every opportunity to succeed, but there is no guarantee of success. If all goes well, they can then expect to be promoted to the highest level their abilities and drive will take them. Some call this pathway "finding their highest and best use."

- **Executive escalator:** If a family member joins, they can expect an easy glide to the top executive ranks. They'll be promoted quickly and treated as a special case. They can "fail" their way to the top, with few, if any, consequences.

It usually makes sense to find a way to offer family members a clear career path, with support, but one in which they know they have to earn their promotions over time. Bringing a family member swiftly up to the executive suite without merit rarely pays off for either the employee or the company. Doing so can be a recipe for resentment, the loss of loyal non-family employees, and, ultimately, failure.

Design feedback and development for family employees

During his four-year tenure with the family business, Omar never once had a review. He tried to learn from his mistakes, but he rarely knew what they were. The lack of candid and constructive evaluation plays out badly in other well-intended families, too. Family members, reporting directly to a parent, are never given any constructive feedback or, worse, are not held accountable for their failures and poor decisions. When a family member is ignored or coddled in spite of poor performance, and when nonfamily employees are afraid to speak up, irreparable damage can be done to both the business and the family. Therefore, the business must deliberately incorporate feedback into a family member's career pathway with the company. Family members *are* special, in good and bad ways. The question is, how to make sure that the family employee has genuine, constructive feedback throughout their employment?

Most families treat feedback and development in one of five ways:

- **Ignore:** The family member will receive no formal feedback and little informal feedback or other attention.

- **Treat the family member according to the company's regular policy:** The family member will be given feedback in the same way that all other employees receive it.

- **Supplement the company's policy:** Family members receive additional feedback and training beyond what is typically provided. The process is often led by independent board directors, an outside firm, or a coach that can provide cover to those providing feedback.

- **Prove yourself:** Family employees will be given a series of very difficult business challenges that they are expected to overcome to demonstrate their worthiness. The only feedback they get is another herculean challenge.

- **Coddle:** With little explicit feedback given the family member, failure is tolerated even as the person is promoted.

The most successful families create some version of a supplemental evaluation approach such as an anonymous 360-degree feedback system in which the family member's boss, peers, and direct reports evaluate their

Are you coddling a family member?

Here's a quick test to indicate whether you have a healthy career path in place for family members or you are at risk of enabling a family member. If you answer yes to at least three of the following questions, then you are probably cocooning, indulging, overprotecting—in short, coddling—a family member:

1. Has a family member worked exclusively in the family's business?

2. Have they reported within their parent's span of control for most or all of their career?

3. Have they never received formal feedback on their performance?

4. Is the family member paid significantly above the market-based compensation for their position and is that compensation not tied to performance?

5. Has the family member been promoted beyond their capabilities?

6. Is the family member's behavior often outside the boundaries of the acceptable value-based behavior of the company?

If you find yourself saying yes to several of these questions, you may be in jeopardy. Here are some remedial steps to be considered by the various players.

Overindulgent parent

Family owners need to set things right. This duty generally involves adopting a merit-based system—carefully and fairly. Such a system isn't easy to put in place. Altering what are often long-standing, implicit family employment policies can be upsetting to the family, but you need to make this change if you want to stop strangling your business. In family businesses, merit-based systems mean both that family employees are in explicit competition for positions with nonfamily employees and that family members receive supplemental feedback to ensure that they learn and grow. If your family business has a board with outside directors, consider enlisting them in the sensitive task of gathering honest feedback and delivering it to family employees.

Coddled individual

You need to get outside of your parent's span of control. Given your special treatment, it is likely that you are now in a job that requires more competence than you currently have. Working in a job that is beyond your capabilities is not good for the business or for you. Continued coddling is toxic to your sense of achievement and self-worth. Find a place in the business where you can employ your talents, an area you have passion for. Or take a leave of absence and work at another firm. Wherever you go, purposefully seek out more honest feedback.

Nonfamily employee

You are in a difficult position. Providing candid feedback to or about the coddled individual can get you fired. However, all is not lost. Most family businesses have long-term employees who have earned the deep trust of the leadership over several decades. If you are one of those people, you may be in a unique position to carefully raise the need for action. If you are not in that position, seek out those who are, and share your concerns. When you do have the dialogue, frame it as concern for the long-term health of the business and for the individual in question.

performance. Otherwise, the family members don't get real feedback on their performance. Coddling, as we discuss in the box "Are you coddling a family member?," is the most destructive of all.

Compensate family employees

Although Omar was paid better than he had been at his previous job, he had no idea how raises or bonuses would happen in the future. How to compensate family members in the business is a tricky topic. Should family be treated as special when it comes to doling out a paycheck for the work they're doing? In some family businesses, the family members are given shockingly generous pay packages with virtually no commensurate career demands. In other businesses, the family members are treated financially no differently—and occasionally more harshly—than any entry-level employee is treated. Neither extreme is healthy for the individuals involved, and both extremes can generate resentment, jealousy, and family tension.

Your decision about compensating family members who work in the business should be based on their *roles as employees*, not as future owners or directors of the business. Family members' pay should not be reduced today because "one day, they will benefit from the success of this business that they're building as an owner." Instead, they are entitled to bring home the fair paycheck that any other employee in that job might earn. This delayed-compensation thinking is often a legacy of the founder's philosophy—entrepreneurs often take little or no salary while they're getting the business off the ground, in part because they know they are building equity for themselves. But after the founder's generation, it's unfair to not pay family members for business roles in which they are serving, not least because nonworking owners benefit from the underpaid work of those in the business. You should also be on the lookout for psychological power games being played out through compensation decisions. It's not unusual for patriarchs to provide intermittent rewards to family members to emphasize who is really in control, for example.

So how should compensation be handled? We have seen five typical compensation models in family businesses:

- **Take what you need:** Family members have no set compensation, but can take what they need from the business to pay their bills or fund their lifestyle. Next-generation family members are expected to come to the senior generation and ask when they need more.

- **Market:** All compensation is at market levels. We define *market* as the compensation level the company would pay to an equally qualified nonfamily employee. Compensation consultants can provide comparisons on nearly all positions.

- **Below market:** All compensation (salary, benefits, bonus) is below market. This approach is frequently seen in family businesses at entry-level positions as a kind of a test to confirm that family members are joining for the right reasons. Below-market compensation for family members is often used as a weeding-out process. Only if the family members know they will not receive special compensation packages, the thinking goes, will they be sincere about joining the business.

- **Above market:** Compensation is above market levels. Some family businesses pay above market to attract family members who may have better-paying career opportunities elsewhere. If you own a foundry in Indiana, for example, you might need to pay more to attract your daughter who has a job at a top consulting firm in Chicago than you would be willing to pay to recruit nonfamily members. Others view above-market compensation as "combat pay" to recognize that working in a family business brings many additional tax complexities. Some expect to be paid more to compensate for the career track they've given up outside the family business.

- **All equal:** Compensation for all family members is equal regardless of their effort or achievement. This approach can be appropriate when all owners are working in the business and contributing in a roughly equal manner, but in general, it should be avoided because it conflates ownership and management compensation.

It can be more difficult being a family employee than others might realize, and both market and above-market compensation often work best. Whichever you decide on, start your compensation decisions by separating management roles from ownership and by compensating family employees according to the job they will be doing, not their current or future ownership position.

Prepare an exit path for family employees

As Omar found out, it is often easier to join a family business than it is to leave one. Perhaps the most sensitive topic of all is how a family member exits the business—whether by choice or not—and on what terms. The stakes for a departing family member are enormous; not only is their job at stake, but their relationship with the family is as well. How should your family deal with deciding when and how a family member must leave the business? It must plan for this eventuality. Your family needs to anticipate separation from the business and have rules in place ahead of time for that exit. A good exit policy might feel something like a prenuptial agreement. It's hard to talk about, but you're much better off preparing an exit policy before you come to the moment of needing one. If both sides know the rules, separation from the company will be much easier—and potentially save the family relationships in the long run.

How does your family handle the departure of family members from the business? The most common models we have seen are as follows:

- **Underperform, and you're fired:** If a family member consistently underperforms (or misbehaves), they will be asked to leave.

- **Up or out:** Family members must be promoted within a designated time frame or will be outplaced.

- **Suitable role:** Family members will be allowed to rise to the highest level of their competence and, assuming strong performance, can remain there through their career. This approach is similar to how nonfamily personnel are treated.

- **Job for life:** Family members are entitled to design and retain a role, regardless of performance.

- **All to the top:** Family members occupy the top roles in management, regardless of performance, and they remain in those roles for their entire career.

The decision about how and when family members will leave the company can be the most emotionally difficult one of all. Family members who are asked to leave (or who leave on their own but do so with bitterness) can feel as if they have been asked to leave the family itself. Family employees who leave the company can take as long as five years to return to their normal relationships within the family.

The business should develop a separation package for family employees. You don't want to negotiate a leave package during the heat of a family member's exit. Such packages often include generous severance, help with career counseling, and thoughtful options on where else in the Four Rooms the exiting individual can contribute. It's difficult, but possible, to outplace a family member without incurring lasting damage to the family, but only if the separation is handled well. See the box "What if it doesn't work out? Should you fire your father?"

Draft your family employment policy

Now it's time to evaluate and build your family employment policy. Do you have one in place, either formal or informal? Is it serving your family well? Is it up-to-date with the complexities of your family's interest in working in the business? Have you addressed all the critical career junctures?

Thinking through your own policy can be a two-step process. First, use figure 10-1 to identify your family's current implicit or explicit policy. Take a moment to review the spectrum of options for each category we have discussed in this chapter. Where do your family policies

What if it doesn't work out?
Should you fire your father?

As brothers, Bruce and Mark were inseparable—they grew up together, only fourteen months apart in age. They took over their family business in their mid-thirties and grew it successfully for decades with Bruce as COO and Mark the outward-facing CEO. When Mark died suddenly, ownership shifted. Bruce, his daughter, and his nephews became partners in their family business.

With Bruce mourning his loss and not seeking more responsibility, his thirty-one-year-old daughter Meredith became the CEO, with her father and cousins reporting to her. As a father, Bruce was terrific. As an employee, however, Bruce underperformed. Product was not shipped on time, employee morale was slipping, and fights between daughter and father were weekly events. Two years into her new position, Meredith came to the painful conclusion that Bruce was no longer up to the job. Meredith called us with a loaded question: "Should I fire my father?"

Family business leaders often agonize about whether to allow a family member to stay in a job even when he is not performing well. Where do you draw the line between the desire to protect and support family members and hard-nosed business decisions? The repercussions of such a decision can be profound. Fired family members can harbor grudges for decades. Family members who are fired from their family business in a way they found unfair often remove themselves from interactions with their family for years, risking long-term relationships in the process.

So the question of whether to fire a family member is particularly important to get right. But the *how* here is just as important. If all parties view it as a fair process, you have a chance to maintain your complex personal relationships.

Therefore, we recommend that you carefully plan and execute a fair process. You may need to defend this process and outcome to yourself and other family members for the rest of your life. That process should include:

- **Clear and written role definition and performance targets** that are mutually agreed upon. It's an awkward conversation to have when your father reports to you, but it's necessary. Bruce and Meredith had never clearly defined his role or targets.

- **Consistent, candid written and discussed feedback** on those performance targets from the boss, peers, and direct reports, also known as a 360-degree review. Bruce had never had a formal review during his entire career. When he finally did, the feedback did not surprise him, but Bruce realized that it wasn't just Meredith who found his performance unsatisfactory.

- **A managerial evaluation from an independent organizational-assessment firm.** You can readily find firms that provide evaluations of employee's motivations, functional skills, and aptitudes. This step provides you with a better and common language to understand strengths and weaknesses. Bruce's issue turned out to be more about motivation than skills or aptitude.

- **A series of performance conversations with the family member, including specific examples of behavioral and performance issues.** Don't expect one conversation to be sufficient for such an important topic. Meredith set up monthly discussions with Bruce in which she shared both things to praise and shortfalls in his performance.

- **Distance from the decision.** Remove yourself as the sole decision maker. Recognize that your managerial instincts may not be at their best with such an emotionally complex decision. As a rule,

(continued)

family members are imperfect judges of their other members' job performance. Often, the complexity of the relationship clouds their normally clear judgment on job performance. Meredith enlisted the help of her board of advisers in discussions with Bruce.

- **A candid conversation with the family member about his future.** In our experience, people who are struggling often know they are. They may trudge on out of pride or a sense of obligation, but it will wear them down. Bruce knew he was struggling, and over time Meredith learned that he, too, was open to the idea of change.

When Bruce and Meredith followed such an approach, he admitted that he was unhappy in his job. Without his brother, he realized, working in the business was never going to be the same—and he was proud of how Meredith and his nephews had stepped up. Bruce gave his notice to leave so he and his wife could take a world tour that they had repeatedly delayed. Meredith, for her part, then instituted a family employment exit policy and a mandatory retirement age in the company to preempt future issues.

No matter what you decide, be clear what "hat" you are wearing—management, board, owner, or family. Not least, this may help preserve your relationship, even in the face of such a difficult situation. Meredith no longer wanted Bruce as COO, but she certainly wanted to preserve her relationship with Bruce her father, Bruce her board member, and Bruce her leading shareholder. As an oft-told story goes, one family business patriarch, wearing his "CEO hat," told his son that he was fired. Immediately afterwards, he put on his "dad hat" and said, "Son, I've heard you've just been fired. How can I help?"

fall on the spectrum? Circle the categories that most closely resemble what you have in place now. It's okay to circle more than one if you're not clearly in a single category. Looking across all the categories, does the sum of your circles represent the family employment policies and values that you want?

FIGURE 10-1

Family employment policy: six key decisions and their options

Attract:

Discourage	Stay silent	Handpick	Publish rules	Recruit

Entry rules:

None in	Glass ceiling	Level playing field	Higher bar	All in

Career path:

Undefined	Branch silo	Company's career path	Custom family path	Executive escalator

Feedback and development:

Ignore	Same as company's regular policy	Supplement company's policy	Prove yourself	Coddle

Compensation:

Take what you need	Market	Below market	Above market	All equal

Exit:

Underperform and you're fired	Up or out	Suitable role	Job for life	All to the top

If you have no policies in place yet, start by crossing out the ones in figure 10-1 that wouldn't work for your family. Then circle those that are most similar to what you have in place now, implicitly or explicitly.

For the second step, begin your family discussion about what you actually want. Your family can agree to have formal, written policies or implicit ones, you must think through and decide what's right together. Who should decide? Each of the Four Rooms should be involved. But the final decision should be made in the Owner Room, since a family employment policy speaks to the fundamental values of the family as owners of the company.

For many family business leaders, their greatest joy is to see their children succeed in their business as employees. But successfully employing the next generation can be a thorny endeavor. As you can see, we are talking about a very different leadership task than in corporate environments. The rewards are different and deeper. Family business leaders can find meaning, money, and mentoring in ways not available in other types of businesses. The most successful family business leaders we know have great wisdom in how they do it: they don't coddle; they challenge. A thoughtful family employment policy can help you provide family members with real jobs, real challenges, and a real chance to thrive.

Summing up

- Issues related to family employment are some of the most common causes of destructive conflict in family businesses. A family employment policy can help you avoid these struggles and set family members up for success.

- An effective family employment policy has to speak not just to the criteria for coming into the business but also to each major element of working in a family business. In particular, your policy should address six dimensions:

    - How, or if, you want to attract family members to the business

    - The entry rules for those who want to join

    - The career path of family members once they have entered the business

    - How you will provide feedback and development to family employees

    - Compensation policies for family employees

    - How you will approach the exit of family employees who are not performing

- The work to build a family employment policy should be collaborative across the Four Rooms, but the final decision should be made in the Owner Room.

11.

How to Be Responsible with the Wealth of Your Family Business

As a thirty-eight-year-old family member working in her family furniture business, Judy knows that more than 90 percent of her personal wealth is tied up in the business. The company has had a great run, creating wealth for her entire family. But now, with people starting to whisper that Judy will be the company's next leader, the wealth of the family may soon be her direct responsibility. How does she continue to build that wealth, ensuring that she doesn't "mess up" what has been three generations of success? Should she focus on continuing to generate healthy dividends for the family rather than investing in innovation that may or may not pay off? Should she consider taking on debt to help grow the business or simply stay the course, maintaining the business's conservative business model?

Judy doesn't want to ruin what the previous generations worked so hard to build. The responsibility weighs heavily on her shoulders.

Your family business has probably made, or will hopefully make, your family wealthy. The idea that the family may be successful enough to be financially independent, provide for multiple generations, and offer benefits to family members is part of the wonderful payoff of building a family enterprise.

This chapter will provide advice on a weighty question: how to be responsible with the wealth of your family business. While there are no one-size-fits-all formulas for success, business families grapple with the same three questions:

1. How do you protect the golden goose?

2. How do you build a portfolio to last for generations?

3. How do you prepare your family to be responsible with wealth?

Plenty of advice exists for dealing with wealth in general (see "Further Reading" for some of the best), but less clear is how to manage wealth specifically from a family business. We offer here some suggestions to navigate the key issues.

Protect the golden goose

Many family businesses refer to their core business as their golden goose. That is, whatever the family does, whatever feuds it has, whatever business decisions it makes, however the members "overexpress" their egos, the family's overriding concern is to avoid hurting the business.

Less talked about, however, because it's harder to see from the outside, is how family businesses responsibly protect their golden goose. Here are the patterns we often see in family businesses.

Survive, profit, then grow

Once, when we were helping a next-generation leader with a growth strategy for her construction company in Florida, her father, the patriarch, called us into his office, asked us to have a seat, and said, "Now, boys, I'm not against growth. But make sure you get our priorities right. They are, in order, one, survive; two, profit; and then, three, grow. If you put revenue growth first, my grandchildren may have no business at all. We don't want that, do we?"

It was a great reminder that aggressive revenue growth always brings risks. If you want your family to own your business for multiple generations, you need to prioritize survival and profits instead of chasing risky revenue growth opportunities. Of course, you hope that your business will have periods of strong growth for many years. But unlike owners of a venture capital firm, which may invest in ten firms, betting that one, maybe two, survive more than five years, you may hope your one company will be "evergreen" and survive for a hundred years or more. (Recently, we have seen an increase in this evergreen philosophy, with such groups as the Tugboat Institute bringing together like-minded owners, many of whom are from family-owned businesses.)

Keep debt low

When we started working with family businesses, we were shocked by their low level of debt. It's common for family businesses to have zero, or even negative, net debt, meaning their cash and cash equivalents on their balance sheet exceed all their debt. For example, one client keeps enough cash on its balance sheet so the business can survive two years with zero revenue. This policy flies in the face of what business schools teach and many private equity firms practice—that debt is both tax-efficient and a good way to increase return on equity. Family businesses that thrive across generations know that too much debt can lead to losing the company to the debt holders (i.e., bankruptcy) sometime in the medium to long term. A global study by Standard & Poor's in 2011 showed that during a ten-year period, default rates are greater than 50 percent for companies with C to CCC bond ratings and about 30 percent for companies with B-rated bonds. In chapter 5, we pointed out that your level of debt is an explicit choice in your Owner Strategy. But too much debt can have existential consequences, as the Covid-19 economic crisis illustrated to many indebted firms.

Keep most of the wealth "in the cave"

If your business is concentrated in one industry, it will probably be more volatile than if you own a diversified portfolio of businesses. While it may seem more rational to diversify with liquid proceeds to weather this volatility, some owners keep their wealth, as they say, "in the cave": they may be wealthy on paper, but their money is tied up in their business. The money might be invested in working capital, a factory, the land the factory sits on, or inventory on the shelf. The owners take this approach for two primary reasons. First, with their wealth in the cave, they can use it to invest in down cycles when other owners can't, boosting their own competitive position. Second, many owners believe that the gold in the cave should stay in the cave. As one matriarch told us, "You have a choice: live rich or be rich." Liquid wealth is easier to spend (or fritter away) than is money tied up in the business. Owners increase risk to the business with excess personal spending because their personal spending habits can become similar to fixed business expenses. For example, people can take out mortgages for expensive homes and then become dependent on distributions from the business for mortgage payments.

Diversifying your wealth out of the cave doesn't automatically mean selling some of your assets so that you can enjoy spending that money (which you are fully entitled to do). Instead, diversifying for long-term wealth creation can mean investing in *other* businesses or investment vehicles but with a focus on investing for the long term.

Build a portfolio to last generations

Successful owners of multigenerational family businesses rarely rely on just a single company to generate and sustain their wealth. That's in part because of the natural life cycle of any business. For ten years or even twenty, a single business may generate significant value, but seldom does this happen decade after decade. At some point, you will most likely need to build a portfolio. Here are tips for how to do so responsibly.

Be in business, not in a particular business

Evolving from your original legacy business can be tough because the owners often have a deep emotional connection to it. Multigenerational family wealth, however, is typically created via a portfolio of related businesses. A study by Shell about corporate longevity found that "many successful moves were made when companies did not see themselves locked into a particular business, but *in business*, with talents and resources that could be used profitably to meet a variety of consumer needs."[1] This *in business* idea perfectly describes how most multigenerational business families work—they systematically, often over decades, extend into businesses adjacent to their current business. One of our clients, for example, began in local coal delivery but then over the decades added heating oil delivery, gas distribution, gas stations, convenience stores (with great fried chicken), and, most recently, real estate. Over time, each adjacency played an important role in diversifying and growing the family's wealth. Successful portfolio creation comes in all sizes and types of family enterprises. For example, another of our clients became well known for a small but celebrated jewelry business in Milan in the 1960s. But the family actually made more money from a corporate-gift business and from real estate owned at the business's primary location. That combination proved to be a responsible portfolio approach for the family in the long term.

Create a portfolio to fit the owners' interests

In multigenerational family businesses, your portfolio approach needs to blend value creation and your family values. Invest in businesses that you want to own together. Each business family has to find its own blend as it balances its unique expression of growth, liquidity, and control.

We learned one of our favorite approaches to a family business portfolio from a highly entrepreneurial family that balanced its interest for long-term financial security, a desire to reward individual passions for building businesses, and its attachment to its core business. Table 11-1 shows the

TABLE 11-1

Joint investment categories of one successful family business's portfolio

Category	Objective	Sample investments
Moonshot portfolio	To generate significant wealth if bets pay off	• Investments in startups, mostly in software, which is a passion for several family members
Core wealth-creation portfolio	To provide wealth-creating opportunities and employment for qualified family members	• Family-owned and actively managed businesses
Income portfolio	To provide acceptable standard of living irrespective of the fate of the wealth creation portfolio	• Real estate in the United States and home country • US municipal bonds
"Hurricane" fund	To provide emergency help to family members in case of natural or political disasters	• Cash in diversified countries and locations • Physical gold • US Treasury bonds

four investment categories the family uses for its collective wealth, listed from the highest risk–reward ratio to the lowest.

Each of the investment categories has a role—both economic and familial. The moonshot investments, for example, were created to both bet on high-risk, high-reward businesses and to let some of the entrepreneurial family members follow their passions. The "hurricane" fund recognized the family's psychological need for highly conservative emergency and liquid funds, reflecting the family's painful history as refugees.

Follow a dividend policy

Owners often keep most of their gold in the cave, but not all of it. Dividends can take several forms:

- **Regular dividends:** Payments from the company to shareholders in proportion to their economic ownership of the firm. Owners set guidelines, or a policy, for how the annual dividend is calculated. The board declares the exact amount annually.

- **Share buybacks:** Option to sell a predetermined number of shares at a calculated price per share to the company in a set time frame.

This approach allows shareholders who want liquidity above and beyond regular dividends to access it (and can help prevent people from feeling trapped) into ownership. One seventy-five-year-old firm we worked with has never paid an annual dividend but instead offers an annual share buyback program. An owner told us, "We like it that dividends are not a right here; we think it should hurt a bit to get some money. Selling shares of our successful firm is painful."

- **Special distributions:** Onetime payments to owners. Owners decide on these payments for various reasons, including situations when the company has more cash than it can invest wisely.

- **Tax distributions:** Payments to owners to cover their tax payments. These distributions reflect the corporate structure and are usually sent to the tax authorities rather than spent. Since they don't end up in the hands of owners, we won't consider them in our discussion of managing family wealth.

Decisions about dividends are among the most important in a family business. They affect the long-term viability of the business as well as the culture of the family. How you treat dividends reflects your values and can therefore be a significant source of conflict. Here's what to consider as you navigate this critical choice:

- **Agree to an annual dividend policy instead of negotiating the amount every year.** Discussions about dividends are rife with conflict and can be financially and emotionally challenging. You're better off not relitigating the dividend decision every year but rather deciding on a policy ahead of time and reconsidering it only when circumstances change or after several years. For example, you could decide on an annual dividend of 10 percent of your firm's free cash flow.

- **Set your dividend policy according to your Owner Strategy.** More liquidity means either less growth or reduced control over your company. Create the policy in your Owner Room and communicate it to your board as part of your Owner Strategy statement. The board should base the annual dividend, which is usually expressed as a formula, on this policy.

- **Treat your dividend like an equity rather than an annuity.** The value of equities goes up and down, while annuities stay the same year after year. Most of the payment should be at risk and tied to the performance of the business instead of a set amount every year. A large set amount creates a dependency and disconnects the owners from the performance of the business. Family members should be prepared to live without dividends in case the company can't afford to pay them without taking extraordinary measures, such as borrowing. Some owners set a floor dividend amount that "guarantees" a relatively small income.

- **Have some level of dividends.** Dividends are a valuable way to reward and encourage long-term ownership, especially when some owners are governors and investors. For example, if some family members work in the business as executives and are rewarded with generous compensation packages, nonoperating owners will question the fairness of zero dividends. Additionally, dividends can increase the financial independence of owners whose wealth is highly concentrated in their family business. As one spouse explained to us, "We want 'emotional diversification'—which for us means our family branch wants to own some assets separately from the broader family. We sleep better at night knowing that not all of our wealth is tied to the collective decisions of our full family."

- **Use the dividend to set expectations of management.** Management should treat your capital as valuable and scarce. Dividends are a valuable lever for owners to maintain discipline in the business. Special dividends should be considered when the business can't make good use of the owners' capital, using agreed-on metrics to measure the value of further reinvestment.

Prepare your family to be responsible with its wealth

Many family business owners worry intensely that their wealth will quickly dissipate with each generation. Several countries have some version of the three-generation rule, such as these three adages:

- "Shirtsleeves to shirtsleeves in three generations" (United States)

- "Pai Rico; Filho Nobre; Neto Pobre" (Brazil)

- "Dalle Stalle Alle Stelle Alle Stalle" (Italy)

Like the three-generation rule discussed in chapter 2, this claim is misleading. Certainly, some families go from rags to riches and back again, but on average, they do not. Gregory Clark, an economist at University of California, Davis, conducted extensive research on social mobility over generations and concluded, that in general, rich families stay rich and poor families stay poor.[2] He found that while there is some "regression to the mean, the process can take 10 to 15 generations (300 to 450 years)."[3] A study conducted by two economists from Bank of Italy looked at tax records in Florence in 1427 and 2011. They discovered that "the top earners among the current taxpayers were found to have already been at the top of the socioeconomic ladder six centuries ago."[4] Though this research is not specific to business families, the findings apply to them as well. Wealth may dissipate over time, but it does not happen quickly. Those who climb to the top of the ladder tend to stay there.

If your business is creating significant wealth, you need to prepare your family for the responsibility of dealing with it, probably for many decades. The good news is that by owning a business, you have several ways to embed the idea that with wealth comes responsibility. We advise you to consider the following approaches taken by other successful multigenerational business families.

Expose your children to the business

Owners have an enormous and often underemphasized advantage in how and when to expose their children to the real heart of their wealth—the parents own a business and have a family narrative. Talking to your children about the business early on will help them understand the hard work that has generated your family wealth.

Top business families make a point to have their preteen and teenage children learn about the people who work in their business, what these people produce, and how they do it. Regina Helena Scripilliti Velloso is a fourth-generation owner of Brazil's Votorantim Group. The family-owned company has operations in more than twenty countries in cement, mining, metallurgy, steelworks, banking, orange juice concentrate, and generation of electric power. Velloso recalled to us how powerfully her grandfather instilled in her the foundation of where the business started:

> *When I was a little girl, my grandfather would take us to visit the sugar cane mills. And I really didn't like the taste of sugar cane juice. It's terrible. But I didn't have the courage to tell my grandfather that I hated this juice, because of what it meant to him. He'd say, "When you smell the sugar cane syrup, you are not going to forget it. This is going to enter your blood and your heart." I didn't understand it at the time, but as an adult, I understood he was sharing with me the passion for the business and the legacy of where we came from.*

Youthful exposures—such as working in the company gift shop, stocking shelves, and walking your orchards—create a lasting appreciation for the craft of a family business. It's an early and important lesson that it's not all about money. Business can be fascinating, even beautiful. Many owners provide their children with a deep appreciation of their family business in age-appropriate ways such as visits to the factory floor and internships.

In some companies, college-aged members of the next generation participate in higher-level Owner Strategy discussions. In one such meeting, a family debated whether it should continue to own a business that made components for assault weapons. Both sides in the argument had deep convictions and respectfully listened to the other's point of view. Seeing how thoughtfully the owners approached an important topic, the next-generation members in the room understood the depth of responsibility of ownership. Eventually, they found a compromise that, though imperfect, they could all live with. They decided to keep the business but pull it out of the main holding company to allow family members who didn't want to participate in it to sell to those who supported it.

All these experiences can help your children appreciate your business instead of your wealth. Show them how the wealth embedded in the business is used: to create things of value for customers, to create jobs, to clarify and express what you value, to give back to the community. With these experiences, your next generation will better understand the responsibility of their family's wealth.

Be open to a variety of stances on your business wealth

People in family businesses relate to their wealth in different ways, and there is no single right way. For this reason, you need to understand and recognize where family members stand on wealth. You don't want each person's relationship with wealth to be held against them, building resentment and creating difficult relationships. Most owners take one of seven stances on the wealth from the family business:

- **Rebel:** You reject wealth and actively speak and act out about the negative effects of wealth and social inequity.

- **Avoid:** You act as if the wealth does not exist; you refrain from actively engaging in its management (e.g., physically and emotionally separating yourself from your family and the family business).

- **Give it away:** You donate the wealth to worthy causes during your lifetime (e.g., Bill Gates as cochairman of the Bill & Melinda Gates Foundation).

- **Steward:** You care for the wealth for the benefit of future generations, your employees, and society. You broadly define wealth financially, psychologically, and socially.

- **Create:** You create more wealth so that you leave more than what you received; you find personal fulfillment in creating great wealth (e.g., Ian "the creator" in chapter 1).

- **Enjoy:** You enjoy the benefits of your wealth through personal spending and philanthropy, while not defining yourself by it.

- **Self-define:** Your wealth defines you. You don't merely enjoy your wealth, but you revel in it. Spending your wealth makes life feel more rewarding.

Family owners as individuals can live happy and healthy lives with any of these stances, except the rebel and self-defining stances in their extreme forms, which can become destructive. Someone rebelling against wealth, for example, will cut themselves off from their wealth and their family, while someone who defines themselves by their wealth will lose sight of the values that created it.

Business families tend to glorify those who create wealth. But a family member is not a bad person for avoiding wealth, giving it away, or seeing themselves as a steward of that wealth. Those are all perfectly healthy relationships with family wealth. "Not all owners have the same financial interests and priorities," observes Ben Persofsky, executive director of Brown Brothers Harriman Center for Family Business. "It could be for no other reason than differences in their stages of life. And that's okay. What matters is not that there are differences, but that you find ways to be transparent about them."

Once you identify where your family members stand, you should have insights for today and a roadmap for the future. If none of the next generation identify with the creating or stewarding stances, for example, you may be more open to selling the business. Or if you have a spread among the stances, you may find that the next generation will naturally fall into different, and important, roles in the future. Of course, a person's relationship to wealth may change during their lifetime. Consider John D. Rockefeller, the founder of Standard Oil Company, who went from one of greatest wealth creators in the nineteenth century to one of its greatest philanthropists.

Avoid creating entitled kids

Want to know what keeps the owners of successful family businesses up at night? Across businesses of all sizes, geographic locations, and industries, these owners share one common fear: the dread that their kids will grow up to be entitled.

Most upper-class parents share this concern, but among family business owners, this anxiety is especially powerful. Will their children and grandchildren end up lazy good-for-nothings who are not contributing to society—trust-fund babies—and whose scandalous antics fill the pages of the tabloids and social media?

But wealth turns out to be a less important factor than you might think in the development of entitlement. Some very rich kids turn out to be highly motivated and engaged—we see people like this in our work every day. Our experience also suggests, however, that kids don't mysteriously end up entitled; parents make choices that substantially increase the odds that the kids end up feeling that the world owes them a living.

Entitlement is not something that kids just fall into. It's a trap—set for them, unintentionally, by well-meaning parents. Your number one instinct as a parent is to protect your children. Entitlement is the result of misguided protection. And family business provides fertile ground for parental protection.

How do you avoid the entitlement trap? There are not pat answers. But we have identified five practices that families have used to foster healthy relationships with wealth:

- **Use your wealth to broaden your community.** Parents who isolate their family in a social circle of similarly wealthy people can be enabling entitlement.

- **Make sure your children have jobs.** There are many ways to contribute to society but at some point every person should have the experience of having a boss, being responsible, and earning a paycheck.

- **Help your children see a path to build a legitimate career.** Parents who coddle their children's careers in the family business are not preparing them to value the parents' own hard work.

- **Allow your children to have setbacks.** When overly protective parents shelter their children from fate's hard knocks, the parents fail to help the kids build resiliency.

- **Instill an attitude of gratitude.** Psychologist Jim Grubman suggests that fostering gratitude is one of the most important practices for parents with wealth. "Gratitude is the antidote to entitlement," Grubman says.

A grateful attitude requires work on the parent's part, however. You cannot simply expect your children to be grateful. Modeling gratitude and thinking out loud with your children about your financial decision-making can help foster appreciation. For example, Grubman points out that, yes, you can simply purchase a fancy new car and tell your children how much you love it. But you can also, instead, speak out loud about how deciding to make this expensive purchase reflects your values and your own thankfulness: "I'm really enjoying the new Porsche. I always feel very fortunate that my parents worked hard, we worked hard, and we have the kind of resources that let us have some of the finer things in life." Without experiencing that explicit and repeated modeling of gratitude, your children may not pick up your values about never taking wealth for granted. Practice being thankful yourselves, and chances are that your children will end up thanking you for it. That's a critical step out of the entitlement trap.

You can have a healthy approach to wealth, one that is neither fawning nor damning. You can start by thinking through the guidance we offer here to see if you are on track. "There's no doubt you can raise incredibly sophisticated and responsible kids in a wealthy family," San Orr, president of BDT Capital Partners, LLC, a merchant bank that advises and invests in family and founder-led companies, told us. "The key is preparing them to assume the mantle of responsibility being placed on them, a bedrock that will serve them well for the rest of their lives."

Summing up

- Concerns about wealth are common in family businesses. On the one hand, owners worry about squandering what has been created. On the other hand, they are anxious about the impact that money will have on the family. Wealth can be an uncomfortable topic for families, but you can't avoid it if you want a multigenerational family business.

- Think about the choices you are making to protect the golden goose. There is a difference between a strategy that maximizes financial value and one that fosters long-term resilience. If you want the latter, you should follow these practices:

  - Prioritize survival and profitability over rapid growth.

  - Use debt carefully, if at all.

  - Reinvest most of your profits back in the business.

- Think about your business as a portfolio. Construct a portfolio that retains the spirit of innovation while still meeting the owners' various needs, such as growth, entrepreneurialism, and security. And use a dividend policy to foster some financial independence from the family business.

- Prepare the next generation for what's coming. Try to create children's personal connection with the company so that they appreciate it rather than treat it as purely an investment. Recognize that there's more than one healthy way to deal with wealth. Instead, encourage family members to find a way to mesh their attitude toward wealth with their personal values. And take actions to prevent the younger generation's feelings of entitlement, especially by fostering an attitude of gratitude.

12.

Conflict in the Family Business

Two brothers sharing ownership in a successful fourth-generation concrete business had a bitter falling-out triggered by an unlikely issue: a sailboat. The older sibling accused his younger brother of dipping into the company till to support his racing habit. The younger brother countered that since he often entertained customers on the boat, he was following the same pattern the older brother had for years by having the company pay for expenses that had both a personal and a professional use. The younger man pointed to the ski house that had long been expensed to the business. This conflict, which revealed long-standing concerns over their roles and contributions to the company, had been simmering just below the surface. As their standoff continued, they refused to be in the same room together, making it nearly impossible for major business decisions to be made and leaving employees caught in the middle. Ultimately, they sold the business at a deep discount and both men went to their graves without speaking another word to one another; their children grew up as strangers instead of cousins. And the family business was gone.

As we have described earlier, family owners wield the power to destroy their businesses. In fact, nothing can undermine a successful company faster than an unresolved conflict among its owners. No organization is immune to narcissistic leaders or difficult relationships among employees. Most nonfamily businesses, however, have rules that govern behavior for everyone from the bottom of the corporate ladder to the top.

But conflict is different in family businesses because the owners make the rules and therefore can also break them. Once a major battle gets started, it can be difficult to stop. Until the owners agree to stand down, conflicts will continue, with potentially devastating implications for the business and family.

Understandable fear about the potential impact of conflict causes many families to focus on maintaining harmony. But the quest for constant peace can backfire. Some disagreement is normal in a family business, and the ability to work through it is healthy. Avoiding clashes at all costs can have dire consequences, too. Both too much and too little conflict are unsustainable. In this chapter, we will help you develop the following skills in working with conflict:

1. Identify the "Goldilocks zone" of conflict

2. Move from fake harmony to constructive conflict

3. Recognize the downward trajectory of the conflict spiral

4. Escape a family feud if you are in one

5. Adopt strategies to avoid family feuds in the first place

Finding the Goldilocks zone of conflict

For most people, conflict is uncomfortable. That can be especially true in families who have watched family arguments tear successful businesses to pieces. Consider the Ambani brothers in India, who bitterly fought for control of the family business, Reliance Communications, after their father died without a will. Or the Adidas founders, whose quarrel led the brothers to separate their German company into rivals Adidas and Puma. Then there is the Redstone family in the United States; the family's battle for control of its media empire has been in the headlines for years.

For many families, the fear of conflict is so pervasive that they go to extraordinary lengths to avoid it. But less often recognized is that *too little conflict* can have an equally destructive impact. In fact, the effects of both too much and too little conflict on the family and the family business are almost identical. In both cases, the business can suffer from limited growth, poor decision-making, a loss of competitive advantage, and, in severe cases, the sale or split of the company. Similarly, at either extreme, families tend to break into factions and suffer poor relationships. The mechanisms are different, but the results are the same.

Conflict is a Goldilocks problem. Both ends of the spectrum are ultimately unsustainable, so the best place is in the middle. While Goldilocks may bring to mind the fairy tale, a better analogy may come from our solar system. The earth is in what astronomers refer to as a Goldilocks zone. Much closer to the sun, and the planet would be too hot to sustain life. Much farther, and the earth would be too cold. Though the causes differ, both extremes would make life uninhabitable on earth.

Conflict in a family business works much the same way. When the dynamic in a family is too hot, the level of shouting, screaming, and outwardly expressed anger makes it impossible to do the work of owning and running a business. When the level of disagreement is too cold, there is quiet seething, a Pandora's box of emotions waiting to be unleashed when opened. Between these two extremes is a healthy middle, where difficult issues can be raised, addressed, and resolved without the parties doing lasting damage to relationships or shared assets.

A family's interests are rarely perfectly aligned. As described in chapter 1, people have different objectives simply because they are in different places in the system. As a result, some conflict of interest is inevitable. Therefore, the priority is to *manage* that conflict, not simply tolerate or eliminate it.

Families on the too-much side of the spectrum struggle with how to reduce the intensity of the conflict so that constructive conversations can occur. Families on the too-little side must learn how to disagree outwardly to release the pressure that builds up internally. In our experience, the too-little side of the spectrum is much more common in families, even though it receives less attention from the media. Most families are conditioned not to fight with each other. Ask almost anyone what matters most to them, and they will tell you it is their family relationships, including the ability to spend time together to celebrate holidays, weddings, and other milestones.

But the pressure to be the perfect family that never disagrees often ends up sowing the seeds of destruction down the road. Whenever families tell us that they get along perfectly, our ears perk up. Most often it is a fake harmony which reflects a lack of discussion on critical issues. Much like an iceberg, the surface seems pleasant enough, but the danger is not far below the surface.

What constitutes excessive conflict (as opposed to constructive disagreement) depends on personal interpretation and the family culture. Some families can more easily tolerate conflict than others, and the extent to which people will stoically put aside their personal interests to support the common cause also varies. But the Goldilocks zone shares some characteristics across all families. Here's a three-part quiz you can use to see if your family has found the zone:

1. **Is there general satisfaction with the direction of the family enterprise?** You may not be happy about every aspect, but you are unequivocally better together than apart.

2. **Are decisions about critical issues being made?** You need not address every single point of disagreement, but everyone would agree that there is no elephant in the room.

3. **Are family relationships good enough to work and celebrate together?** You don't have to be best friends to own significant assets together. Instead, you have to be good business partners, which means you agree on the big issues and can enjoy each other's company, at least most of the time.

If you answered yes to all three questions, you are likely to be in the Goldilocks zone. If not, you have work to do, either to lower the temperature or to raise it.

Moving from fake harmony to constructive conflict

Sierra Nevada Brewing Co. is a family-owned beer company. Its tagline, which shows up on every can and bottle, is "Family Owned, Operated & Argued Over." Ken Grossman, Sierra Nevada's founder, told us, "It's funny, but it's the truth. We can get together and argue over what's best for us as a company moving forward, but we all do it in good faith, knowing that everyone wants what's best overall."

Can you say something similar about your family business? If not, you may find yourself in a difficult position precisely because you have avoided conflict. Take, for example, the experience of one family in the retail business. Throughout the years, tempers would begin to flare—not because there was too much disagreement, but because leaders were avoiding important decisions rather than dealing with potential disagreement. For example, although every member of the third generation worked in the business, there was a major discrepancy in their commitment levels and contributions. Those who worked overtime to get their work done began resenting those who showed up at their leisure, but the family resisted setting any standards that might alienate someone. Eventually, the leaders of the business decided to sell the company rather than tackle the disagreements that would threaten to disrupt family harmony during the transition to the third generation. Unfortunately, selling the business did not solve the problem. There were grievances about how the proceeds were divided and a feeling among many that they had given up the family legacy too easily. And without the business to keep family members together, they started to drift apart. Within a few years, many members looked back on the sale as a mistake. Both the business and the close relationships were gone.

If, like this family, you find yourself on the too-little side of the conflict spectrum, here's some advice on getting into the Goldilocks zone:

- **Agree on meeting ground rules to help guide healthy discussions.** For an example, see the box "Sample meeting ground rules." You should agree on these ground rules before you get into substantive discussions. And then review them before each meeting. When someone's behavior deviates, gently but directly use the specific ground rule to call it out.

- **Start with building shared purpose.** Talk about what you are trying to accomplish by owning the family business together. Doing so helps create the foundation for collective action and sacrifice. You can also articulate a *negative purpose*—identifying outcomes you are trying to avoid by dealing with them now. Use this shadow of the future to help motivate action and retain cohesion.

- **Create beachheads to build momentum.** Often, the sheer scale of change is daunting, and it can be valuable to have a small place to start. It's usually better to be evolutionary rather than revolutionary. With one family, we were exploring ways to integrate in-laws into the governance structures. There was a reluctance to put them in the family council, so we used a next-generation taskforce to create a starting point. Make sure you work with the current sources of authority rather than trying to overthrow them.

- **Focus on principles rather than people.** Try to avoid making decisions with particular people in mind, since each person's position will be shaped by how it affects them. Instead, start with broader principles that you can then apply to a particular situation. Try to develop the principles before you need them. For example, businesses wisely come up with a family employment policy well before the next generation is ready to enter the workforce and before people start advocating for their children. If you are having to deal with a "live" issue, try to frame it as a precedent that could ultimately affect anyone in the future.

- **Graft new ideas onto existing ones.** In the plentiful research on how ideas spread, one of the key findings is that new ideas are more acceptable if they are added onto existing ones rather than being seen as brand-new.[1] Change is hard for most families and is more readily accepted when it is perceived as being connected to already-embraced wisdom. This practice employs the notion of *grafting*, or consciously integrating a new idea into what is already in place. For example, we were trying to help a family to change a rule set down by the father. It was easier for family members to accept it when they could connect this change to exceptions he had made previously on the same subject.

- **Affirm the value of what came before.** In a change process, leaders should resist the tendency to make the case for a new idea by denigrating the current one. This negative approach often creates defensiveness among the people who created the current system. Instead, start with identifying why what exists today is entirely rational given the prevailing set of circumstances when the choices were made. Then explain why the change in circumstances makes those approaches no longer viable.

No one aims to have conflict in a business and, even worse, in a family. But some disagreement is actually healthy. It provides a chance to clear the air of lingering resentments and potential issues and perhaps to even find a productive process for disagreeing and still making decisions. Conflict doesn't have to destroy a family—managed well, it can make the bonds even stronger. But when bad feelings are allowed to fester, the descent to irrevocably broken relationships can be swift.

The conflict spiral: from diverging interests to family wars

As we have discussed, conflicts in family businesses can spiral out of control like mighty tornadoes that destroy everything in their paths. No family sets out expecting to get into a feud. And yet fights do happen. That conundrum led us to explore how family feuds unfold. We discovered seven standard stages of conflict (figure 12-1). While people tend to believe that if

Sample meeting ground rules

To ensure that your discussion encourages constructive conversation, have the participants agree in advance on some basic meeting guidelines. Consider posting the ground rules in the room as a reminder.

- Presume good intent. If there are multiple interpretations of someone's comment, give them the gift of assuming that they meant the most positive one.

- Understand that we will deal with difficult issues and the goal is to talk about how to move forward rather than assign blame.

- Speak only for yourself, not on behalf of anyone else.

- Avoid the temptation to say "you always" or "you never." Instead, use the ABC format:
  - A: "When this situation occurs . . ."
  - B: "I feel/experience . . ."
  - C: "I would like . . ."

- Focus on active listening to, and learning from, each other.

- Use a "parking lot" to address issues you cannot resolve today.

- Stay in the right room. For example, this is an Owner Room meeting, so put Family Room topics in the parking lot.

- Make sure everyone is heard and has time to speak.

- Limit the use of electronic devices to meeting purposes (e.g., taking notes).

- If you feel either you or the rest of the group needs a break, call it.

- Express appreciations for each other.

FIGURE 12-1

The conflict spiral

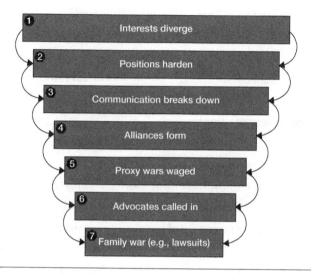

<figure>
1. Interests diverge
2. Positions harden
3. Communication breaks down
4. Alliances form
5. Proxy wars waged
6. Advocates called in
7. Family war (e.g., lawsuits)
</figure>

you leave a conflict alone it will stay the same, we have found that far more often, it will worsen over time. Major conflicts have a gravity to them, pulling families down the spiral, as each step makes sense after the previous one failed to resolve the situation.

1. **Interests diverge.** In their book *Getting to Yes*, Harvard negotiators Roger Fisher, William Ury, and Bruce Patton define an interest as a broad desire that a person or group of people have for something. Some interests are shared; others are individual. Most business families are united primarily in their wanting to protect the golden goose—to keep the business healthy. However, given that family members have different roles and responsibilities as the family business grows, interests naturally diverge. Some family members work in the business, and some are owners. And some members both work in the business and own it, while others belong in none of these groups. Those employed in the business will be more inclined to channel profits into reinvestment and bonuses, while owners not in the business may be disposed to pay higher dividends. Where

anyone stands on an issue will be influenced by where they sit in the family business system.

2. **Positions harden.** Once interests diverge, individuals or groups typically adopt different positions on issues. A position is the specific way that people try to get what they want, and positions become clear when decisions must be made. Again, all families have to make important decisions (such as where to live and where to send the kids to school), but business families are called on to make significant decisions more frequently. Because these decisions often involve the allocation of resources, people's choices can degenerate into zero-sum games: they want more; therefore, we get less. Positions harden, and suddenly everyone feels that the matter can be resolved in only one way—their own way. Positional bargaining begins, and even if a solution is reached, one party often comes away feeling that the solution is unfair. Consequently, positional bargaining typically leads to outcomes that are neither successful nor sustainable.

3. **Communication breaks down.** When the parties fail to recognize common interests and when positions harden, communication becomes badly muddled. Family members start shunning one another or sending flaming emails. Typically, the situation is neither a silence nor all-out fighting but rather a tense dynamic where people break away and don't talk for a while. Then the tension bubbles up to the surface again, and things explode. In one client family we worked with, three brothers would get into huge screaming matches, hurling verbal abuse, before lapsing into silences that threatened the business because no decisions would be made. Although the brothers were effectively the CEO, the chief operating officer, and CFO, they wouldn't talk to one another for months after a fight, not even on business matters.

4. **Alliances form.** When people stop talking directly to each other, alliances inevitably begin to take shape. Everyone feels forced to

take sides, and partisan camps spring up, often starting with the spouses of the "wronged" family member. Alliances harden as confirmation biases set in. All actions of the other side are interpreted through a lens that confirms the righteousness of the alliance's view. In this stage, things get very personal, and each side labels the other as irrational, stupid, lazy, or worse. This polarization makes compromise even more difficult. In business families, five kinds of alliances are common: (1) family branches (e.g., brother's side versus sister's); (2) owner groups (e.g., voting versus nonvoting shareholders); (3) participation levels (operators versus investors); (4) gender; and (5) generations (current versus next).

5. **Proxy wars are unleashed.** As alliances become entrenched, the opposing sides look for ways to bolster their positions, and inevitably they entangle other people in the battle. Family members enlist insiders, nonfamily managers, and employees, for example, to serve as pawns in a game that nobody will win. Proxy wars take multiple forms. In a very large firm, businesses aligned with, or led by, the other side are sold; aligned senior managers are fired; and dividends are withheld to hurt a few investors at the expense of many other people. At one client family, for example, a board member threatened to unleash an out-of-the-ordinary audit of the work of a CFO aligned with the other branch, not too subtly accusing him of fraud.

6. **Advocates are called in.** After involving innocent insiders, the next move down the conflict spiral is to bring in expert outsiders as advocates for a particular point of view or position. For example, at one family, warring co-CEOs, who were cousins, called in a compensation consultant, whom one cousin accused of being biased. The cousins dismissed the consultant, but the tension between them mounted. Even worse, family members lawyer up. Since lawyers are obligated to advocate for their clients, they make the strongest possible, uncompromising case for why their side is in the right and the other side in the wrong. The nature of the dialogue changes, too, as the search for unlawful behavior takes center stage over

reconciliation. For this reason, even the best-intentioned lawyers almost always ratchet up the conflict. We remember one painful board meeting with seven family board members, each with a personal counsel sitting behind them. As the meeting degenerated into one legal objection after another, all attempts at making important decisions were smothered.

7. **Family war begins.** The final stage is the all-consuming fight for supremacy, where only one side can win and where the ends justify virtually any means. Often, these family wars take the form of lawsuits. The suits are almost always counterproductive and expensive both financially and psychologically. Recall the Market Basket grocery chain feud earlier in the book. Our colleague, Steve Salley, himself a former attorney, summed up the situation: "Family litigation is the ugliest form of warfare: civil war. Hostages and casualties vastly outnumber apparent winners, and the scars are permanent. Any victories end up being tragically unsatisfying." When families think of lawsuits as the remedy, they are not taking into account the likely regret they will feel for the next five to ten years, or longer, as well as the impact on their employees and the community.

These stages are predictable, but they're also avoidable if the owners of family businesses are aware of them and know how to extricate themselves when they get caught up in a spiral. As one client told us, "Conflict is inevitable, but combat is optional." Not every situation follows the pattern precisely, but families in a conflict situation have found it useful to understand where they are in the spiral. It helps them to recognize that the conflict has not been caused by any one individual but is an escalating process that affects all of them. Understanding where you are in the spiral can help you address the situation with the other members of the family business, since continuing down the spiral could mean that all of you could easily lose control and end up in a family war that no one wants.

Escaping a family feud

Unfortunately, many business families see the tragic unfolding of these seven stages of conflict. We have observed great anguish and frustration, families fractured, careers and businesses ruined. But that doesn't have to be your fate. There is a difficult, but possible, path out of the conflict spiral—a few important steps that can get you on the right path again.

Create alignment for change

As a rule, conflicts do not end until interests change. That is, the combatants need to conclude that their common interest in finding a solution outweighs the competing interests they were fighting over. Usually this kind of change happens through some level of suffering, whether it's financial, emotional, or both. If family members feel enough pain, then they become willing to see their interests in a new light. When those interests shift, warring factions can come to the table and find compromises that didn't exist before. At some point, whatever people are fighting about becomes less important than ending the conflict.

If you find yourself in this situation, look for opportunities to agree on common interests. That doesn't mean you suddenly put aside everything that had brought you to this point. You don't have to agree on much other than, as one family we worked with said, "the status quo is not an option." Often there is some residual family bond that can be accessed. Families can tap into a visceral, almost biological, reservoir of family connection, usually one focused on preserving family ties into the future. As one family member put it, "Let's work out our differences so that we don't poison the next generation."

Put all options on the table

With alignment on the need to change, the next step is to identify a path forward. You must put every option on the table. Resolutions that may have been unthinkable before may be the only way out now, since the alternative is a return to the suffering of being stuck in a family feud.

Start by trying to surface all the available options. They will generally fall into these main categories:

- Sell the family business to an outsider

- Have one part of the family buy out the rest

- Divide up the company—or its assets—among the owners

- Construct a "grand bargain" that keeps the family together as owners but under a new agreement

The first three of these paths represents an attempt to solve the underlying conflict by changing the family's relationship as owners of the business. Tragically, there are times when families just can't turn their pain to their advantage. They can't go back and find a commonality of interests; they can't forgive the mistakes of the past. The pain is too profound. Then it's time to sell or divide the business and to save whatever remains of family relationships.

The last path keeps the ownership group intact but changes the nature of their relationship to the business. We call it a *grand bargain* because it usually involves addressing multiple issues at the same time, with each side getting what matters most to it and compromising in other areas. This path will often involve changes across all of the five rights of owners described in part 2.

One family we worked with found itself in a deadlock because of several disagreements about the future of the business. After the family worked its way down the conflict spiral, the company's performance stagnated as the formerly close family relationships suffered. Realizing that the members all wanted to stay as owners despite what they had been through, they agreed on a grand bargain that included several decisions:

- Moving from a Partnership to a Distributed type of family ownership. This meant that family members who didn't work in the business could now be owners.

- Building out Owner, Board, and Family Rooms to replace the loft they had been working in. This distributed decision power into groups better suited to make good decisions.

- Creating a new purpose for building the business. They shifted their Owner Strategy from liquidity control to growth control.

- Communicating to the next generation about the business so the new people could make informed decisions about whether they wanted to be part of the company as employees, board members, or owners. The improved communication substantially increased the engagement of the next generation.

- Agreeing on an estate plan that would ultimately equalize owner-ship across the branches. This decision resolved a decade-long feud between two branches.

Each grand bargain that we have helped construct looks different, depending on the needs of the family at that moment. If you are trying to construct a grand bargain in your own family, avoid the temptation to look for a silver bullet. Major conflicts are invariably caused by a huge constellation of factors, so a single solution is not likely to do the trick.

Rebuild trust over time

In the midst of a family feud, some members will refuse to come to the negotiating table because they don't feel as though they can trust those who would be sitting on the other side. The lack of trust is entirely reasonable. In chapter 6 we provided a definition of trust: "one party's willingness to be vulnerable to another party based on the belief that the latter is competent, open, concerned, and reliable." Since trust is about being vulnerable, as the conflict worsens and people feel less safe, they often have a much more difficult time trusting each other.

The challenge is when trust becomes a precondition for making progress. That requirement is unrealistic. Greater levels of trust are likely to be the *consequence* of resolving conflict, not the *cause*. Because a feeling of trust reflects the behaviors of the other person, it can be reconstructed over time. In fact, before you even begin to negotiate details in a conflict, you should take concrete actions to build trust by demonstrating competence, openness, concern, and reliability to others. That includes defining guidelines that tie to those four behaviors to lay out how everyone will treat one another. With these actions, the level of trust will slowly start to rise. In turn, the increased trust will not only open up other options, but also raise the likelihood that you can ease strained family relationships.

Get outside help

Managing your exit from a family feud on your own is an incredibly difficult task. When trust is low, you are likely to need an honest broker who can bridge the communication back and forth and facilitate tense conversations. It also helps to have someone who can bring ideas for how to resolve the situation.

The outside help may come from your personal network, a trusted adviser, a relative, a clergy member, or a mutual friend. If you don't have someone who can serve in that role, a number of experts, such as mediators, therapists, and family business advisers, can help. "There are some systems where relationships (e.g., brother–brother) are so toxic, often for historical reasons, that trivial comments produce explosive reactions and draw attention away from a decision and onto the two individuals," Harvard Business School's David Ager told us. "To avoid paralyzing the system, the only way to move forward on any significant decision is through the use of a trusted, neutral third party whose responsibility is to manage the conversation between the family members, often by reframing and interpretation, with the goal to avoid misattribution in every statement uttered by the other family member."

Avoiding the conflict spiral

Even better than knowing how to exit a battle that is spiraling downward, however, is knowing how to avoid it in the first place. If you and your family want to avoid the disastrous spiral of conflict, keep an eye open for the seven escalation points. When people disagree, they often think that the best solution is to leap into action. And the tricky thing is that this reaction is often rational. If someone in the family is not honoring a written deal, the logical step is to turn to a lawyer. It's also reasonable that the other person will hire their own lawyer. Taken individually, all these steps make sense. Ironically, such rational actions provoking further rational reactions can send business families down the devastating spiral.

We advise you, therefore, to take a deep breath before allowing yourselves to jump to the next stage. Recognize that whenever anyone says, "I think this is the only way to do it," you've taken a step toward escalating conflict in your family business system. Whenever you give up truly trying to communicate, you're moving toward all-out war. Each of the seven stages of conflict is a step that a family member or branch can take or not take—there is a choice. All-out war is not inevitable. Each of you has many chances to keep the family and the business from self-destructing. That's a huge opportunity and responsibility.

So, take the time to learn about conflict, both why a healthy family business needs it and how it can spiral out of control. If the situation starts to go south, get everyone on the same page about the potential impact of failing to reach a consensus. A thorough understanding of the cost of litigation—for example, how ugly it is and how much you will regret it later—can go a long way toward avoiding a vicious war. Few families remain intact after battling each other in court.

Beyond being aware of the downsides of excessive squabbling, get out ahead of the issues most likely to cause a family feud. If your family business has been successful for any period, you have clearly found the right balance between too much and too little conflict. Your success has been based on some agreement on how you exercise the five core rights of family owners. But family businesses are dynamic—people die and others join the family, families disperse and come back together, businesses go through ups and downs. These changes can create shocks that undermine what had worked brilliantly in the past. When times are good, install "shock absorbers" by carefully considering what changes will be needed to handle the likely future disruptions. For example, creating a family employment policy long before any next-generation member is considering joining the business will ensure that the decisions about any one person are not personal. Similarly, revisit the five rights of ownership with an eye to future disruptions. These forward-looking exercises are no criticism of what works today or was effective in the past. You are simply recognizing that some approaches may not work in the future. By agreeing on the changes required in advance and taking gradual steps toward them, you will significantly increase your family business's odds of staying in the Goldilocks zone.

Conflict is necessary for any business to survive. Well-managed conflict doesn't make for good headlines. When handled well, conflict can build up a family business rather than tear it apart.

Summing up

- Conflict in family businesses is different because of the presence of the owners. Since the owners can make the rules, they can break the rules.

- Conflict is a Goldilocks problem. Both too much and too little lead to similarly unhealthy outcomes for the business and family. While family feuds receive most of the media attention, fake harmony, where true disagreement is shoved under the rug, is much more common. In those situations, families need to learn how to disagree constructively.

- Major fights in family businesses often follow a pattern, which we call the *conflict spiral*. You may think that the situation will either stay the same or get better, but more often it will get worse if left unresolved. Conflict has a gravitational pull; common actions to resolve it can instead further entrench the dispute.

- If you are in the midst of a family feud, you will probably need to look for a grand bargain that addresses a series of issues rather than looking for a silver bullet. Aim to identify the core needs of each participant in the dispute, and put all options on the table as you look for a way for everyone to resolve the conflict.

■ To prevent feuds from happening in the first place, get ahead of the situation. Most major conflicts arise because changes in the family business system have upended how things had long worked. For example, the death of a matriarch or the entry of the next generation into the business or ownership can sow discord. As you experience those changes, or see them coming, take a comprehensive look at how you are exercising the five rights of family owners. For example, consider changes to your governance structure or Owner Strategy.

13.

The Family Office in a Family Business

"I hate to say it, but we keep coming back to the need for a family office." With great reluctance, Phil recognized that the family business had to formalize the support services the company had long provided for family members. He was one of the leaders of the second generation of a thriving family business, one that had always had staff dedicated to supporting the tax, financial, philanthropic, and other needs of its owners. The company accountant would handle, say, the members' personal tax filings, mortgage payments, charitable donations, and so on. That structure worked just fine for Phil's father, the founder, and Phil's siblings, all of whom dedicated their lives to growing the company. For them, there was little separation between the business and the family. And they liked the lack of bureaucracy and the informality in their current setup, which fit with their lean-and-mean approach to running the company.

But they realized that eventually, the lack of structure could trigger problems for the next generation. Phil and his sister Natalia had always relied on company resources to help with the logistics of their lives, for instance, making free use of company planes and cars. Could the business sustain that kind of structure in the next generation of seven? As he looked ahead, Phil recognized that this free-form approach was already causing conflict in the next generation, which included members who were working in the company and others who were not. Despite the cost and additional bureaucracy, it was time to formalize the support services that family members were receiving from the company so that the distribution was fair.

As your business and family grow, one challenge you will face is how to manage all the stuff that is not associated with operating the business but can be vital to its success. These activities can include paying taxes, creating life insurance policies, giving to charity, coordinating family and owner meetings, overseeing a vacation home, or investing the money distributed through dividends. These issues are personal, but they can have a major effect on the business either directly (e.g., an owner doesn't prepare for estate taxes, forcing the business to be sold when they die) or indirectly (a family fight over the vacation homes spills over into the business). A family office can be a solution to the complexity that comes with owning a family business.

When a family office is mentioned, people often think about large pools of investment assets controlled by spectacularly wealthy families, but that is not at all what Phil had in mind. His family business reinvested almost all the company's profits for growth. The company had liquid wealth, but it was kept in the company and invested in an extremely conservative way. The owners had no need for asset managers. Instead, they simply required a way of ensuring that the complicated taxes of each owner were done correctly and that their shared property, donations, security needs, and funds for family education were being properly overseen.

The term *family office* has become so broad that it has lost much meaning. We have been part of several benchmarking efforts with our clients to learn more about family offices. The primary takeaway seems to be that every family has a different version of this function. As a client summarized after one such effort, "If you have seen one family office, you have seen one family office."

The number of family offices has exploded since around 2010. Campden Wealth and Ernst & Young estimated the number of single-family offices globally somewhere in the seven thousand to ten thousand range.[1] And now a huge array of service providers, best-practice networks, and educational courses are aimed at serving this demand.

As a family business owner, how do you navigate this growing, often confusing, landscape? Do you need a family office? If so, what kind? Do you already have one without really knowing it? If you have one, is it serving your needs or adding the kind of cost and unnecessary layers that Phil feared?

In this chapter, we will describe the main roles that a family office can play. We will then help you decide if your family is ready for such an office and will outline the different types of these offices. Finally, we will provide guidance on building out your family office—and on how to know if it's time to shut yours down.

The functions of a family office

Part of the confusion about family offices comes from people's use of the same term to describe very different functions. Family offices have typically been created to serve three main purposes.

Investment

Family offices can be formed to manage family wealth outside the operating business. You may have sold one of the businesses in your portfolio or taken one public, creating a liquidity event. Or you might have a business that generates more money than you can effectively reinvest back into it. Or perhaps you have consciously decided to take money out of the operating company to diversify your risk. You might also have created a fund to pay for family education and health needs or to donate to charities.

In these cases, a family office operates like the endowment of a major university or hospital. There is an investment strategy, which often consists of a mix between stocks and bonds as well as so-called alternative investments such as private equity and hedge funds. Some family offices only hire managers to invest their funds, while others have employees that search for operating businesses to buy. The majority of the service providers in the field are aimed at supporting those who have money to invest, measuring themselves by their "assets under management."

Support

A second function of family offices is to provide a range of services that help the family address the complexities that come with owning significant assets together. Many of these support services relate to the tax implications of ownership. Many family businesses are held in *pass-through entities* (e.g., S-corporations and limited liability companies in the United States), where the profits and losses flow directly into the personal taxes of the individual owners. That arrangement creates incredibly complicated tax returns that require real expertise to complete. If your family business is held in a trust or a series of trusts, you will face similarly involved tax and other financial situations that a family office can address.

Support offices can also be formed to manage the family's noninvestable assets outside of the business. Many families have houses, cars, planes, artwork, or other valuables that require care and oversight. These assets are often a disproportionate cause of conflict among families (especially shared property; see the box "Managing shared family property"), so management of these resources may take on a high priority. Some offices also support families in their personal lives, whether by paying bills or administering their philanthropic activities.

Some family offices have internal experts provide these services. Others primarily outsource the work, but the family office takes on the responsibility of identifying and managing the network of service providers.

Governance

A third purpose of family offices is to implement governance structures and processes. As the family and business grow, the work involved in the Four-Room model of governance can expand beyond the family's time, talent, or interest. Family offices can fill the gap. They can support the structures that have already been put in place. For example, a family office can organize meetings for family councils, owner councils, and family assemblies. One family office leader describes the annual family gathering as her Super Bowl, since she is on the hook to organize the event from the time the family arrives to when people depart.

Family offices are also often involved in keeping the machinery moving. Some offices serve in a role analogous to the shareholder relations function of a public company, managing the communication between the company and the owners. One family business we have worked with has made its family office leader the point of contact for any family questions or requests about the business. It is up to that leader to field those queries and figure out the right way to resolve them, coordinating with the board and management as needed. The liaison person acts as both a bridge and a buffer between the company and the family. Other family offices are in charge of creating the family's communication platform, whether that's a family website or a document storage program. Many family offices work on finding educational programs to train people for the roles they are or will be playing across the Four Rooms.

A family office can help in any or all of these three categories. As you begin thinking about the idea of a family office, use these categories to clarify your needs. Table 13-2 lists examples of services for each category. You can start your group discussion by checking those that are relevant to you, both now and as you prepare for a transition to the next generation.

These categories can also help you in finding relevant service providers and comparable family offices. When you approach providers, frame your questions according to the functions you are looking to fill.

How to know if you need a family office

How will you recognize that your family has reached the point where it could benefit from a family office? You'll know it when your activities or

Managing shared family property

Barney Corning and Laird Pendleton surveyed the more than one hundred members of their family office network, CCC Alliance, and asked them, "In the broad range of family activities where your family office engages, list three activities that create family harmony and three that create dissension." Family vacation homes and compounds appeared on both lists. At their best, shared properties provide a hub for family members to gather and foster relationships with each other across generations. Many families we work with point to the formative time spent with siblings or cousins during weekends or vacations while they were young as helping them build the trust that allowed them to work together effectively as adults.

At the same time, because they hold such sentimental value, these properties can also cause some of the nastiest fights we have seen. For example, we advised one group of five siblings who owned a business going through difficult times. They needed to collaborate to make some tough decisions about how to turn the company around or whether to sell it. However, at every meeting, they spent most of the time arguing about issues related to the vacation home they had inherited from their parents: who was using it too much, who was making changes without permission, who wasn't paying their fair share, and so on. The house embodied the spirit of their parents and some of their happiest childhood memories, so we understand the emotion. But something that represented less than 5 percent of their common assets was rendering them incapable of doing the work required to deal with the remaining 95 percent.

To avoid this kind of situation, you'll want to create a plan for any shared family property that has significant financial value or emotional resonance. You can use the core structure of the five rights of ownership as a basis for the plan, as shown in table 13-1.

TABLE 13-1

Developing a family shared-property plan

Design	• What is included in the shared family property? Are there parts that belong to individual family members? • Who can be an owner of the property? • Which owners can participate in decision-making?
Decide	• What governance structures do you need to oversee the property? Use the Four-Room model as a starting point. • What policies do you need to put in place? Focus on policies about usage. For example, who can use it? Who has priority, and what expenses are owed?
Value	• What is the purpose of owning this property? • What are your family's goals for it? • Are you expecting the asset to appreciate in value? • Do you want to generate income or break even, or are you willing to contribute money to fund it? • Would you consider selling some of it to outsiders or borrowing to pay for major expenses? • What guardrails should you put in place for the property? For example, is there a maximum budget each year?
Inform	• How do you educate family members about the property's financials, ownership, rules, etc.? • How do you communicate guidelines about the use of the property?
Transfer	• What are the rules for selling and donating interests in the property? Are they captured in a shareholder agreement?

One family we worked with had jointly owned a farm for seven generations. It was the source of many memories, as well as several disagreements. Using this structure outlined in the table, they developed a shared property plan that has helped the farm remain a source of family harmony while minimizing the degree of dissension.

TABLE 13-2

What can a family office do for you? A sample of possible services

Investment	Support	Governance
• Investment strategy • Asset allocation • Manager selection • Performance measurement and benchmarking • Investment policy • Investment reporting • Investment opportunity sourcing and due diligence • Cash management	• Accounting administration • Tax planning and management for individuals and entities • Financial, estate, and insurance planning • Administration of family giving • Payment of family bills • Management of family assets (planes, houses, etc.) • Management of service providers	• Family events and meetings coordination • Communication across the Four Rooms • Shareholder relations (meetings, proxy statements, questions) • Education (courses, resources, etc.) • Career development and progression • Family website or portal

concerns have grown to the extent that can't easily be handled by existing family members acting in leadership roles or by the support of company executives. Kathryn McCarthy, who has spent several decades advising leading family businesses in their formation of family offices after a career at Rockefeller Trust Company, cites some clear signs that it's time to consider a family office:

- **Pressing needs are not met.** You have identified issues that need professional management, such as the diversity and liquidity of your investments, the interface between the company and family members who either do and don't work in the business, or issues related to shared assets such as family vacation homes.

- **Professional expertise is lacking.** Your family's assets and needs extend beyond what, say, a competent CFO within the business can manage. For example, you need a sophisticated level of services for family trusts. In one family business we worked with, the family required expertise in taxation from both a business and a family perspective. The CFO raised the concern that her team was trying to fill both roles but was not doing it as efficiently as would two teams: a team inside the company for the business's taxes and a team outside the company for the family's personal taxes.

- **Family or owner governance needs support.** A family office can play an important administrative role in keeping orderly Four-Room governance. Who calls the shareholder meetings? Who ensures that family members are informed of important developments? Who will take responsibility for educating and mentoring the next generation? Even when a family member plays a leadership role on these issues, it can be helpful to have professional support to organize the calendar and logistics.

Types of family offices

So far, we have been operating under the idea that there is an actual distinct family office with a physical location and dedicated staff. In fact, there are four main types of family offices, each of which has its advantages and disadvantages (table 13-3):

- An **embedded family office** is integrated into the operating company. There may be a department dedicated to serving the types of needs described earlier. Or, more commonly, those services are provided alongside support to the business. For example, in Phil's family business, a treasury department is responsible for both the cash needs of the company and those of the owners. The tax department is in charge of both corporate and personal tax returns, which are connected, since Phil's company has a pass-through corporate structure.

- A **single-family office** (often called an SFO) is a separate entity dedicated to serving the needs of a specific family. These offices usually have their own staff and office space, though sometimes they have contracts for one or both with the operating business.

- With a **virtual family office** (or VFO) a family hires one or more external companies to address its investment, support, and governance needs. For example, in one family business, the owners have contracted with an accounting firm to do all their personal

TABLE 13-3

Pros and cons of different types of family offices

Family office type	Pros	Cons
Embedded family office	• Leverage company resources • Simplicity of governance	• Restrictions on what can be provided • Conflict over varying levels of usage
Single family office	• Dedicated services • Expertise customized to family needs	• Cost of dedicated staff • Complexity of additional entity to govern
Virtual family office	• Select best providers for each category • Only pay for what you use	• Complexity of multiple providers • Onus on family to provide direction
Multifamily office	• Breadth of services • Depth of expertise in a variety of areas • Flexibility	• Bundled services, not all of which may be needed • Lack of customization • Not under family control

tax returns, which were formerly done by the operating company CFO's team. The accounting firm works directly with the CFO to ensure that the right information is shared back and forth.

- A **multifamily office** (or MFO) is a company established to serve the needs of several families. These offices employ professionals across a wide range of disciplines, such as accounting, estate planning, family governance, and philanthropy, and clients can access these experts as part of joining. Many multifamily offices, such as Bessemer Trust and Brown Brothers Harriman, started out serving one family and eventually opened their doors to others.

Most family businesses start out with an embedded family office. In fact, many times it exists without even having a name; it's just the way the business works. Costs are run through the business, just like any other operating expense. This loft-like model is especially common in the founding generation, which often makes no distinction between business and personal assets. The company may own houses, cars, planes, artwork, and so on, and is responsible for managing all of it.

Once the scope or scale of services becomes substantially larger, a formal family office structure is often created inside the company. Again, the arrangement may not be called a family office, but there are people who are dedicated to serving family and owner needs. This office will often start charging family members for services if they are not business-related or are provided at different levels of intensity across the family.

At some point in this evolutionary process, the family office will usually separate itself from the main business. Family office employees may still be on the company payroll, but the office will have its own leadership and governance. Specific triggers, including the following events, spur this separation:

- The company goes public, and this new structure changes reporting requirements and accounting rules.

- There are multiple types of owners—for example, operators, governors, and investors—each with different needs (as in Phil's situation).

- Family members start to value privacy over their financial affairs, rather than having them known by company personnel and kept on company systems.

- The complexity of the governance system requires new types of expertise (e.g., trust administration) that typically doesn't reside in a company.

Before continuing, pause to assess your current situation. Do you have a family office, even if you don't call it that? If so, which of these four types is it? What services does it provide? How well is it meeting your needs? If you don't have a family office, do you need one? If so, which of the three main roles—investment, support, or governance—has the highest priority?

Building out your family office

There is no one right way to form your family office or to expand on what you have already created. Each family office exists to serve the needs of a business-owning family, and these needs will vary both across families and within families over time.

With that in mind, here are some suggestions as you consider creating or expanding your family office:

- **Take a long-term view.** Pendleton and Corning, whom we intro-duced earlier, are the heads of the CCC Alliance, a leading network of family offices. The two leaders have also launched their own families' offices. In their role at CCC, they have had a window on over one hundred family office launches. In their experience, they told us, "it is a mistake to get started without the end in mind. Think about what you want it to be and look like over the very long term, meaning twenty to fifty years. New families often start mak-ing investments, building structures, and hiring staff before they have a clear idea of their long-term vision." Pendleton and Corning see education as one objective that family offices should focus on early, since "an uninformed, disengaged next generation, even with the best tax, legal, and investment planning, can destroy the wealth in ten to twenty years."

- **Identify the leader before you finalize the structure.** Family office adviser McCarthy told us that families should "look for the leader (either from within the family or outside) before or parallel to building the structure. You can't build an office and then hand it to someone to run." When asked what makes for a good family office leader, she points mainly to soft skills: "They have to be really good communicators. They have to want to get out there and interact with the family and company, rather than sitting in an office. They have to bring a presence that commands respect from all parties and allows them to build trust. They should be humble—arrogance does not play well. And they have to be able to handle the ambiguity that comes with the job. You are stuck in the middle, so deal with it. You can always buy technical competencies; this role is all about personal characteristics."

- **Create a separate legal entity.** Having the family office set up its own profit-and-loss statements helps create greater accountability and transparency, which may not be vital in early generations, but will be over time. There can be value in keeping the family office under the company umbrella, which can be accomplished by making it a subsidiary. Or, have service-level agreements that allow the company to pay for the family office's expenses. If the family office is not a separate legal entity, it must at least have a separate identity within the family business, according to McCarthy.

- **Establish good governance for the family office.** Some family offices struggle because they lack clear accountability. Or they are accountable to the business leaders rather than to the family itself. Governance can help address these issues. Be clear about who the family office leader reports to—is it the family council, the owner council, or its own board? In most cases, we recommend forming a board specific to the family office to ensure that the family office receives appropriate guidance and oversight. That board can consist of a mix of family members, outside advisers, and company leaders.

- **Foster a culture of respect for the family office role.** According to McCarthy, there is a risk that family office employees will be "treated like second-class citizens. They may not have the authority to act within the business and so are not always respected. They are sometimes seen as getting the jobs no one else wants to do." When this kind of culture is created, the family office employees may have difficulty doing their jobs. It also becomes difficult to attract and retain good talent. The owners should communicate the importance of the family office's function and back up their words by showing respect, especially when in the presence of other leaders in the family enterprise.

- **Prepare to adapt your family office over time.** As Pendleton and Corning put it, "Families evolve, so the family office needs a flexible structure so it can change as the family does." McCarthy says that a number of changes to the environment will affect family offices. These changes include the impact of technology, multiple generations existing alongside each other as people are living longer, and the spread of many families across multiple countries. Finally, she cautions that "you should not assume that the same person will lead the family office for twenty-five years. You need changes in leadership every now and then to keep up-to-date."

Deciding when to close your family office

Family offices do not necessarily last forever. There are several reasons that they may end up being shuttered, according to McCarthy, including these:

- **Service-level inadequacies:** At the end of the day, a family office is only as good as the services it offers. With a small staff and limited budget, service levels may not meet family expectations.

- **Difficult staff and family relationships:** It can be challenging to recruit and retain competent, trusted family office staff who meet the ever-present needs of a large, diverse family—and to pay them what their services command on the open market. Families can't necessarily expect to hire, say, a world-class investment adviser and compensate them commensurate with what you pay top employees in the business. Top family office professionals can command much higher remuneration. That is not always easy for families to accept.

- **The family's diverse needs are too broad for one office:** As nice as the idea of one-stop shopping is for a family, sometimes one family office can't handle the range of requirements for a given family.

There are numerous other reasons that family offices get phased out, but many of them add up to the difference between high expectations for the office and reality. Sometimes, one generation values the office more than the next. In other cases, family members agree to a family office to please an aging patriarch but want independence when it's their time to call the shots. Or family relationships are too fraught to continue to be tied together in decision-making. It's possible (and sometimes advisable) for family offices to be unwound, McCarthy says, or shifted to a multifamily office where there is more flexibility for individual family members.

Summing up

- A family office can be a helpful way to manage the multiple functions that come with a growing business and family. Even if you don't have a formal family office, you probably have some of its functions built into your operating company.

- Family offices serve three main functions. They manage family *investments*, provide *support* services, and implement *governance* structures and processes. As you explore the creation, or reassessment, of a family office, start with identifying what types of needs it will address.

- Consider forming a family office when your investment, support, or governance needs are unmet because business leaders lack the time or expertise to address them. If you are going to create a family office, think about your long-term needs and design it with those in mind. And remember that these offices need dedicated governance, such as a board, to stay on track.

- Family offices come in different shapes and sizes, each with its own pros and cons. An *embedded family office* sits within the operating company, often without centralized leadership. A *single-family office* is separate from the business and dedicated to your family. A *virtual family office* can be assembled by identifying one or more service providers to fill key functions. And a *multifamily office* is dedicated to supporting a group of families with a range of expert resources.

- If you have a family office, take time to reassess whether it is meeting your needs. If not, you should consider adapting it, switching types (e.g., from a single-family office to a virtual family office) or closing it down.

14.

The Dangers of Losing What You've Built

Stories of bitter family feuds that end up ruining the business and the family are the stuff of tabloid fodder and made-for-TV movies. But in reality, families often lose what they have cherished for generations in far less dramatic, but equally insidious, ways. Three main pathways lead to this loss:

1. You lose control by explicitly or implicitly ceding your fundamental rights as owners.

2. You lose your way as family owners with an erosion of your guiding values.

3. You lose your business because of a failure to adequately respond to an economic crisis.

What these three scenarios share in common is that they are the consequence either of action or inaction on the part of the owners. The loss may seem to come out of nowhere, like a rogue wave that takes down an unsuspecting ship. However, in each case, there are moments when action can be taken to avoid the danger. Here is how to head off that fate.

Recognizing warning signs that you might be losing control

For years, Devin and his family members had been detached and disengaged owners in their third-generation family business. No family member worked in the company, and those who sat on the board rubber-stamped management's decisions. But they were still shocked when the nonfamily CEO said that they had to live without dividends—or sell the business. How did that surprise sneak up on them? They had been increasingly passive owners until faced with the reality that they were at risk of losing the business that had been in the family for three generations. In truth, they had brought this fate on themselves with their indifference to their rights and responsibilities as owners.

While the details vary, stories of family owners unintentionally losing control of their businesses are common. Consider what happened when a relatively young patriarch died unexpectedly, leaving no succession plan in place. The children were unprepared to take over, and the widow had no business experience. She brought in a nonfamily CEO who, unfortunately, recognized the family's weakness as owners. So he came to treat the business as his personal fiefdom. Eventually he tried to buy the business himself at a deflated price. The family managed to hold on, pushing the CEO out, but the experience damaged the family emotionally and financially.

While a nonfamily CEO sometimes plays the role of villain in these situations, the blame lies more often with the owners, who created a power vacuum for others to fill. Lacking substantive direction from the owners, these executives understandably followed their own self-interests. But even when families are fortunate enough to find that selfless, protective nonfamily leader—and there are many—owners still need to speak with a single voice about what they want. Otherwise, there is no way to ensure that their interests are being served.

Here are five red flags signal that you might be on the path to losing control of your family business:

- **Dividends never change.** If you receive stable dividends year after year, then you should grow concerned. Dividend targets are fine, but the dividends of a well-run company are always uncertain and should vary with the company's performance and its future opportunities. Every year, there should be some discussion about the company's profits and what to do with them. If you grow accustomed to receiving annual dividends—in the worst cases, treating them as an entitlement—then you forfeit an essential mechanism for controlling the business, namely, deciding how much of your money should be reinvested annually. You have effectively placed your Owner Strategy on autopilot.

- **Board meetings are a formality.** For larger family businesses, a board of directors (or advisers) is used to ensure that the business is pursuing the owners' objectives. At their best, independent directors bring wisdom, expertise, and a willingness to challenge management. Owners must see to it that the board is properly formed and empowered. Do you have a paper board that rarely meets or that essentially rubber-stamps the recommendations of management? Is the board filled with family friends or with the CEO and the executive's allies? Is the board's role murky? If you answer yes to any of these questions, then you're giving away a key lever to maintain control.

- **Too much or too little business information is provided.** As an equity owner, you should receive information about business performance in a timely and appropriate way. Both fifteen-minute updates ("The business is great!" or "Enjoy your dividend!") or 200-page "summaries" should set off alarm bells. If you don't work in the company, you are already at a disadvantage, lacking first-hand knowledge of what's happening. When management either skimps or drowns you in details, it's very difficult to understand your business's performance and potential.

- **The CEO seems irreplaceable.** Some business leaders can run your business and deliver outstanding results while also cultivating proper family engagement. Do what you can to hold on to these people. Watch out, however, if you (and they) talk and behave as if they are irreplaceable. Respect and appreciation for a job well done are healthy. Fear and dependency are not. Irreplaceable executives can begin to make decisions independently, believing they know better than you do. They may even refer to you as "the kids." If your family ownership group walks on eggshells around your nonfamily CEO, your behavior may signal a dangerous imbalance of power.

- **Family members are shut out of the business.** Sometimes, family owners lose control of the business because the previous generation has shut the door to them during the succession process. There is a perceived lack of talent among the next generation—or fear about the dangers of family conflict. As a result, employment policies are put in place that either prevent or make it very difficult for family members to work in the business. Sometimes this "professionalization" of the family business may make sense. But be aware that the family's direct link to the operations of the company will be severed. You don't need to run the business, but having owners employed there helps the family keep a finger on the company's pulse.

Course-correcting: getting back in control

If you realize that you've lost some or most of the control over your company, then it's time to ask yourselves whether you wish to continue to own your family business. You may decide it's time to sell. But if you want to keep it in more than a technical sense, then you should start by engaging as owners. You don't have to suddenly start micromanaging executives or meddling in operational decisions. You do, however, need to renew and reassert your owner rights.

If you haven't created an owner council or if yours has become an "empty structure" (see "Further Reading") it's time to start one. Your owner council can shape or reshape your priorities as owners and enables you to speak to the board and management about these priorities in a united voice. Create an Owner Strategy statement to help guide your prioritization. Put in place clear financial policies for dividends and debt levels and establish financial and nonfinancial guardrails, such as return-on-investment targets or bans on some investments (e.g., tobacco). You, as owners, then need to hold the board accountable to choose a CEO who supports your owner agenda, not the executive's.

You may never become an expert on return on invested capital or other financial details. That you and your co-owners aren't necessarily experts only underscores the importance of structures that let you rely on the knowledge of people who appreciate your values and follow your agenda. But for each generation, your presence as active and effective owners allows you to let go of many decisions—without losing control of your family business in the process.

Maintaining your family values

Although you can relinquish some decisions to the experts, you can't afford to let go of your family values, which form the bedrock of your business. They are the reason you choose to stay together, in business, as a family. They have to be cultivated and transferred from one generation to the next. Family values provide important ethical guardrails to keep the business on track.

Take, for example, the legacy passed on by Robert Pasin's grandfather. When he was attending his grandfather's funeral, Pasin, now CEO of Radio Flyer, was overwhelmed by the outpouring of affection and respect for the family patriarch, who had founded the third-generation toy manufacturer. "All these people who worked in the factory," he told us, "all these suppliers, they told me stories about my grandfather. His word was his bond. One supplier told me that they had never even had a signed contract, just a handshake agreement. I remember feeling proud and grateful that that kind of person had established this company." It was a lesson that Pasin had absorbed over the years watching both his grandfather and his father run the business, one that became part of his DNA. "When you start out with really good values, it's much easier to maintain them," Pasin says.

With so many advantages going for your family business, how do you make sure that you don't unintentionally let your values drift and damage the business your family has spent generations building?

In *How Will You Measure Your Life?*, Harvard Business School professor Clayton Christensen and his coauthors argued that the road to ruin happens one step at a time. Each individual choice that moves further from the moral high ground makes it easier to take the next one. This is the theory behind marginal thinking: you make what seem to be completely rational choices about the immediate decision in hand, without ever considering the full costs of that decision over time. For example, in 2005 General Motors decided not to redesign a faulty ignition switch that was linked to car crashes, because it would have added $1 to the manufacturing cost of each car.[1] The decision to keep the defective switches would eventually lead to $4.1 billion in repair costs, victim compensation, and other costs, not to mention the toll of congressional hearings and the ensuing public relations debacle.

The same marginal thinking happens in our personal integrity as well. Just this once, I can make an ethically questionable choice or ignore the rules. Just this once. Except for most of us, Christensen and coauthors argue, "just this once" repeats itself over and over again. In our experience working closely with multigenerational family businesses, the risk of marginal thinking can clearly play a big role in leading a family business away from the values it once stood for. Many family businesses find themselves in situations they never intended to pursue, because of an accumulation of small, logical, incremental decisions. Staying true to those values requires work and vigilance from each generation. Six warning signs suggest that your family business may be heading down the wrong path.

You lose your family narrative

Family values are passed down from generation to generation through stories. But don't just tell the triumphant tales. You need to share both the successes and the failures in family business history, what Emory University professor Marshall Duke calls "the oscillating narrative"—an acknowledgment of both the good times and the bad. Understanding why the family came to face difficult challenges and how it overcame them can provide guideposts to help future generations avoid temptations to compromise on their values for short-term gains.

You think "professionalizing" the business means taking the heart out of it

Steve Shifman, who became CEO of his wife Julie's family business, Michelman Incorporated, a specialty chemicals manufacturer, struggled to balance maintaining the qualities that made his third-generation family business special and the need to remain competitive when he first took over the business in 2003. "I was hell-bent on professionalizing the whole business," Shifman shared with us. "But then I slowly realized that I had created a false binary between 'family business' and 'professional business.' Part of what made us able to recruit and retain our amazing talent was also what made us special as a family business. We are driven by purpose and values, not just by markets. This isn't just a wealth-generation machine to us; it's something more. I realized there was something magical about that."

You only allow "credentialed" people in the room for key decisions

As family businesses grow, they often build boards with outside professionals. The members who supposedly fail to measure up (often, family members) are ignored or excluded. The external professionals usually assume that total shareholder return is the ultimate goal—and these people advocate for choices consistent with that goal. As we discussed earlier, allowing these professionals to determine the owners' goals can lead to disaster, not least because the choices made by an executive or a board member who is not an owner may look good on paper but be inconsistent with your family values.

Protecting those values often requires a family member with an outsider's perspective in a position to ask important "why" questions. In fact, some of the best family business board members we have seen have no traditional experience but always ask the hardest questions. In one striking instance, a family member who had been relatively uninvolved in the business during the past decade challenged the board to justify why it had agreed to use unsustainably sourced raw materials for the company's industrial manufacturing business. The marginal economic rationale was clear—the materials were cheaper than sustainably sourced ones—but the underlying family values didn't support the investment. Without a fresh perspective to pause the conversation and make sure that such a step was consistent with the family's values, the company might have found itself heading in a direction it would regret in the long run.

You start defining yourself and your family through money

As discussed in chapter 11, individual family members sometimes start defining themselves through their money and the attendant public attention. Worse still is when the entire family starts defining itself that way, lending their name to buildings, parks, and other public areas. There can be lots of good civic reasons to support charitable causes, but if the underlying motivation is about showing off your money, the family has started down a slippery slope. When the need for outsider adulation dominates decisions, those outsiders—rather than family members—start defining your values. And once you've given others the right to define your own family values, you may feel the pressure to cut corners to make ever-grander gestures that maintain your public image.

Profit becomes your primary motive

Academics and thought leaders have been telling us for years that the purpose of a corporation is to maximize shareholder value. This observation may be accurate for public companies, but family businesses are free to be different. They have an advantage in that the owners can choose what to prioritize—be it profit, family harmony, social responsibility, or some other dimension. When family businesses overemphasize profit to the detriment of their customers or the communities in which they live, they can find themselves heading down the wrong path. But companies that can clearly articulate their motives beyond profit can help reinforce values and strengthen family harmony. At one family company we worked with, the owners chose to run one of its businesses at a loss because it provided careers for family members and a much-needed public service to the community.

Because family companies face so little scrutiny from the outside world, it might be all too easy to take "just this once" baby steps down a path that can eventually destroy the values you hold dear. Radio Flyer's Pasin recalls one such moment with his father, years ago, when he questioned his father's decision not to use less expensive materials for one of the company's trademark red wagons:

> I remember my dad making the decision whether to use cheaper steel and cheaper tires on one of our wagons years ago. And I said to my dad, "Does it really matter? Will consumers know?" And my dad said, "I'm not sure. But when in doubt, I like to overbuild stuff because I can sleep at night. There will be a lot of things you will lose sleep over running this business, but this won't be one of them." I think about that every day. It's one of the most important lessons my dad ever taught me.

You relinquish your values in an effort to avoid conflict

When family businesses lose sight of their owner responsibilities, it's often the result of a misguided effort to avoid conflict in the family. With their very human tendency to skirt confrontation, owners might hesitate to ask each other challenging questions. They let the elephant remain in the room. They think to themselves, "I won't challenge the professionals, who probably know more than I do." Too often, owners have been inadequately prepared for their roles and don't know how and when to speak up when they are struggling with a decision. So instead, they say nothing even when their gut is telling them something's not right.

Ultimately, the healthiest family businesses don't avoid the hard discussions. Nor do they rubber-stamp decisions. And most importantly, they understand that owner rights also have attendant responsibilities. Taking those responsibilities seriously is the best way to preserve the family legacy for many generations.

Responding to an economic crisis

A third major risk to your family business is not responding effectively to an economic crisis. Occasionally, a disruption makes it impossible to practice business as usual. Events like the Great Depression or the 2008 financial crisis can affect the viability of even healthy companies. For example, almost every family business we know was seriously disrupted by the Covid-19 pandemic. Nearly 90 percent saw some negative impact on their business, according to a survey we conducted in mid-2020 at the height of the coronavirus pandemic. Some of these companies were fighting to stay alive.[2]

Owners of family businesses have the unique ability to take critical actions that can help their company through such difficult times. As discussed in this book, your five rights give you the ability to change almost every aspect of how the company works. Under normal circumstances, these are powerful rights, but in a business crisis, the power of owners is magnified.

A crisis forces family businesses to make trade-offs that would have previously been unimaginable. The stress, anxiety, and fear that come out in a crisis can amplify already-challenging dynamics, paralyzing decision-making throughout the enterprise or causing conflict to spiral out of control. Or the challenges can be a call to action, prompting family owners to rally around the flag, put aside their differences, and work hard to make sure that the business survives. The ultimate impact of such a crisis on your family business will be substantially shaped by how you respond. Through your choices, or lack of them, you will influence how the crisis is managed and what kind of company, if any, emerges on the other side.

If you've done the work to exercise your five owner rights, you should find yourself in good shape to face challenges that come your way. But in a crisis, you need to consider specific actions under each right to ensure that company leaders have the proper guidance and tools to respond to the crisis.

Design: define what type of family business you want to preserve

A business crisis may force you to reconsider the core design choices you have made about what you own together, who can be an owner, and how owners exercise control. You need to clarify to company leaders whether any of these choices can be revisited if doing so would help them respond to the crisis or whether the leaders need to work within those design constraints. To make this decision, you should consider discussing these topics in the Owner Room first:

- Which assets in the family enterprise must be maintained, and where do you have flexibility to sell or starve some parts to save the whole?

- Under what circumstances would you consider opening up ownership to employees, in-laws, or outside investors to bring in new forms of capital?

- Should you consider changing what type of business you are (e.g., from Partnership to Distributed to bring in additional family owners)?

Decide: review your governance structures and processes

Managing through a crisis requires the ability to make major decisions faster than ever. Actions that might have seemed drastic several months ago can quickly become insufficient to meet the challenges faced by the company. Embedded in your family business is a way of working that may need to change. It's up to you to "decide how you will decide" during trying times. As the pace and magnitude of decisions increase, so does the risk of losing control. Ensure that the owners are appropriately involved in the big decisions. Ask yourselves these questions:

- Do you have the forums you need for all Four Rooms? If you're lacking an important venue needed to make critical decisions during the crisis, how will you fill the gap?

- How will you make upcoming major decisions? Are there certain decisions that the owners should be more or less involved in during this period? Are you clear about who has authority to make key decisions?

- Do you need to revisit any policies you have set (e.g., dividends, family employment)? Or do you need to set new policies for these unique circumstances?

Value: revisit your Owner Strategy for the company

Update your Owner Strategy statement for the current situation. In a crisis, company leaders need to be clear on what matters most to you so they can do their best to achieve it. Your Owner Strategy will probably change in a crisis. Among the questions you should consider are these:

- What values will inform how you act during the crisis?

- What goals will you set for the business? If survival is primary, what are you willing to give up to achieve it? Around a third of respondents to our survey have cut dividends or plan to cut them.

- How will you make trade-offs among your stakeholders? For example, how do you prioritize the needs of employees (wages, benefits), customers (staying open, extending credit), and suppliers (paying bills)? Are you willing to lose money for some objectives (e.g., retaining employees, supporting the community)? In our survey, two-thirds of survey respondents say they have reduced or shifted operating expenses to preserve cash.

- Are you open to changing the company's capital structure? Will you raise your borrowing limits if the company needs additional debt? Are you willing to recapitalize the company? More than 40 percent of the survey respondents are raising cash through new debt or equity.

Inform: use communication to sustain trusted relationships

In a crisis, your key stakeholders need to see and hear from owners and company leaders more than they might during normal times. You may have to share information that you typically withhold. For example, you may need to calm fears about the company's viability by talking about cash reserves or profits. Help company leaders determine what can be shared with each of your main constituencies. Consider these questions:

- How will you stay connected with each other and with the rest of the family?

- How will you remain informed about what's happening at the company, and how will you voice your questions and concerns?

- What should be shared with employees about the state of the business and your commitment to it?

- How will you manage communication with the public and press, especially if tough decisions need to be made?

Transfer: consider the implications for the transition to the next generation

Family businesses that want to last for generations keep one eye on the present and the other on the future. In general, a crisis is a time to narrow the gaze. But it might also be the window in which to make changes that have been a long time coming. Company leaders will be looking to the owners to see whether to put your transition plans in motion or to shelve them. Discuss these questions as a group:

- Do current family leaders need to remain longer than planned to steward the family business? Or do they need to make way for fresh ideas and untapped energy?

- Should you accelerate current estate plans because of lower valuations? Or should you put them on hold because of the cost or distraction?

- How can you use this opportunity to teach future generations about your core values and principles by involving them in the key owner decisions?

Owners should collectively review each of these five areas and address the most important actions in each area to help the company leaders navigate the current crisis and prepare for the long term. Alignment is vital—companies with a unified ownership group can act decisively, while a house divided will not stand.

Start by organizing yourselves to get the work done and to stay united. How often will you meet? In what venue (in person, conference call, video)? Who is in charge of setting the agenda and facilitating the meeting? Who else should be in the room when you meet (e.g., company CEO or CFO, board chair, family office director)? In a crisis, the facts on the ground change rapidly. You'll need to find the right cadence that allows you to stay on top of the situation without overburdening the management team.

As you and your co-owners do your work, acknowledge your emotions and help each other through the ups and downs. Focus on your common purpose in getting the company through to the other side intact. Staying together during the current crisis is essential to sustaining what you have already built.

Family businesses have characteristics that allow them to outcompete other kinds of companies in normal and crisis environments. They are great employers, positive contributors to their communities, financially disciplined, and have committed owners. Productively harnessing the power of family ownership will help weather any storm.

Summing up

- There are moments in the family business life cycle when everything is on the line, when you will either consolidate another generation of success or hasten the end of your journey together.

- Watch out for three main types of dangers:

  - **A loss of control by the owners places managers in the driver's seat.** Keep an eye out for such warning signs as an irreplaceable CEO, never-changing dividends, rubber-stamp meetings, and a family that is locked out of the Management Room. If you see things like these happening, reassert your role as owners if you want to keep the business. Organize yourselves to assert your five rights.

  - **A loss of the guiding values of the family creates a business you still own but are not proud of.** Family values are usually lost not with a giant leap but rather in a series of small steps that together lead you toward ethical deterioration. To avoid this path, focus on what makes a family business different. Don't define success only by money. Avoid the false dichotomy between having a business that is professionally run and one that has a soul. Teach each generation that there have always been ups and downs, so that new owners won't act out of desperation when the inevitable rough patch arrives.

  - **An economic crisis places your business in jeopardy.** Use the crisis as an opportunity to come together around the shared goal of survival. During this time, you will have to consider changing standard practices and may need to redefine what success means. Use the five rights to identify the work to be done.

- As you face these or other dangers, remember the power of family ownership. You can make the rules, and you can break them. Much of your long-term success depends on your being thoughtful about when to do the making or the breaking.

Conclusion

The Good Journey, Together

In this book, we provide you with many ways to understand and improve your family business. But what do you do now? Where you do start your work?

As an individual, you play an important role in your family business. Start by recognizing how you can be a better owner, future owner, member of the business family, trusted employee, or adviser and how you personally can build better relationships. What specific behaviors could you change to improve these roles and relationships? It may not be easy, and it won't always be fun. But we promise you, you will never regret working harder on the relationships that matter to you.

Although you can apply some of the lessons of this book directly, remember that family business is a team sport. As we have discussed throughout, your family business is a *system*—one that involves (and requires) collaboration to accomplish your goals. Build a change roadmap with others. We propose three steps to start:

- Conduct an assessment of how your system is working

- In the problem areas, clarify what is missing, messy, or mostly working and what maybe can be worked on later

- Build a roadmap and select two or three areas to redirect your journey, together

First, you need to agree on how you assess your system. Below, we offer a simple assessment framework based on the chapters in parts 2 and 3. Gather members of your system together, and ask them to individually assess each aspect of your system and then collectively discuss your ratings (table C-1). You are not judging or assigning blame for any issues of the past; you are looking forward about how to improve. Remember that the way you have done things before has been central to getting where you are today, but it may not be sufficient to achieve the goals of tomorrow. You should find that the discussion itself helps participants find points they can support.

In discussing your assessment, guide your group to focus their change efforts on one or two areas where the system is not functioning well, as indicated by many "strongly disagree" or "disagree" ratings, and where your group can influence change.

But what to work on in those areas? For the areas you assessed as needing work, reread the related chapter for ideas on what to tackle in that area. It helps to classify potential changes into activities that are missing, messy, mostly working, or maybe later. Table C-2 shows how you can classify the key activities involved in creating a plan for transferring ownership of the family business. You could add rows to this table for the other owner rights, such as the right to decide on governance and the right to design your type of business.

Finally, build your roadmap. On a broad level, a roadmap outlines the changes you would like to make to your system during the next two or three years, with the nearer-term changes more specific than the later ones. Unless there is an emergency such as an unanticipated death in the family, don't rush or take on too many changes at once. Instead, select a

TABLE C-1

Assessment of your family business

Statement (chapter number)	Strongly disagree	Disagree	Neutral	Agree	Strongly agree	Don't know
Design: The type of family ownership we have designed is appropriate to meet our future needs (3).						
Decide: We have the right governance structures (e.g., owner council, board) and processes (e.g., dividend policy) across the Four Rooms to consistently make great decisions (4).						
Value: We have a compelling purpose as owners, have agreed on what goals we want the business to accomplish, and have set clear guardrails for those running the business (5).						
Inform: We are communicating effectively to build the trusted relationships that our family business needs to succeed (6).						
Transfer: We have a well-constructed continuity plan for how to transition our assets, roles, and capabilities (7).						
Disruptions: Our business family is prepared for disruptions such as deaths, new spouses, inequalities, and behavioral health issues (8).						
Career path: Family members, spouses, and nonfamily employees can reach their full potential while working in the business (9).						
Family employment policy: We have an appropriate and well-understood family employment policy (10).						
Wealth: We are taking the right steps as a business and family to treat our wealth responsibly (11).						
Conflict: We have found the Goldilocks zone of conflict in our family business (12).						
Family office: We have the infrastructure in place to address our investment, support, and governance needs (13).						
Dangers: Our family owners are in control of the destiny and the values of our business (14).						

TABLE C-2

What do you need to work on?

Sample classification of the key activities involved in creating a plan for transfer

Area	Missing	Messy	Mostly working	Maybe later
Transfer	• Plan to transfer roles • Plan to build capabilities • Estate plan (self)	• Plan to transfer assets • Tax planning	• Estate plan (sister)	• Glide path for current leaders

few items in the "missing" and "messy" categories that you and the other owners together want to improve and can influence. Remember that in a system, changing anything can have unintended consequences. Let those consequences emerge before tackling another big change. Working on a few relatively straightforward changes can give your group some experience in working together and increased confidence to tackle harder challenges. You should find that, with success, your ability to manage conflict and know and appreciate each other rises intrinsically. Once your group tackles your first set of actions, turn your attention to the next.

Family businesses require a ton of work to sustain. But perhaps counterintuitively, this work requirement is a blessing. The work in a family business, when the members do it well and do it together, can be exceptionally rewarding. Connection to your family, personal growth in how you relate to others, pride in your contributions, financial success, closeness to long-term employees, and an expression of your values in the larger community—it all can happen. One of our clients calls the work "the good journey, together." And we can't agree more.

Notes

Introduction: Understanding Your Family Business

1. Although family relationships are more fluid today and some people have long-lasting personal relationships with someone they refer to as a partner rather than a spouse, we use the term *spouse* in this book to refer to anyone's permanent partner.

Chapter 1: Decode Your Family Business

1. Throughout this book we use the "G" to refer to generations. For example, a G2 is part of the second generation.
2. This concept draws on Robert Jervis, *System Effects*. See "Further Reading."

Chapter 3: Design: Choose the Type of Family Ownership You Want

1. We have worked with some family businesses that, like the one just mentioned, want neither to grow their shared assets nor to sell them. Although such families own a business collectively (and want it to succeed), they are more focused on creating wealth outside the business. We refer to this type of ownership as a *nested* structure. A nested approach is worth considering when the owners disagree on how to grow a business but see value in keeping it. A nested approach might also be appropriate when families want to deliberately limit the scope of what they own together. Everything beyond the core business—philanthropy, investments, new ventures, and the like—is done on an individual or branch basis. A nested structure opens up major questions. For example, how does the business retain its vitality when its fuel is being siphoned off for other activities? Or how long can a company stand in place, especially in a rapidly changing business environment? But in certain situations, a nested structure can solve a situation that will otherwise result in destructive conflict or a premature sale of the business.
2. The survey took place in 2020 and had 190 respondents.

Chapter 4: Decide: Structure Governance to Make Great Decisions Together

1. The owners exercise their power directly through their rights as shareholders or indirectly through a board, which they control. Of course, owners must act within the legal, tax, and compliance laws and regulations of the countries they operate in and the rules set by whatever trust or other vehicles are set up to hold their shares.

2. In some family businesses, the owner council has no legal authority and can only recommend decisions to the shareholders. When all owners are present in the meetings, which is often the case when all the owners are first- and second-generation members of the family, there is no meaningful distinction between a council's recommendation and a decision. In some owner councils, the rest of the shareholders legally delegate the council to make certain decisions. In such cases, the owner councils are sometimes referred to as owner boards rather than councils.

3. A **tag-along** clause requires the majority shareholder or shareholders to allow the minority owners to join in on a sale. The **drag-along** clause requires the minority owners to sell their shares if the majority agrees to a sale. Both clauses give to the minority owners the rights to receive the same price, terms, and conditions received by any other seller.

Chapter 6: Inform: Use Effective Communication to Build Trusted Relationships

1. Ownership brings with it the potential for a virtual monopoly on information about the business. This right can be seen in the protections that have been established for minority owners. In most jurisdictions, any owner has the right to access a wide scope of information—organizational records, financial statements, customer contracts, and so forth—within some basic limits that protect the company. For example, owners may be able to demand to see a list of customers, but only if they promise not to sell the list to a competitor. Unless the owners give these rights up to others (e.g., by signing bank covenants), only the owners of a company have these rights.

2. A. K. Mishra, "Organizational Responses to Crisis: The Centrality of Trust," in *Trust in Organizations: Frontiers of Theory and Research*, ed. A. M. Kramer and T. R. Tyler (Thousand Oaks, CA: Sage, 1996), 261–287.

3. Jack Stack and Bo Burlingham, *The Great Game of Business: The Only Sensible Way to Run a Company* (New York: Currency, 2013).

4. Daniel Victor, "Trump Tweet About L. L. Bean Underscores Potential Danger for Brands," *New York Times*, January 12, 2017, www.nytimes.com/2017/01/12/us/politics/linda-bean-ll-bean-boycott.html.

5. 2019 Edelman Trust Barometer, "Implications for Family Business," https://www.edelman.com/sites/g/files/aatuss191/files/2019-06/2019_Edelman_Trust_Barometer_Implications_Family_Business.pdf.

6. International disclosure laws are increasingly forcing even privately held international businesses to disclose their financial statements and ownership. This trend appears in many guises in different countries as requirements of transparency of "ultimate ownership."

7. Eric Berne, *Games People Play: The Basic Handbook of Transactional Analysis* (New York, Ballantine Books, 1996).

8. DiSC is a behavior assessment tool based on the DiSC theory of psychologist William Moulton Marston. This theory was then developed into a behavioral assessment tool by industrial psychologist Walter Vernon Clarke. https://www.discprofile.com/.

9. Sarah Ellison, *War at the Wall Street Journal: Inside the Struggle to Control an American Business Empire* (Boston: Houghton Mifflin Harcourt, 2010), 59.

Chapter 7: Transfer: Plan for the Transition to the Next Generation

1. Vikram Bhalla and Nicolas Kachaner, "Succeeding with Succession Planning in Family Businesses," BCG, March 25, 2015, www.bcg.com/en-us/publications/2015/leadership_talent_growth_succeeding_with_succession_planning_family_businesses.aspx.

2. Bill Taylor, "Hire for Attitude, Train for Skill," *Harvard Business Review*, February 1, 2011.

Chapter 8: The Business Family: Four Disruptions You Will Face and What to Do about Them

1. We thank our colleague Marion McCollom Hampton for her insights and wisdom in helping us build this chapter. See Diane Coutu, "Embracing the Complexity of Families: A Conversation with Marion McCollom Hampton," Banyan Global, https://banyan.global/wp-content/uploads/2019/10/2019_Updated_Partner-Interview_Marion_Embracing-the-Complexity-of-Families.pdf.

2. To calculate the number of relationships and the growth in your family, use this formula: the number of relationships (R) for a number of family members (N) is $R = N \times (N - 1)/2$. See Peter K. Gerlach, "Family Relationships," in *Break the Cycle!*, accessed July 12, 2020, http://sfhelp.org/fam/pop/formula.htm.

3. Martin E. P. Seligman, director of the Positive Psychology Center at the University of Pennsylvania, conducted research on this issue. See "Giving Thanks Can Make You Happier," *Healthbeat*, Harvard Health Publishing, accessed July 12, 2020, www.health.harvard.edu/healthbeat/giving-thanks-can-make-you-happier.

Chapter 11: How to Be Responsible with the Wealth of Your Family Business

1. Shell study cited in Arie de Geus, *The Living Company* (Boston: Harvard Business School Press, 1997), 150.

2. Gregory Clark, cited in Stephanie Pappas, "Surname Status: Elite Families Stay Elite for Centuries," *Live Science*, December 2, 2014, www.livescience.com/48951-surnames-social-mobility.html.

3. Gregory Clark, "Your Ancestors, Your Fate," *Opinionator* (blog), *New York Times*, February 21, 2014, https://opinionator.blogs.nytimes.com/2014/02/21/your-fate -thank-your-ancestors/?referringSource=articleShare.

4. Guglielmo Barone and Sauro Mocetti, "What's Your (Sur)Name? Intergenerational Mobility over Six Centuries," *Vox* (CEPR Policy Portal), May 17, 2016, https://voxeu .org/article/what-s-your-surname-intergenerational-mobility-over-six-centuries.

Chapter 12: Conflict in the Family Business

1. Richard Price, "Reversing the Gun Sights: Transnational Civil Society Targets Land Mines," *International Organization* 52, no. 3 (summer 1998): 613–644, www .jstor.org/stable/2601403.

Chapter 13: The Family Office in a Family Business

1. Alastair Graham, "Single Family Offices—Who Knows the Numbers?," *Family Wealth Report*, Clearview Financial Media, London, July 26, 2019, www .fwreport.com/article.php?id=184381#.Xubb_WpKjPh; and Hilary Leav, "How Many Family Offices Are There in the United States?," *Family Office Exchange*, Chicago, August 9, 2019, www.familyoffice.com/insights/ how-many-family-offices-are-there-united-states.

Chapter 14: The Dangers of Losing What You've Built

1. Paul Lienert and Marilyn Thompson, "GM Avoided Defective Switch Redesign in 2005 to Save a Dollar Each," Reuters, April 1, 2014, https://www.reuters.com/ article/us-gm-recall-delphi/gm-avoided-defective-switch-redesign-in-2005-to -save-a-dollar-each-idUSBREA3105R20140402.

2. The survey had 190 respondents across six continents and more than twenty-five industries.

Further Reading

Chapter 1: Decode Your Family Business

Doud, Ernest A., Jr., and Lee Hausner. *Hats Off to You 2: Balancing Roles and Creating Success in Family Business*. Santa Barbara, CA: DoudHausnerVistar, 2004.

Gersick, Kelin E., John A. Davis, Marion McCollom Hampton, and Ivan Landsberg. *Generation to Generation: Life Cycles of the Family Business*. Boston: Harvard Business School Press, 1997.

Jervis, Robert. *System Effects: Complexity in Political and Social Life*. Princeton: Princeton University Press, 1997.

Kerr, Michael E. *One Family's Story: A Primer on Bowen Theory*. Washington, DC: Bowen Center for the Study of the Family, 2003.

McGoldrick, Monica, Randy Gerson, and Sueli Petry. *Genograms: Assessment and Intervention*. New York: W.W. Norton & Company, 2008.

Schuman, Amy, Stacy Stutz, and John L. Ward. *Family Business as Paradox*. London: Palgrave Macmillan, 2010.

Chapter 2: The Power of Family Ownership

Baron, Josh. "Why the 21st Century Will Belong to Family Businesses." *Harvard Business Review*, March 28, 2016.

Gaddis, John Lewis. *On Grand Strategy*. New York: Penguin Press, 2018.

Kachaner, Nicolas, George Stalk, and Alain Bloch. "What You Can Learn from Family Business: Focus on Resilience Not Short-Term Performance." *Harvard Business Review*, November 2012.

Kiechel, Walter. *The Lords of Strategy: The Secret Intellectual History of the New Corporate World*. Boston: Harvard Business Press, 2010.

Miller, Danny, and Isabelle Le Breton-Miller. *Managing for the Long Run: Lessons in Competitive Advantage from the Great Family Businesses*. Boston: Harvard Business School Press, 2005.

Reeves, Martin, Knut Haanaes, and Janmejaya Sinha. *Your Strategy Needs a Strategy*. Boston: Harvard Business Review Press, 2015.

Chapter 3: Design: Choose the Type of Family Ownership You Want

Aronoff, Craig E., and John L. Ward. *Family Business Ownership: How to Be an Effective Shareholder.* New York: Palgrave Macmillan, 2011.

Caspar, Christian, Ana Karina Dias, and Heinz-Peter Elstrodt. "The Five Attributes of Enduring Family Businesses." *McKinsey and Company,* January 1, 2010.

Poza, Ernesto J., and Mary S. Daugherty. *Family Business.* Mason, OH: South-Western Cengage Learning, 2014.

Chapter 4: Decide: Structure Governance to Make Great Decisions Together

Hampton, Marion McCollom, and Nick Di Loreto. "Empty Structures Syndrome: Losing the Energy That Drives Governance." *Trust & Estates,* August 2018.

International Finance Corporation. *IFC Family Business Governance Handbook.* 4th ed. Washington, DC: International Finance Corporation World Bank Group, 2018.

Lorsch, Jay W., and Colin Carter. *Back to the Drawing Board: Designing Corporate Boards for a Complex World.* Boston: Harvard Business School Press, 2003.

Pendergast, Jennifer M., John L. Ward, and Stephanie Brun De Pontet. *Building a Successful Family Business Board: A Guide for Leaders, Directors, and Families.* New York: Palgrave Macmillan, 2011.

Rogers, Paul, and Marcia W. Blenko. "Who Has the D?: How Clear Decision Roles Enhance Organizational Performance." *Harvard Business Review,* January 2006.

Salley, Steve, Devin Bird, and Judy Lin Walsh. "Family Business Boards: The Arbiter of Fairness." *Owner to Owner* (Brown Brothers Harriman), quarter 1, March 1, 2016.

Chapter 5: Value: Create an Owner Strategy to Define Your Success

Bungy, Stephen. *The Art of Action: How Leaders Close the Gap Between Plans, Actions, and Results.* London: Quercus, 2011.

Burlingham, Bo. *Small Giants: Companies That Choose to Be Great Instead of Big.* New York: Penguin Group, 2005.

Frankl, Viktor E. *Man's Search for Meaning.* Boston: Beacon Press, 2006.

Liddell Hart, Basil Henry. *Strategy.* New York: Meridian/Plume, 1991.

Chapter 6: Inform: Use Effective Communication to Build Trusted Relationships

Berne, Eric. *Games People Play: The Basic Handbook of Transactional Analysis.* New York: Ballantine Books, 1996.

Harris, Thomas A. *I'm OK—You're OK.* New York: HarperCollins, 2004.

Tierney, John and Roy F. Baumeister. *The Power of Bad: How the Negativity Effect Rules Us and How We Can Rule It*. New York: Penguin Press, 2019.

Stack, Jack, and Bo Burlingham. *The Great Game of Business: The Only Sensible Way to Run a Company*. New York: Currency, 2013.

Chapter 7: Transfer: Plan for the Transition to the Next Generation

Bhalla, Vikram, and Nicolas Kachaner. "Succeeding with Succession Planning in Family Businesses: The Ten Key Principles." *BCG Perspectives* (Boston Consulting Group), March 25, 2015.

Korine, Harry. *Succession for Change: Strategic Transitions in Family and Founder-Led Businesses*. New York: Palgrave Macmillan, 2017.

Lansberg, Ivan. *Succeeding Generations: Realizing the Dream of Families in Business*. Boston: Harvard Business School Press, 1999.

Sonnenfeld, Jeffrey A. *The Hero's Farewell: What Happens When CEOs Retire*. Oxford: Oxford University Press, 1991.

Stalk, George, and Henry Foley. "Avoid the Traps That Can Destroy Family Businesses: An Emerging Set of Best Practices Can Turn Age-Old Problem of Generational Succession into an Opportunity to Thrive." *Harvard Business Review*, January–February 2012.

Chapter 8: The Business Family: Four Disruptions You Will Face and What to Do about Them

Brown, Fredda Herz. *Reweaving the Family Tapestry*. North Charleston, SC: BookSurge, 2006.

Brown, Fredda Herz, and Fran Lotery. *The Essential Roadmap: Navigating Family Enterprise Sustainability in a Changing World*. Tenafly, NJ: Relative Solutions, LLC, 2020.

"Drug Addiction (Substance Use Disorder)." MayoClinic.org, October 26, 2017. https://www.mayoclinic.org/diseases-conditions/drug-addiction/symptoms-causes/syc-20365112.

Kaye, Kenneth. *Family Rules: Raising Responsible Children*. New York: Walker and Co., 1984.

Kerr, Michael E., and Murray Bowen. *Family Evaluation*. New York: W.W. Norton & Company, 1988.

Kets de Vries, Manfred F. R., Randel S. Carlock, and Elizabeth Florent-Treacy. *Family Business on the Couch: A Psychological Perspective*. West Sussex, UK: Wiley, 2007.

Libby, Ellen. *The Favorite Child: How a Favorite Impacts Every Family Member for Life*. Amherst, NY: Prometheus, 2010.

National Alliance on Mental Illness. "Warning Signs and Symptoms." Accessed July 12, 2020. https://nami.org/About-Mental-Illness/Warning-Signs-and-Symptoms.

Ruiz, Don Miguel. *The Four Agreements: A Practical Guide to Personal Freedom*. San Rafael, CA: Amber-Allen Publishing, 2001.

Chapter 9: Working in a Family Business

Walsh, Judy Lin, and Aline Porto. "Is It Time to Leave the Family Business?" *Harvard Business Review*, January 24, 2020.

Chapter 10: Family Employment Policy

Walsh, Judy Lin, and Ben Francois. "When Should You Fire Your Child from the Family Business?" *Harvard Business Review*, July 24, 2019.

Chapter 11: How to Be Responsible with the Wealth of Your Family Business

Gallo, Eileen, and Jon Gallo. *Silver Spoon Kids: How Successful Parents Raise Responsible Children*. New York: McGraw-Hill Education, 2002.

Grubman, James. *Strangers in Paradise: How Families Adapt to Wealth Across Generations*. Burlington, VT: Family Wealth Consulting, 2013.

Hughes, James E., Jr. *Family Wealth: Keeping It in the Family*. Princeton, NJ: Bloomberg Press, 2004.

Levine, Madeline. *The Price of Privilege: How Parental Pressure and Material Advantage Are Creating a Generation of Disconnected and Unhappy Kids*. New York: HarperCollins, 2006.

Lucas, Stuart E. *Wealth: Grow It and Protect It*. Upper Saddle River, NJ: Pearson Prentice Hall, 2006.

McCullough, Tom, and Keith Whitaker. *Wealth of Wisdom*. West Sussex, UK: Wiley, 2018.

Perry, Ellen. *A Wealth of Possibilities: Navigating Family, Money, and Legacy*. Washington, DC: Egremont Press, 2012.

Stovall, Jim. *The Ultimate Gift*. Colorado Springs, CO: David C. Cook, 2001.

Chapter 12: Conflict in the Family Business

Baumoel, Doug, and Blair Trippe. *Deconstructing Conflict: Understanding Family Business, Shared Wealth and Power*. Beverly, MA: Continuity Media, 2016.

Fisher, Roger, and Daniel Shapiro. *Beyond Reason: Using Emotions as You Negotiate*. London: Penguin Books, 2006.

Fisher, Roger, William L. Ury, and Bruce Patton. *Getting to Yes: Negotiating Agreement without Giving In*. London: Penguin Books, 1983.

Chapter 13: The Family Office in a Family Business

Campden Wealth and UBS. "Building a Family Office: The Global Family Office Report 2019." September 24, 2019. www.campdenwealth.com/article/global-family-office-report-2019.

Fidelity Investments. *Evolving the Family Office*. 2019. https://clearingcustody.fidelity.com/app/proxy/content?literatureURL=/9884440.PDF.

Chapter 14: The Dangers of Losing What You've Built

Chernow, Ron. *The House of Morgan*. New York: Simon & Schuster, 1991.

Christensen, Clayton M., James Allworth, and Karen Dillon. *How Will You Measure Your Life?* New York: HarperCollins, 2012.

Ellison, Sarah. *War at the Wall Street Journal: Inside the Struggle to Control an American Business Empire*. Boston: Houghton Mifflin Harcourt, 2010.

Index

Acknowledgments

Throughout this book, we celebrate the power and joy of working together toward common goals. We found that our joint writing process reflected this belief. We shared our experiences and poked and prodded each other's ideas, practices that led to a much stronger book in the process.

While this book lists just two authors, the work reflects the contributions of many people important to both of us. First, we thank our clients, whom we can't name. But we can say that it has been a prodigious privilege to work with and learn from them. Next, we thank our team of Banyan colleagues for their feedback, which taught us so much, and for sustaining us through the writing of this book—Natalia Amaya, Lauren Ayres, Vlad Barbieri, Devin Bird, Fernanda Brasil, Sam Bruehl, Carlos Costa, Rob Davies, Nick Di Loreto, Natasha Falke, Henry Foley, Ben Francois, Lisa Frelinghuysen, Marcos Herszkowicz, Sharon McDermott, Seth McLaughlin, Marcella Mendonca, Philip Moore, Kelly Nealon, Meredith Nealon, Aline Porto, Sarah Reichert, Ana Resende, Laureen Robinson, Omar Romman, JoEllen Ross, George Stalk, Bruce Stevens, Hilla Talati, Leigh Terhaar, and Judy Lin Walsh. We can't imagine a better team of professionals. We hope we didn't mess up.

While everyone at Banyan contributed in some way, we want to single out our Banyan partners Marion McCollom Hampton and Steve Salley, who each "volunteered" to be internal peer reviewers and generously offered their profound expertise. Our colleague Megan Hayes tirelessly helped keep us organized and on track, and Alison Hiler spent hours providing an eagle-eyed edit of our manuscript. Our editor at Banyan, Karen Dillon, wisely, gracefully, and tirelessly guided us to deliver the best of our thinking and writing. Our champion at *Harvard Business Review*, Susan Francis, was a true partner from start to finish. Patricia Boyd and Jen Waring both made the book much better as a result of their keen eyes and expert touch.

Top family business professionals provided their wisdom and experience in countless ways. They include David Ager, Rodrigo Amantea, Ari Axelrod, Jorge Becerra, Gifford Booth, Brad Bulkley, Barney Corning, Jim Coutre, Diane Coutu, Sebastian Ehrensberger, Ken Foraste, Kathryn George, Jim Grubman, Ute Hagehulsmann, Fredda Herz Brown, Dennis Jaffe, Ellen Libby, Heinrich Liechtenstein, Luiz Lima, Doug Macauley, Kathryn McCarthy, Dave McCabe, Arden O'Connor, San Orr, Laird Pendleton, Jennifer Pendergast, Thiago Penido, Ben Persofsky, Michael Preston, Andrew Tanner, Daniel Van Der Vliet, and Dave Whorton. We also thank our anonymous reviewers for their helpful feedback.

Josh: I thank my parents, Pam, Sol, Sara, and Art, for a lifetime of love and support; Kathryn, Melissa, Elisa, and Mark, my four extraordinary siblings; my students at Columbia Business School, especially from Family Business Management in the spring and summer of 2020, for being guinea pigs for a draft of this book; my wife Beth, for making everything possible and life wonderful; and our twins Eloise and Charlie, the lights of our lives and the greatest source of our joy.

Rob: I thank my father and mother, Gus and Ruth Ann, and in-laws, Eugene and Patricia, who all taught us invaluable lessons about raising a strong, loving family; my brother and sister, Bruce and Kathy, who are my sibling besties; our three daughters, Anna, Elena, and Sophia, who bring such joy to our life; and most of all, my wife, Catherine, for her patience, wisdom, and love.

About the Authors

DR. JOSH BARON is a cofounder and partner at BanyanGlobal. For over a decade, he has worked closely with families who own assets together, such as operating companies, family foundations, and family offices. He helps these families define their purpose as owners and establish the structures, strategies, and skills they need to accomplish their goals. Before Banyan, he worked at Bain & Company and the Bridgespan Group. Baron teaches family business courses at Columbia Business School in the MBA, Executive MBA, and Executive Education programs. He publishes and speaks frequently on family enterprises and is a regular contributor to the *Harvard Business Review*, including "Why the 21st Century Will Belong to Family Businesses," "Why Family Businesses Need to Find the Right Level of Conflict," and "Every Business Owner Should Define What Success Looks Like." A graduate of the University of Pennsylvania, the University of Cambridge, and Columbia University, he is also the author of *Great Power Peace and American Primacy: The Origins and Future of a New International Order.*

ROB LACHENAUER, a cofounder, partner, and CEO of BanyanGlobal, has been an adviser, a business leader, and a writer throughout his career. As an adviser, he was a partner at the Boston Consulting Group, where he helped family-controlled and other businesses set and implement growth strategies. While at BCG, he coauthored *Hardball: Are You Playing to Play or Playing to Win?* with George Stalk. Published by Harvard Business School Press in 2004, *Hardball* was subsequently translated into ten languages. As the founding CEO of Banyan, Lachenauer has worked closely with scores of family businesses throughout the world, helping them navigate the decisions they face as owners while strengthening family relationships. He is an expert in leadership and governance for family businesses. A graduate of Harvard Business School and Cornell University, Lachenauer has also made frequent contributions to *Harvard Business Review*, including "Making Better Decisions in Your Family Business," "What Happens When You Lose Your Mentor," and "Why I Hired an Executive with a Mental Illness."

Invaluable insights
always at your fingertips

With an All-Access subscription to
Harvard Business Review, you'll get
so much more than a magazine.

Exclusive online content and tools
you can put to use today

My Library, your personal workspace for sharing,
saving, and organizing HBR.org articles and tools

Unlimited access to more than 4,000 articles in the
Harvard Business Review archive

Subscribe today at hbr.org/subnow

The most important management ideas all in one place.

We hope you enjoyed this book from *Harvard Business Review*. For the best ideas HBR has to offer turn to HBR's 10 Must Reads Boxed Set. From books on leadership and strategy to managing yourself and others, this 6-book collection delivers articles on the most essential business topics to help you succeed.

HBR's 10 Must Reads Series

The definitive collection of ideas and best practices on our most sought-after topics from the best minds in business.

- Change Management
- Collaboration
- Communication
- Emotional Intelligence
- Innovation
- Leadership
- Making Smart Decisions

- Managing Across Cultures
- Managing People
- Managing Yourself
- Strategic Marketing
- Strategy
- Teams
- The Essentials

hbr.org/mustreads

Buy for your team, clients, or event.
Visit hbr.org/bulksales for quantity discount rates.

Harvard Business Review Press